ROCK 'N' ROLL PLAYS ITSELF

ROCK 'N' ROLL

Plays itself

A SCREEN HISTORY

JOHN SCANLAN

REAKTION BOOKS

Published by
REAKTION BOOKS LTD
Unit 32, Waterside
44–48 Wharf Road
London N1 7UX, UK
www.reaktionbooks.co.uk

First published 2022

Printed and bound in Great Britain by TJ Books Ltd, Padstow, Cornwall

A catalogue record for this book is available from the British Library

ISBN 978 1 78914 572 4

CONTENTS

Bob Dylan in D. A. Pennebaker's *Don't Look Back* (released 1967) peels off lyric cards to 'Subterranean Homesick Blues'. Allen Ginsberg stands to the left with Dylan's road manager, Bob Neuwirth (out of shot), London, 1965.

PROLOGUE:
GET BORN

Grappling with a large wad of notecards that have been carefully decorated in stylized lettering, Bob Dylan – a skinny young American with frizzled hair – stands in a London alleyway holding in his hands a selection of words from a new song he has written, which bears the curious title 'Subterranean Homesick Blues'. Once the camera is rolling, he will begin to peel off the cards, trying to keep time with a recording of the song, whose words are transformed with the help of music into a welter of images that marry the sound of rock 'n' roll to his kaleidoscopic consciousness. Off to his right stand Allen Ginsberg and Bob Neuwirth, the latter accompanying Dylan as his road manager on this short 1965 tour of England, which will end in a few days, two weeks before the singer turns 24. Ginsberg and Neuwirth act like they are taking a break from picking up litter as Dylan readies himself. Unusually, he does not attempt to sing along or mime to these words as he is being filmed. He simply stands rooted to his position. It is rock 'n' roll, but not as it had ever presented itself before.

Such is the iconic beginning of one of the most celebrated rock films ever made, D. A. Pennebaker's *Don't Look Back* (filmed in 1965 and released in 1967). It is probably as familiar to anyone reading this book as any other moment from the screen life of rock 'n' roll. But within that memorable movie beginning lies another beginning, a new sound and attitude, as the singer, fed up with the demand that he somehow always be the Bob Dylan that his audience has come to expect, stands there *not* pretending (as you are supposed to do in the movies). As 'Subterranean Homesick Blues' clatters along, the sound of a rock 'n' roll jalopy on bumpy ground, this is Bob Dylan playing himself: the film existing as evidence of how he was able to wipe out a version of himself that the public had until now carried in their minds.

Across the broad scope of many stylistic variations since its origins in the mid-twentieth century and through several distinct eras in its history, rock achieved its maximum intensity – although not always its greatest popularity – when it was at the point of some new beginning. In film, the image of these points in time, as they relate to rock's performers and the wider society, is often crystallized into something akin to birth moments, as if rock 'n' roll emerges as a fully blown self-generated phenomenon that takes shape in the form of particular individuals, or can be seen to permeate the culture and attitudes of particular times and places, always seemingly waiting to be found or discovered again in a new guise. But while undergoing changes as a musical form, rock has from the start always moved backwards and forwards in time, consuming its own past as it reaches to the future in search of new beginnings and the renewed spirit that marks another point of origin.

Rock 'n' roll film has sometimes been associated most readily with films of the 1950s, perhaps because rock 'n' roll itself – or certainly the use of that label – is often associated with that decade. But the earliest rock films showed nothing of what *Don't Look Back* would introduce in the form of the artist as the author of their own often complex and contradictory public image. Instead, the 1950s films usually did little more than attempt to capture the excitement of the music or its performers at the peak of their popularity, when they would be able to help sell tickets to a picture show, and so some of the originators of rock 'n' roll often appeared in what were more or less cameo roles, miming to hit songs. In this way, the early films in which rock 'n' roll features reflect the fact that popular music itself was viewed as ephemeral, something to be milked to death for the few short months or years that its stars remained capable of capturing the imagination of a youthful audience; an audience of teenagers always likely to be diverted by the next thing that would come along. Aside from Elvis Presley – the only rocker to be the top-billed star of almost every movie he appeared in – the stars of the 1950s existed in a market-driven era when the commercial imperatives of television and Hollywood determined how they would appear on screen. Because they did not control how their image was disseminated to the same extent as rock artists of the following decade and beyond, their ability to break out of the expectations of the age was very limited, almost non-existent.

And unlike those 1950s films that were made by the big Hollywood studios, *Don't Look Back* was a low-budget production that initially found its audiences in the kind of theatres that were more used to showing nudie films; where the dark, cheap and grainy black-and-white look of Pennebaker's movie was judged to be in keeping with what the people who frequented those cinemas might be willing to look at.

From the start, Dylan had concocted fanciful tales of his origins – something not exactly unusual in the entertainment business, where self-invention (even if it extended little further than assuming a new name) was as old as showbiz itself – and throughout his recording career he would shift and change styles, all the while remaining who he was. But in *Don't Look Back*, he and Pennebaker – who could be described as Dylan's co-conspirator, wielding his own jerry-built equipment to allow him to get close to his subject – were not only reinventing the rock film but inventing the idea of the rock star as the central figure in their own mythology, one in which the screen image became all-important. No rock film before had so revealingly gone behind the scenes and into the private world of a rock performer. And in the years ahead, American documentary film in the style of Pennebaker, the Maysles brothers and a few others would become a kind of template for capturing rock on screens, big and small.

And so, the post-1950s rock star, in control of their image and able to express themselves in the full range of their work in ways that were uncommon the decade before, was already in some sense acting. But the difference was that to succeed in rock – unlike acting in the movies – the trick was to play oneself. What, then, do more than five decades of rock on screen tell us about what happens when an artist in one medium moves into another? Equally, when taken as the expression of a wider culture that also grew into something socially transformative in a more lasting way, rock's dependence on the visual – whether experienced in person or through the medium of screen culture – allowed it not only to be represented in film, TV and other media but to actively extend its own life: to, in a sense, play itself on screen.

We might wonder how something like rock 'n' roll, which in its early years took form as throwaway teenage culture, managed to endure in the way it has, and what its life on screen can tell us about the many changes, or reinventions, it went through to survive for so long.

1
EXPLODING TOMORROW

elevision, more than radio and records, was the medium that first exposed mass audiences to rock 'n' roll. To begin with, the producers of the various entertainment shows that would channel this new musical phenomenon into millions of homes had only the hit parade to guide them. If a record was a hit, there was a chance that whoever performed it would make it to the screen. The most successful of these was *The Ed Sullivan Show*, broadcast on Sunday nights across the United States, which featured an early sighting of rock when Bo Diddley, purveyor of a unique sound that blended a juddering rhythm with a guitar drenched in outer-space echo, made his one and only appearance on the show. A one-of-a-kind artist, when Diddley got into his stride he made a sound that was capable of shaking loose anything that wasn't fixed in place, people included. It was a music meant for the body that actually worked its way from the ears to the limbs and nerves.

When the show's producers signed Diddley up for an appearance in November 1955 it was purely because he was hot on the charts at the time. It had nothing at all to do with Sullivan or his producers having any particular enthusiasm for the music. Quite the contrary – this was a music almost entirely alien to them. This fact may account for the speed with which they were taken aback when they saw Diddley rehearsing his act, driven on by a hypnotic beat that seemed to belong somewhere less salubrious than the TV studios of a family show. The song being rehearsed, titled 'Bo Diddley', was a homage to its architect and a prime example of the libidinous force of the rhythm he concocted. Light entertainment it was not. As Charlie Gillett wrote of this particular song, 'the rhythm was a bump-and-grind shuffle' made doubly profane by its suggestive lyrical braggadocio, which seemed to lay out Diddley's rules of sexual conquest.[1] Sullivan was having none of it. Some say that he grabbed a piece of sheet music from his orchestra and instructed Diddley to perform it instead. Allegedly, it was the score for 'Some Enchanted Evening', a popular song from the Rogers and Hammerstein musical *South Pacific*, one of the biggest hits of the time. Other accounts describe Diddley also being persuaded to rehearse the popular Tennessee Ernie Ford tune 'Sixteen Tons', simply because they thought he looked like the kind of rough-hewn character who could pull it off convincingly.

This unwillingness to let Diddley perform his own bona fide hit gave a strong hint of something that would become apparent with subsequent attempts to bring rock to the screen in its early days: the entertainment establishment didn't really understand rock 'n' roll. They still thought that the hit parade, and the popularity of its various singing stars, was about the song.[2] Songs were usually written by professional songwriters, shadowy figures sequestered away in dark rooms. The performers? They were just interchangeable. The problem was that rock 'n' roll really upended that idea. What separated it from the pop music of earlier decades was the individual stamp that each of its performers brought to bear on the music, even when they were performing other people's material.

When the Sullivan show rolled on to the Bo Diddley segment during the live broadcast that night, the studio orchestra struck up the monumentally un-Diddley-like sound of 'Some Enchanted Evening'. The audience would have recently heard it being performed by Perry Como – a popular singer, no doubt, but one who occupied a place on the musical and attitudinal spectrum somewhere at the opposite end of where Diddley would be found. At first, Diddley seemed to go along with it, but, as David Halberstam recounts, 'the audience began to giggle' at the obvious discomfort they saw in this man acting out a part that was entirely foreign to him. It was enough to spark the real Bo into life. 'Suddenly Bo Diddley went into his song about the heroic Bo Diddley,' while the orchestra continued to play Rogers and Hammerstein.[3]

While *The Ed Sullivan Show*, with its eye on ratings, would continue to feature rock 'n' roll, the seemingly irascible host did not understand that this music, perhaps to a much greater extent than the music of previous generations, was bound up in the personality, appearance and public image of the performer themselves. Bo Diddley having a giant hit with a song called 'Bo Diddley' was just the most obvious example of that fact. This was a music of self-creation, itself brought about through its enactment in performance. There was no faking it. These weren't mere entertainers who had learned to knock off the standards; they were people possessed by a spirit that was channelled through not only words and music but physical embodiment. To be the embodiment of a one-off, to be original – no matter how slight the musical, stylistic or sartorial departure from others – was what drove rock 'n' roll's stylistic innovations, both then and into the future.

While Diddley would not reappear on *The Ed Sullivan Show* after this performance, Elvis Presley would be able to use the show as a means of translating his status as a music phenomenon into film stardom. Presley became one of the most iconic figures of the twentieth century by virtue of the power of television and film, and not least by the way that these changed, and were ultimately transformed themselves by, rock 'n' roll. As the most visually alluring manifestation of the new music that had captivated the young, he embodied something that they were only too ready to gobble up. He was wholesome enough and more acceptable to advertisers than his black musical contemporaries like Bo Diddley. Change was slow in the world of television in the 1950s. The three networks that broadcast in the USA did not yet reach the entire nation, and the medium seemed strangely attached to the past, acting as the focus for a kind of 'collective memory', evident in the countless western series about cowboys on the range that filled out its prime-time schedules.[4]

But the elements of R&B and hillbilly music that Presley blended were a unique creation, something inflected with his own personality and performance style. This was also a time when all of the major emerging figures – Chuck Berry, Little Richard, Jerry Lee Lewis and Presley – sold records in huge quantities to both black and white audiences alike, despite the airwaves being essentially segregated. This early crossover appeal was dramatized in the 2008 film *Cadillac Records* – a fictionalized account of Chess Records – when Chuck Berry's 'Maybelline' is played by DJ Alan Freed in a moment that integrates the airwaves. When we later see Berry (portrayed by Mos Def) turn up for a club date he is refused entry because he is black and therefore couldn't possibly be *the* Chuck Berry. 'Chuck Berry is a country and western singer,' the club owner says, as he stands in the way of Berry's bemused bandmates.

The crossover appeal of rock 'n' roll reflected its mixed origins and presented a challenge to radio formatting along racial lines that had long kept black and white artists within separate listening spaces. The power of television, as far as rock 'n' roll went, was not fully apparent, but what it did offer was a reach that far surpassed America's system of regional radio licensing and broadcasting, along with its segregated broadcast audiences.

In 1948, there were an estimated 500,000 television sets in America, mostly confined to cities in the north, and this was to increase dramatically to 19 million sets in 1952.[5] By the time Presley made his first appearance on *The Ed Sullivan Show* in 1956, he was watched by an estimated audience of 60 million viewers (the population of the United States was around 166 million), which accounted for 82.7 per cent of the total American TV audience.[6] Together, the new music and television would spearhead the advance of rock 'n' roll as a cultural phenomenon in that decade and eventually spawn a host of 'rocksploitation' movies released before 1960.[7] These would feature cameos or performance interludes from the likes of Chuck Berry, Little Richard, Frankie Lymon & The Teenagers, Gene Vincent, Fats Domino,

Mos Def as Chuck Berry in *Cadillac Records* (2008) tries to prove his identity after being refused entry to a club where he was booked to perform.

The Platters, Eddie Cochran and countless artists lesser-known today. But of all these, only Presley would end up a movie star, albeit one who seemed to feature in a new and unusual genre that could only be described as The Elvis Movie.

Under the guidance of his manager, Colonel Tom Parker, Presley was nothing if not willing to do what it took to make it in the movies. As the living embodiment of rock's youthful exuberance, not to mention its best-selling artist, Presley had no match as a saleable commodity. While his early regional fame in the South had much to do with the fact that he was a white man singing in a style more often heard on R&B records, Presley's nationwide appeal quickly went beyond the merely musical and became inseparable from the way he looked and moved, as well as the fact that 'he became the subject of extraordinary female sexual fascination' for a significantly large segment of the population, who, according to the prevailing norms, 'were not supposed to express or even possess such sexual desires'.[8] Beyond the musical world of Memphis, where he cut his first sides with Sun Records, the Elvis of the early days struck a pretty unusual figure; as alien or 'out-there' looking in his own time as anyone who followed in later decades was in theirs. He 'bought his clothes at Lansky's on Beale Street', Stanley Booth writes, 'where the black pimps traded'.[9] He was about as weird looking as it was possible to get on nationwide TV in 1955, although in his hometown of Memphis he was no longer such a freak: 'Duck-tails were becoming common, along with sideburns and a change in the style of dress. What had been latent in the relationship between black and white music was becoming overt; each was groping for the other.'[10] Frank Sinatra, who had inspired a passion-ate following the decade before, used his appeal as a springboard to Hollywood, mapping out a path that Presley could follow. One major difference was that Presley came up through a different route, one that existed beyond the purview of mainstream entertainment, defined by regional influences and entrepreneurs like Sam Phillips, who ran the Memphis Recording Service where Presley was discovered. Like many of these figures who released records on independent labels, he was a *sui generis* character. In the words of one witness, Presley and his like were people who seemed to have 'come in on the midnight train from nowhere ... it was like they came from outer space'.[11]

The elements of self-creation in rock 'n' roll can be very subtle, and they manifest themselves in a number of ways, but in performance and recording it was often found in the kind of off-the-cuff, on-the-spot improvisation that gave the records the stamp of the real that could recommend them to an exploding teenage audience on the lookout for excitement.

The moment of Presley's discovery in 1954 by Sam Phillips in Memphis is found in a number of the screen recreations of the singer's early days. It is there in the 2005 miniseries *Elvis* (with Jonathan Rhys Meyers as Presley); in the inventive 1990 series also titled *Elvis* (with a lookalike Michael St Gerard in the role), which utilized a home-movie aesthetic to make the viewer feel as if they were watching the actual events; and finally in *Elvis*, a 1979 TV movie directed by John Carpenter, with Kurt Russell in the starring role (the only actor to have both played Elvis and appeared alongside him in film, as he did as a child star in *It Happened at the World's Fair* in 1963). The key moment in Presley's self-creation as seen in these versions of his rise is the moment of validation that occurs when Phillips realizes that there is more to this young singer than meets the eye. Presley had been fascinated with 'Mystery Train' by Little Junior Parker, a record that Phillips had produced in 1953 and which was a big hit on the

Memphis radio show *Red, Hot and Blue*, which Presley listened to religiously, becoming acquainted with the blues and R&B stylings of the likes of 'Louis Jordan, Wynonie Harris, Rosetta Tharpe, Roy Brown, Big Boy Crudup'.[12] Some say that Presley had already learned 'Mystery Train' by the time he came to record a novelty record for his mother's birthday at the same Memphis studio in 1953, although Phillips had no inkling of this at the time.[13] Whatever the origins of the decision to cut this song, it is on the Presley version as recorded by Phillips – and released in mid-1955 – that we can hear some of what the later movie representations of that moment seem ultimately unable to recreate. The Presley version is not as heavy on the rhythm as Parker's version. The latter is also built on an instrumentation of piano and saxophone. Presley's version is more country, more suggestive in its sound of the lithe figure Presley cut as he sashayed across the stage, as seen in 1955 newsreel footage. It achieves a strange kind of weightlessness, more of a glider than the train of the title in terms of its ability to convey a sense of movement. As Larry Birnbaum writes, it was 'smoother, faster and more mellifluous than Parker's, dispensing with the Blue Flames' chugging rhythm and train-whistle sax'.[14] For years afterwards Phillips would say it was the greatest thing he ever did with Presley. And therein lies one of the main problems of translating rock 'n' roll to screen as re-enactment: nothing but the real, live thing can adequately mimic those personal touches, such as the sound of Presley yelping in delight as the recording fades out. That sound is the spirit of rock 'n' roll.

Elvis Conquers America

The peak of Elvis mania before he disappeared into the army in early 1958 was played out on his tours of the United States between 1955 and 1957, and not much evidenced on screen. In August 1956, before anyone dared label him the King of Rock 'n' Roll, one local paper, observing the effect that he had on teenage girls, described him as the 'king of cacophony', the sound of his performance often being buried beneath the screaming voices of the kind of unhinged audiences not found in the TV studios.[15] The inability or unwillingness to convey precisely what his appeal was perhaps reflected the lack of understanding that defined the so-called generation gap that emerged with rock 'n' roll and would continue to separate the young from their parents' generation in the decades ahead. Presley's 'tortured moans', one report complained, 'have found a vast audience in a tin-eared nation'.[16]

Describing the kind of sight that television would soon decide to censor when *The Ed Sullivan Show* filmed Elvis from the waist up, the *San Francisco Chronicle*'s reporter noted that it was his legs that drove them wild:

> The crowd was quiet as he sang, in lyrics verging on the unintelligible – until one of his black-denim clad knees shot out. When the screams subsided, the right knee picked up where the other left off and gradually, as the movement spread upward, the famous voice was lost in bedlam.[17]

Something of this dangerous animalistic phenomenon – minus that amped-up atmosphere created by the huge crowds – was what was seen on TV when Presley appeared, first on Tommy and Jimmy Dorsey's *Stage Show*, then on *The Steve Allen Show* and finally *The Milton Berle Show*. From late January 1956, his first TV appearance, to his July turn on Allen's show, Presley made nine nationwide television appearances, with viewing figures rising all the time. The Dorsey brothers' *Stage Show*, for example, was of a variety that belonged in an era that was now about to be eclipsed by rock 'n' roll. Its hosts Tommy and Jimmy Dorsey were well-known bandleaders in their own right – Frank Sinatra made his name singing with the Tommy Dorsey band – with Tommy once the best-selling artist on RCA Records until Presley came along to claim that distinction.

On that first appearance, on 28 January 1956, Presley performed two Big Joe Turner songs: 'Shake, Rattle and Roll' and 'Flip, Flop and Fly'. Musicians in the Dorsey band, whose musical talents had been formed in the 1930s and '40s, fell about laughing at what they were hearing and seeing during Presley's rehearsals. They thought he was a rube. 'He looked dirty,' one said.[18] The way he dressed and the way he wore his hair, when taken alongside the 'leering smile' and 'unabashed sexuality' of

Elvis Presley and his trio on the Dorsey brothers' *Stage Show* (1956).

his movements, left TV audiences 'alternately shocked, terrified, and delighted'.[19] Clearly, then, a winning prospect under any circumstances. It would be some months before most of those who had laughed and mocked came to realize that Presley in 1956 was a cultural watershed. A generation gap had appeared; but it was more than that, as one of Dorsey's biographers noted: 'It was the raw against the cooked, postwar prosperity versus prewar propriety, an atomic burst of sexual vitality obliterating the palled remnants of Depression-era glamour.'[20]

In the wake of this TV success, Presley's manager was quick to run flattering 'thank you' adverts in the trades – anything that he thought would move things in favour of his artist – while also using it as an opportunity to state for the public record what a success Elvis on television had proven to be, despite the wave of disapproval coming from some quarters. 'Thanks "Mr. Television" Milton Berle, for having me on your show,' ran one advert, signed with the words: 'Elvis Presley – The Nation's Only Atomic Powered Singer.' From here onwards, Presley's name would be lodged in the national consciousness with an image derived in equal parts from sound and moving pictures. It seemed inevitable that the exoticism he exuded would find a place on the big screen.

But the show that pushed his popularity over the edge was the biggest of them all, *The Ed Sullivan Show*, the site of the Bo Diddley showdown a year earlier. Fronted by the eponymous host, a halting, wooden screen presence who seemed to lapse easily into a grumpy demeanour and who shifted stiffly around the stage as he introduced the acts, it was regularly watched by tens of millions across the United States. 'His body language was that of someone frozen and not yet thawed out,' wrote David Halberstam of Sullivan.[21] But it didn't matter: he was the king of Sunday night TV. Over the next decade and a half, in fact, his show would provide one of the main showcases for any rock act intent on making it to the top of the charts. Such was its status as a gateway to massive audiences that many performers felt that it was easier to go along with whatever Sullivan wanted, simply as a means of gaining nationwide exposure.

Sullivan paid a record-breaking $50,000 for three Elvis appearances after he was deluged with requests from fans all over the country. Before the agreement was reached to book him, Sullivan personally checked out the supposedly risqué act by looking over what was known as a kinescope – a recording of a broadcast, made by filming the TV monitor – of Presley's appearance on the Dorsey show that had so outraged some, before declaring that he 'found nothing objectionable' in it.[22] No doubt his opinion would have been influenced by the fact that *The Steve Allen Show* received such a boost to its viewing figures after Presley's appearance that it was enough to temporarily knock Sullivan's own show from the top of the ratings chart for the first time.[23]

But when he appeared on *The Ed Sullivan Show* for the first time, watched by those 60 million Americans, it was once again the image of his sexually charged gyrating that left its mark on the TV audience, prompting further dire warnings of his baleful influence on the young from ministers, teachers and other protectors of public morality. The rock writer Richard Meltzer later identified the seismic effect of Presley's TV performances as the 'birth of a revolutionary consciousness' that swept through his school:

> everybody in the home room would go *nuts* reliving
> it the next morning. Usually we'd file in stoically with
> our hundred pounds of books ready for another day

of torture but after an Elvis appearance there'd be a buzz . . . Black kids, white kids, Puerto Ricans, everybody was uncontrollable, it was total anarchy.[24]

Perhaps most famous of all of these performances was the last of *The Ed Sullivan Show* engagements, when the network decided that it would be prudent to defuse the effect Presley was having with his hootchy-kootchy moves. The only solution was to position the cameras to cut off that which offended the most – his legs – and film Elvis from the waist up.

Presley soon moved to Hollywood and appeared in a handful of films before the end of the decade, including *Love Me Tender* (1956), *Loving You* and *Jailhouse Rock* in 1957, and *King Creole* in 1958 – dramatic roles that exploited his popularity as a singer and appealed mainly to his female following. As the music historian Michael Ochs recalled of seeing *Love Me Tender* as a young man, when Elvis suffered his first screen death, 'all the males in the audience cheered, and all the females cried.'[25]

Both *Loving You* and *Jailhouse Rock* present versions of the rock 'n' roll origin story, with the former being almost a biopic but with the names changed. Crucially, though, Presley was not playing himself but rather a Presley-like singer on the rise. It was yet another example – like Ed Sullivan trying to make Bo Diddley sing a Perry Como hit – of the entertainment business not really grasping what made rock such a potent force, which was the fact that it was not an act. Each time Presley appeared in the guise of a cowboy, racing car driver, playboy or other character, in the dozens of movies he would make, it actually diminished his potency as a rock 'n' roll figure.

In *Jailhouse Rock* he plays Vince Everett, a regular working guy who is goaded into a bar-room brawl, accidentally landing

Presley suffers his first screen death in *Love Me Tender* (1956).

fatal blows on his tormentor. In prison he finds himself sharing a cell with a once successful but now washed-up country singer, Hunk Houghton. Vince takes an interest in the guitar that hangs on the wall of their cell and reveals a talent for singing. When a local TV station plans a visit to the prison to look at the life of the inmates, Vince agrees to perform in a show that is being put together by Hunk for the cameras. When the broadcast goes out, Vince is a hit with viewers and receives sacks of fan mail, which he doesn't see until he is released from prison some months later. Hunk, who works in the prison mail room, has seen the impact that Vince has had and decides to play up his connections in the music world to sign him up to a partnership agreement before he gets wind of how popular he already is, and 'talks him into signing an exclusive contract allowing for a 50-50 split of either's future earnings'.[26] Vince, unaware that Hunk's star is falling just as his own is rising, signs the contract. This theme of a rapacious manager or similar figure out to take whatever they can get would recur in rock movies over the decades, as we will see.

Presley's 1950s film efforts were arguably his best, however, and would give way to a veritable conveyer belt of formulaic movies throughout the 1960s; following his spell of almost two years in the U.S. Army between 1958 and 1960, three per year was not unusual. For the TV audiences denied sight of his gyrations in 1956, there would always be the key musical set piece of *Jailhouse Rock* to keep them happy. Alongside a few other scenes – a surly, guitar-smashing, rude Elvis, and a sexually precocious Elvis who comes on to women with the immortal words, 'it's just the beast in me' – it is the best sequence in the film. Presley (as Everett) performs the title song on a spare set constructed of jailhouse doors in an expertly choreographed number that – hootchy-kootchy moves aside – would not be out of place in many Hollywood musicals of this or previous eras.

Jukebox Musicals

Beyond the confected dramas of the Elvis movies, the first rock films had no real interest in the actual origins of the music; that would come much later. Perhaps there is no reason why they should have, given that it was viewed as merely another passing fad. In most of the rock films made between 1956 and 1958 – the point at which the phenomenon looked to be on the wane – the most iconic figures of the age were represented in isolation from the real context in which they had developed as artists. In an important sense, what did make it onto screen in the 1950s was often a diluted version of the real thing.

The one attempt to present the discovery of rock 'n' roll was 1956's *Rock Around the Clock*, which – playing up an aspect of its faddishness – identified the music with a dance craze. It was not the first time that the sound of Bill Haley had appeared on film. *Blackboard Jungle*, released a year earlier, was the first film to use rock 'n' roll in a cinematic context, becoming a point of origin for a whole genre of films that revolved around the theme of teenage delinquency. The movie skilfully deployed Bill Haley & His Comets' 'Rock Around the Clock' (1954) to maximum effect, placing it in an entirely novel context that would effectively shape the public perception of rock 'n' roll in the years to come.

The film opens with a scrolling text of white letters on a black background, mimicking a school lesson on the nature of the problem with which the film is concerned. As the screed rolls up the screen, a simple snare drum rattles out a military-style rhythm, gradually transforming into something looser and less martial, more akin to the kind of beat that might be heard in a nightclub. Then, with a double crack of the snare, it merges into the beat that begins 'Rock Around the Clock', and the screen opens out on to a schoolyard scene. Standing outside the building is a new teacher, Mr Dadier (played by Glenn Ford), apprehensively eyeing up the situation. Two teenage toughs let out a lewd whistle in his direction – an implicit challenge to his masculinity. Off in another corner, a gaggle of delinquents are throwing dice against a wall. While the setting takes form before our eyes, 'Rock Around the Clock' is not merely projected outward, towards the viewer; it actually seems to permeate the atmosphere of the schoolyard on screen.[27]

Before Dadier, whom the kids will disrespectfully address as 'Daddy-O', finally begins his first day in the classroom, he meets with some of the other teachers in the school gym; as one of them limbers up for the day on a punchbag, they discuss problems in the classroom:

'You can't teach a disorderly mob.'
　'That's right, you've got to have discipline, and that means obedience.'
　'How you gonna get that?'
　'With a ruler . . .'
　'Take a ruler to one of these delinquents, he'll beat you to death with it. This is the garbage can of the educational system.'

Rock Around the Clock's treatment of Haley as the source of the music that instigates the dance craze is standard Hollywood fare: the star out of nowhere who hits the big time due to the intervention of canny, business-minded talent scouts at small-town sock hop in some anonymous part of Middle America. A band promoter and a friend, on the lookout for new talent, go along to a dance one evening to check out the new sound that has captured the locals. As they approach the dance hall, Bill Haley & His Comets kick off 'See You Later, Alligator', with the saxophone blowing out the song's main riff. Cocking an ear to this, the unconvinced promoter says to his friend: 'They're slaughtering cattle – did you hear that?'

Inside, bemused by the sound, they notice young couples are spinning each other around the room, the men throwing female partners in the air, dragging them through their legs, all done with wild abandon to accompany the music. 'What is that outfit playing up there?' one says to the other. 'I don't know. It isn't boogie, it isn't jive, and it isn't swing. It's kinda all of them.' He approaches the commotion in front of the band and comes face to face with a girl who at that moment has just been swung over the shoulder of her dance partner, her head dangling upside down, and asks her the same question. 'It's *rock and roll*, brother, and we're *rockin'* tonight!' she exclaims.

Bill Haley's most enduring record from this point until he passed away at the age of 55 in 1981 was the title song, 'Rock Around the Clock'. When it had first been released in 1954 and become a minor hit, the record label, as they often did in those days, identified the dance that was supposed to accompany it when it was spun at record hops. At the time of its original release, it was – strange as it now seems – identified as a 'foxtrot', a dance that did indeed conform to the four beats to the bar that was characteristic of rock 'n' roll music, but which had reached the peak of its popularity in the 1930s. If the moves that were choreographed in the film seem far from that, it was still true that Haley really had one foot in the pre-rock swing era. Slimmed-down bands like the trio of Bill Black, Scotty Moore and D. J. Fontana that accompanied Presley – with guitars becoming more prominent than the saxophone and other brass instruments that had driven swing-era bands – also made rock 'n' roll visually distinct. A singer who played guitar with the instrument slung round the neck, even if it was often little more than a prop (as with Elvis), could move and strike poses that just weren't available to other instrumentalists. Haley himself looked old enough to have been a holdover from another era; although almost middle-aged in appearance, he was only thirty years old. There was none of the blazing sex appeal of Presley, whose 'dark, heavy features, greasy black hair, and surly expression became elements of an image that producers everywhere sought or attempted to re-create'.[28]

In the earliest example of the way in which rock 'n' roll would become bound to its own representation on film, *Rock Around the*

Clock presents what amounts to a set of instructions on how to behave when the music kicks off, even inspiring cinema audiences to get out of their seats and start dancing and jiving in the aisles. The film makes the most of the way that the camera could capture the action on the dance floor from numerous angles to see more than a mere throng of bodies – it saw from above, below and even right in the midst of the commotion, with its pictures revealing how the novel dance steps and acrobatic moves were executed.

If this fictional discovery of rock 'n' roll was somewhat fanciful, in truth there was little else to go on by way of evidence, and the makers of early rock films 'had no inkling of how to connect the story organically with the rock acts'.[29] In the aftermath of *Rock Around the Clock*'s popularity, however, there followed a succession of cash-in 'jukebox musicals': *Don't Knock the Rock* (1956), *Shake, Rattle and Rock!* (1956), *Mister Rock and Roll* (1957) and *Go, Johnny, Go!* (1959), all of which registered appearances by major new performers of the day. 'In contrast to the traditional screen musical, in which the songs had at least a formal relevance to the development of a narrative,' Charlie Gillett wrote, these films offered little beyond 'a succession of filmed singing performances, strung together on a tenuous story', such as teenagers seeing rock 'n' roll on TV.[30]

Performances like Chuck Berry's 'You Can't Catch Me' in *Rock, Rock, Rock!* (1956), which featured the performer essentially miming and acting out the song, were precursors of the short clips that would later be made as TV appearance stand-ins. The storyline of another 1956 film, *Don't Knock the Rock*, revolved around attempts to bar rock 'n' roll as a consequence of the public disorder that it inspired, with the music all but banned until the star of the film, rock DJ Alan Freed, convinces everyone that it is a force for good. On the day after the film opened in New York, the papers carried a handful of stories about this phenomenon and the speed at which it was spreading everywhere. One piece likened it to a kind of 'medieval lunacy' and the so-called St Vitus dance, 'its victims breaking into dancing and being unable to stop'.[31] Around the globe, in London, Sydney, Australia, Jakarta, Indonesia and Japan, audiences were gripped with the rock 'n' roll frenzy. Even the Soviet Union could not remain immune from the spread of this contagion. 'In Leningrad,' another of these stories revealed, 'recordings by Elvis Presley cut on discarded X-ray plates sell for $12.50.'[32] The *New York Times* film critic Bosley Crowther reported from the opening night of *Don't Knock the Rock*, an event followed by an Alan Freed-curated concert, stating that somehow, amid the tumult of dancing in the aisles and fighting for seats, 'the roof stayed on': 'What is 'rock 'n' roll'? Well, to one comparatively middle-aged man who made the awful

LaVern Baker and band in the 1956 'jukebox musical' *Rock Rock Rock!*

mistake of grabbing a seat down front, it goes thump, *thump*, thump, *thump*.'[33] Parents the world over would have recognized what he was getting at. But the fact was that the teenage audience for rock film represented a new and lucrative market once it became apparent that this was no flash-in-the-pan trend. And where there was a dollar to be made, there was no shortage of entrepreneurs looking for a way to exploit the situation. The year 1956 would be a pivotal one in the story of rock film. In the wake of hit records that had elevated Elvis Presley, Chuck Berry, Little Richard and others to national fame throughout 1955, it was clear that major studios – which had always drawn on a talent pool of musical performers in previous decades – began to see the commercial potential of these new acts. At the same time, in the face of what would soon become a rising tide of media hysteria about the evils of rock 'n' roll, *Billboard*, the trade journal of the record industry, was about the only outlet in which the new music was discussed in a non-sensationalist manner, its writers and industry analysts keen to try to figure out what this emerging style – and, more specifically, its market – was going to be. 'The shouting and tumult has died, but rhythm and blues or, as the teen-agers call it, rock and roll, has not departed,' one February 1956 report claimed: 'Rather, it may be stated that it has achieved respectability. The true measure of this development is the extent to which the idiom is being used in more or less pedestrian areas of the entertainment and advertising world.'[34]

Rock Around the Clock was the most significant marker in the 'mass acceptance for rock and roll'.[35] Yet the success of rock film was still taken to be indicative of little more than an explosion of energy that was bound to subside.[36] Aside from the music itself, which sold in vast quantities (Presley sold more than 15 million records in the United States alone in 1956), everything from jeans and other clothing to rugs for dancing on and, indeed, dance lessons to learn the moves that were so expertly deployed on *Rock Around the Clock* were being sold to an audience of rapacious teenage consumers that had snapped up 'more than $20,000,000 worth of Presley products' alone, not including his records. These included:

> jackets, skirts, T-shirts, jeans, hats, nylon scarves, charm bracelets, sneakers and nylon stretch bobby sox . . . Chain, drug and novelty stores now feature lipsticks in autographed cases bearing color names for such Presley hit tunes as Hound Dog orange, Love You fuchsia, and Heartbreak pink.[37]

The financial rewards for tapping such a market underlined that whatever else it was, rock 'n' roll was also a new consumer phenomenon, driven in large part by film and television. 'Rhythm and blues', the older term that had been used to describe many artists now assimilated within this newer and more marketing-friendly category of rock 'n' roll, was not wrapped up in the teenage consumer market in the same way as rock 'n' roll would become. Rock clearly appealed to an audience that might be sold numerous commercial spin-offs from records and films.[38]

It was a process that effectively domesticated and repackaged the music in ways that not only met the needs of Hollywood but identified it as something to be targeted at teenagers. Yet, at the same time, the cinema experience, in terms of its blend of image and sound, presented a much better way of experiencing rock 'n' roll as a visual phenomenon than anything besides witnessing it in person. Cinema in the 1950s has to be seen as existing alongside the TV broadcast, which, with all of its attendant technological limitations, was far inferior – the small screens, the black-and-white images, the poor signal reception and how all this affected the presentation of the total package. In the cinema, things could be seen on a bigger scale, heard at higher volume and expanded into something unforgettable.

This was best illustrated in Frank Tashlin's 1956 musical comedy *The Girl Can't Help It*, ostensibly the story of a gangster's attempt to turn his talentless girlfriend (played by platinum-blonde bombshell Jayne Mansfield) into a nightclub singing star. As Mansfield threatens to burst out of her dress, a host of rockers burst into life, assisted by the widest of Cinemascope presentations of the alluring Mansfield and her glamorous surroundings, with the Technicolor pushed to a gaudy maximum. In terms of style alone, the film might be described as 'loud', and it was therefore perfect as a vehicle for rock 'n' roll. Little Richard, Eddie Cochran, The Platters, Fats Domino, Gene Vincent & His Blue Caps and others provided a soundtrack to match. The musical star of the bunch, though, was the irrepressible Little Richard, whose repertoire of wild shrieks and falsetto whoops matched the visual excesses of the film, commanding this expanded screen in a way that few others could have.

Content, presentation and a good deal more irreverence in character and plot made *The Girl Can't Help It* one of the quintessential 1950s rock movies. Others never quite delivered a screen experience that could match the thrill of rock 'n' roll in purely musical terms. Sometimes they couldn't even match their own publicity. A case in point would be *High School Confidential* (1958), for which an impressive print ad appeared in the newspapers the week of its release and screamed the promise, 'EXPLODING TOMORROW . . . A Teacher's Nightmare. A Teen-Age Jungle'. Yet in truth the film was a mundane tale of teenage misbehaviour that featured a comparatively tame Jerry Lee Lewis in a cameo role shoehorned in as a gimmick to sell tickets. This was doubly unfortunate considering that no one so embodied the sense of anarchy that haunted parental nightmares about rock than the self-styled 'Killer'. The mere mention of his name was enough to spread alarm in the nation. When the *New York Times* reported the return of Lewis to America after he was chased out of England following the revelation that he had married his fourteen-year-old cousin, it ran with the headline 'JERRY LEE LEWIS IS BACK', which some thought rather appeared to suggest something like 'the return of a viral strain'.[39] The writer Nick Tosches recalled that the mother of one of his teenage friends would totally lose control at the mere mention of Lewis's name, describing him as 'the garbage of the earth'.[40] And so it came to be, Tosches adds, that 'of all the rock-and-roll creatures, he projected the most hellish persona. He was feared more than the rest, and hated more too. Preachers railed against him.'[41]

Something of this Jerry Lee Lewis is seen in the 1980s biopic *Great Balls of Fire!*, in which the Killer is imitated with demented enthusiasm by Dennis Quaid and seen as prone to tip pianos off the edge of the stage just to get a reaction from the audience. The film's most iconic scene, trading on one of those near mythical rock 'n' roll moments, shows Lewis casually set his piano on fire – almost a decade before Hendrix did the same with his guitar at the Monterey Pop Festival in 1967, itself one of the iconic moments in rock film. In Lewis's case, such wanton destruction was the result of being slighted by Alan Freed, who had preferred Chuck Berry over Lewis to close out one of his jamborees at the Brooklyn Paramount Theater.[42] At this concert, with his wild hair falling over his face, and wearing a 'jacket trimmed in the fake fur of some jungle cat', Lewis tore through hits such as 'Breathless' and 'Whole Lotta Shakin' Goin' On' with additional fury.[43] The audience went wild, and police began to gather at the front of the stage to discourage a rush to the front. Then, in the words of Lewis biographer Rick Bragg, 'he reached inside the piano, took a small Coke bottle of clear liquid, and poured gasoline across the top of the instrument.'[44] In *Great Balls of Fire!*, Quaid, as Lewis, casually sets it alight and continues to pound away as the flames rise before finally ambling offstage, his head held aloft as if he has won the school prize for student of the year.

BY 1963, the motorcycle outlaw look that Marlon Brando had popularized ten years earlier in *The Wild One* was recontextualized in a rather different kind of film that fused rock music and moving image to make something that had never been seen before. Kenneth Anger's *Scorpio Rising*, shot in dreamlike colour, presented an occult vision of rock 'n' roll, homoeroticism and

Dennis Quaid as Jerry Lee Lewis in *Great Balls of Fire* (1989). 'He set the piano aflame and the kids went utterly, magically berserk with the frenzy of it all.'

biker culture. This short film, all of 28 minutes long, mixed images of a Brooklyn motorcycle club shot over a period of several months with the sounds of Elvis, The Crystals, Ricky Nelson and others, mixing in images of Adolf Hitler, Jesus and Brando in *The Wild One* for added hallucinogenic effect. Unlike the Hollywood film-makers, Anger – who grew up in the Hollywood milieu (and authored the scandalous tome *Hollywood Babylon*) – was not trying to make a buck from rock 'n' roll. The only thing he was selling, he later said, was Aleister Crowley, whom he described as 'the 20th-century's most misunderstood genius'.[45]

Through its use of music, *Scorpio Rising* helped introduce the developing underground cinema to 1960s audiences for whom music would become much more securely established in a developing 'counterculture' and the attitudes and values it espoused as the decade rolled on.[46] It was a work that offered a new glimpse of the cinematic possibilities of the music once freed from the strictures of the lip-sync as the method of representing musical performance on screen. Its influence would extend far further than any rock movie of the previous decade, simply by virtue of the fact that it influenced a generation of rock fans who went on to become film-makers.

Before *Scorpio Rising*, when a song or a musical number was heard in film it always had to be seen; performers sang, mimed, danced and sought to animate a song as a performance that was acted out. In this respect, the early rock 'n' roll films had much in common with the kind of musicals that had already proved popular, the star vehicles that a Judy Garland or Gene Kelly would be seen in.[47] The Presley movies, for instance, could be seen as a simple continuation of that earlier kind of film musical. The Civil War-era Presley character in *Love Me Tender* pulls out a guitar and breaks into song in the parts of the film where the

Kenneth Anger's 1963 short film *Scorpio Rising* marked the beginning of a new era in rock film, with the music released from the constraints of being used to accompany visuals of its performers and refashioned into something more phantasmagorical. While harking back to the more innocent rock of the mid-1950s and early '60s, the transgressive sexuality of *Scorpio Rising* cast the music in a new light not only in terms of how it would be used in cinema of the 1960s and beyond, but in its influence on the later decadent mood of rock.

producers felt it appropriate to shoehorn in some music to please the fans.

Such uses of rock 'n' roll did a good job of assimilating the music into the entertainment mainstream, drawing it back to long-established formulae. In the period between around 1958 and 1963, aside from faddish beach movies and several Chubby Checker dance-related vehicles (*Hey, Let's Twist!* and *Twist Around the Clock*, both 1961, and *Don't Knock the Twist*, 1962), Hollywood studios were not lining up to make films about the essentially faceless songwriters and producers who were the unseen driving force behind much of what counted as rock 'n' roll. It would not be until decades later that this period was reflected in a number of film dramas, such as *The Wanderers* (1979), in which East Coast rock of the kind pioneered by The Four Seasons made up the soundtrack to the life of a street gang; *The Idolmaker* (1980), loosely based on the rise of Fabian; *Grace of My Heart* (1996), loosely modelled on the career of Carole King; and *Telstar: The Joe Meek Story* (2008).

The most notable of these semi-anonymous songwriters who were dominating the charts in the first years of the 1960s was Phil Spector. Spector was the most influential figure in this period, but he was not a performer. This meant that if the audience had any awareness that it was him behind the various vocal groups who recorded the songs that he wrote and produced, it was still nothing like the kind of recognition that could be considered translatable to the screen. He was, nonetheless, the brains behind songs like The Crystals' 'He's a Rebel', used to brilliant effect in *Scorpio Rising*. It was only historical distance that made Spector, and other songwriters of the era associated with the Brill Building hit factory in New York, figures of dramatic interest in film.

In *Grace of My Heart*, a Spector-like writer and producer, Joel Milner (played by John Turturro), brings a promising new songwriter, Denise Waverly (the Carole King character, played by Illeana Douglas), into the Brill Building fold, where writers working alone and in pairs in cramped little rooms knock out songs for vocal groups. Waverly, we learn, has already been rejected in her efforts to make it as a performer, but is persuaded to forget about her singing ambitions for the time being. She is a writer, and that is a better gig than being the singer of someone else's songs. 'You're either a singer or a writer,' Milner tells her. 'You can't be both.'

Theirs was the music that Kenneth Anger took – music perhaps not so burdened with the image of its performers – to push his film-making further into the realms of the 'magick' that he pursued as an adherent of Crowley. What he showed was how the music could be reimagined in combination with carefully chosen visuals. His interest was in exploring and plunging the viewer into a place where fantasy and reality might collide to produce the desired magickal effect, a psycho-sexual revelation. Beneath the Crowleyesque and homoerotic invitation, the biker symbolism was drenched in the most intense colours, allowing it to open up another, more ambiguous perspective on rock 'n' roll delinquency.[48]

The film had an immediate influence on New York's avant-garde after it premiered there in October 1963. As the *New York Times* reported in a 1967 profile of Anger, the film attracted a diverse metropolitan crowd of 'in-the-groove psychoanalysts, artists and art critics'.[49] Perhaps more significant, however, were the 'hairdressers, dress designers and decorators' who carried the visual influence of the film into their own realms beyond the movie theatre:

Almost overnight, display windows of elegant uptown boutiques had wicked motorcycle chains throw over plush velvet couches, and models in couture dresses, poised between the handlebars of motorcycles, casting enigmatic glances at dangerous-looking drivers.[50]

Scorpio Rising may have had more of an influence in these artistic and intellectual circles than among devotees of rock music at the time. But along with some of his other short films, such as *Kustom Kar Kommandos* (1965), the marriage of music and image would be something that Anger continued to pursue through closer connections to rock artists of the 1960s and '70s, and some would accord him the status of 'the inventor of MTV and the music video'.[51] Anger, then living in London, would become acquainted with The Rolling Stones in the late 1960s. They could be fleetingly glimpsed in his film *Invocation of My Demon Brother* (1969), an eleven-minute piece for which Mick Jagger supplied an experimental synthesizer soundtrack. Anger's major work, *Lucifer Rising* (1980), completed over a span of two decades, was initially to be scored by Led Zeppelin's Jimmy Page – a fellow Crowleyite whom he met at an auction of Crowley artefacts – although in the end the Page soundtrack was never sufficiently finished enough to be used in the film.[52]

2

UNTAMED YOUTH

I n Britain, the way that showbusiness values were able to assert control over rock 'n' roll, such as it was, is laid out with cold precision in the 1959 film *Expresso Bongo*. Set amid the Soho traffic of strippers, musicians, record business hustlers and prostitutes, Laurence Harvey, as Johnny Jackson, finds his prize: a young singer whose trick is playing bongo drums. In a certain light, the bongo-bashing Bert Rudge (played by Cliff Richard), although slightly chubby-cheeked, has a touch of Presley about him, and Johnny soon wins him over with promises of fame.

Johnny, we learn, had been a musician in a jazz band himself, but that is over – all the youngsters are now interested in is the new music, rock 'n' roll. Like his real-life counterpart Larry Parnes, who bestowed his charges with showbiz names (Marty Wilde, Billy Fury, Vince Eager and so on), Johnny gives Bert his new showbiz name, Bongo Herbert, and tries to sign him up to a management contract. Bongo is all for it, but he is not yet an adult, which means his parents will have to sign the contract. Things don't go as planned, however, since Bongo's mother suspects that nothing good will come of it. 'I ain't signing. It's all a swindle,' she exclaims, 'whenever I sign, it's always a swindle.' Johnny instead persuades Bert to sign the contract. They will simply ignore the issue of his age – he will soon be eighteen anyway – and it is something that no one need ever find out about. 'From now on,' he tells the guileless Bongo, waving the contract in the air to ensure the

Laurence Harvey as dodgy impresario Johnny Jackson (centre, in hat) signs up teenage sensation Bongo Herbert (Cliff Richard, far right) in *Expresso Bongo* (1959).

ink is dry, 'half of everything you earn is going to go to you.' Just as Bongo's mother predicted, it's a swindle.

Expresso Bongo, which had originated as a stage musical a couple of years earlier, was regarded as a satirical sideswipe by the savvier old order at the new rock 'n' roll culture that had swept into Soho.[1] Unusually for a rock-'n'-roll-themed movie of the 1950s, it was X-rated by the censor (due to its images of semi-nude Soho nightclub dancers in performance), and, as such, was not primarily aimed at the younger teenage audience that made Cliff Richard so popular. Although not top billed, Richard was well on his way to becoming the British equivalent of Elvis – the movie-star Elvis, that is – and was quickly established as the most successful of Britain's early rock 'n' roll singers. He would take the starring roles in a couple of big hits that appeared in the coming years, including the *The Young Ones* (1961) and *Summer Holiday* (1963), but the arrival of The Beatles later that year completely altered the musical landscape in Britain, pushing the likes of Richard into more middle-of-the-road terrain.

The influence of *Expresso Bongo* came through the representation of the rapacious manager on the lookout for talent to work towards their own ends. Both Andrew Loog Oldham, who went on to manage The Rolling Stones, and Malcolm McLaren, who did likewise for the Sex Pistols, saw Laurence Harvey's cunning impresario as someone they could emulate as a means of working their way into the business. As Oldham later admitted, the film became almost like a guidebook of how to make it in the London music business. 'It showed you how to do it,' he admitted. 'I took it chapter and verse.' Thus, just as in the movie Johnny Jackson 'walks in and gets a deal for Bongo', Oldham said, he would 'walk in and get a deal for the Rolling Stones. It's as simple as that.'[2]

IN FEBRUARY 1964, film-makers Albert and David Maysles found themselves in a rush to get to the New York airport recently renamed in honour of the assassinated John F. Kennedy. They were on a mission to capture The Beatles on their first visit to America for England's Granada Television.

The subsequent scenes of chaos and ecstasy revealed in their documentary *What's Happening! The Beatles in the USA* (1964) were a precursor to what would be seen later in the year in the more conventionally fictionalized movie treatment of *A Hard Day's Night*. Both films serve to underline the unprecedented nature of the Beatlemania phenomenon while revealing something not seen in any rock film that had gone before – namely, real people. The way that the four subjects of this adulation managed to remain witty and irreverent as all those around them – from reporters to fans to the hyper-enthusiastic DJ Murray the K – fell under the sway of a collective madness is remarkable. The adulation was no doubt of the same order as that which greeted Elvis when he was making his way through the USA on his last concert tour in 1956. The one crucial difference was that Presley did not have a film crew following him to document the offstage moments for a TV audience.

What's Happening! was the first of a kind in that it was able to get up close and personal with its subject in a manner unlike any film before it, providing an insight into the maelstrom surrounding a rock 'n' roll band at the peak of fame. From inside the limousine that carried The Beatles through the streets of Manhattan, we see things briefly from their point of view. On the other side of the window, fans try to run alongside the car and are overtaken by mounted police galloping past. We see how fascinated the band members are with everything that is going on around them, as they mimic the sounds coming out of their portable radio. As they relax in their hotel suite, screaming fans gather outside. Later in the evening, Ringo dances wildly in a nightclub with local women.

The sense of the frantic pace of the life of a Beatle runs through the film, as the band are whisked between cities without even seeming to know where they are going. 'It's great to be in New York,' Ringo says to a reporter who thrusts a microphone at him as they disembark from their train, which has just arrived in Washington, DC. None of what we see in *What's Happening!* would have been possible without the Maysles' ability to move around unencumbered by the kind of bulky equipment that was normally used in film-making. They were able to 'go up and down elevators and in and out of hotel rooms with their portable equipment' just as quickly as their subjects.[3]

The most significant event for The Beatles on this first visit to America was the appearances they made on *The Ed Sullivan Show*, which now went out to even more households than it had eight years earlier when Presley caused a sensation on it. Due to union rules, the Maysles were not allowed to film inside CBS's Studio 50 theatre. They really wanted to get some behind-the-scenes footage of what was likely to be a major moment for The Beatles, but it was not to be; instead, they decided to search out nearby apartment blocks and gamble on being able to gain entry to a home where a family might be watching the show. In a street just around the corner from the theatre, they entered a building and began moving along the corridors, listening for the sound of Sullivan's show. Amazingly, they struck lucky with the first apartment door they knocked on and were able to enter and film the reaction of a father and his three teenage kids to The Beatles on television. It was one-of-a-kind footage of the moment when The Beatles went stratospheric in America and began – just like Elvis the decade before – their capture of America by TV.

The arrival of The Beatles in America was, for many, the moment that kick-started the 1960s. The sense of one thing coming to an end and another beginning was evident in some of the incidental footage that the Maysles brothers shot, and none more so than the sight of Phil Spector among the throng as the band disembark at the airport. If anyone might have laid claim to the rock 'n' roll crown in the years between 1958 and 1964 it was Spector, whose 'wall of sound' hits dominated the airwaves. As it happened, Spector was on The Beatles' flight from London, returning home after spending a few weeks on a promotional trip, during which he had spent time with the band as well as The Rolling Stones. In Regent Sound studio on London's Denmark Street, right in the heart of *Expresso Bongo* terrain, he joined the Stones and Oldham in the studio as they drank duty-free cognac that another visitor, Gene Pitney, had brought to the session, while the band cut their next single, 'Not Fade Away'.[4] Spector was interested in licensing the Stones' records for release in America on his own Philles label and had become friendly with Oldham during his stay in London. During the session he couldn't help himself and started making suggestions to Oldham and the group. He told them to add maracas to the song. Somewhere in the mix, Spector himself is there adding to the percussion by 'tapping a coin on the cognac bottle'.[5]

Spector knew what was stirring in Britain and thought The Beatles had the favour of the gods. The band had already probed him for details of what to expect when they went to America and wanted him on their flight, where they could get more information out of him.[6] Spector had a fear of flying, and, paying heed to his superstitious nature, decided that it would be a good idea to travel with The Beatles, convinced that no flight on which they travelled could possibly come to any harm.[7]

To look at *What's Happening!* now it is easy to blink and miss Spector as he mingles with the people gathered around The Beatles as they step off the plane. But there he is, exchanging looks with John Lennon, who seems to be communicating something or other to the man who would end up producing The Beatles' final album, *Let It Be*, in 1969. As Mick Brown wrote in his biography of Spector, he could have had little idea that this moment was 'to prove the harbinger of his decline'.[8]

THE IMPACT of The Beatles' arrival in America was later re-enacted in a 1978 comedy, *I Wanna Hold Your Hand*, directed by Robert Zemeckis. It is one of very few films that succeed in getting inside the phenomenon of fame from the perspective of the fans, something that might explain why it is not as widely known as more conventional rock movies the interest of which has predominantly been the figure of the star.[9] The film concerns the attempts of a group of friends to gain entry to *The Ed Sullivan Show* to see The Beatles in person. As they are making their way from New Jersey to Manhattan on the afternoon of the show, Sullivan is seen briefing the studio and theatre staff about the group. They're like 'Elvis Presley times four', he says:

> I want you to be prepared for excessive screaming. Hysteria, hyperventilation, fainting, fits, seizures, spasmodic convulsions, even attempted suicides – *Allll purfectleee . . . nooormal.* It merely means that these youngsters are enjoying themselves.

What *I Wanna Hold Your Hand* reveals is the almost contagious nature of teenage rock 'n' roll obsessiveness. As fans gather outside The Beatles' hotel, a cop patrolling a barrier that holds the expectant fans in place accidentally tramples the foot of

Set amidst the chaos of Beatlemania, Robert Zemeckis's *I Wanna Hold Your Hand* (1978) looked at events from the perspective of the fans. Here, Nancy Allen, as Pam, breaks into The Beatles New York hotel suite while they appear on *The Ed Sullivan Show*.

someone on the other side as he walks past. No sooner has the owner of the foot let out a yelp than hysterical screaming has spread to the crowd, now seemingly convinced that a Beatle must be within reach. Nearby, a local TV reporter is interviewing a sobbing teenage fan:

'And, little lady, you have come all the way from . . .'

'Buffalo. I stole money from my mother so I could come here, because I love John . . . Someday I'm gonna marry John.'

'Isn't John already married?'

'But he could get a divorce . . . or his wife could get in a plane crash . . . or she could drown, or anything could happen because John has to marry me. He has to, or I'll kill myself.'

The reporter turns to address the camera: 'There you have it, ladies and gentlemen – Beatlemania.' It is not only The Beatles fanatics who are driven crazy in *I Wanna Hold Your Hand* but those for whom they represented everything bad about what was happening to the music scene. One such figure is Tony, a wisecracking tough who has ridden along with his New Jersey pals so he can goad the stupid kids he sees losing their minds to The Beatles. Outside the group's hotel it is soon Tony who is losing his mind, as he accosts Murray the K, now The Beatles' biggest cheerleader: 'The Beatles are a bunch of wimps. Everybody that listens to their music are wimps too!' he yells, as dozens of small Beatles fans gather around him, 'What're they trying to prove with this long hair? . . . WINS used to be the best radio station in town until you started playing all this Beatles junk. Now that's all I ever hear! Whatever happened to The Four Seasons, Elvis?' Convinced that he alone can stop this madness called Beatlemania, he decides to take decisive action and ascends the roof of the television theatre with a fireman's axe he has stolen. Finding the transmitter tower, he is just about to bring the blade down on the cables when he is blown off his feet by a bolt of lightning. As Phil Spector could have told him: The Beatles were now untouchable.

Back in the actual as opposed to imagined reality of 1964, Richard Lester's Beatles film *A Hard Day's Night* marked a revolutionary shift. Unlike Presley or their near contemporary Cliff Richard, The Beatles played themselves in the film.[10] In formal terms, the film had few traces of the old-style Hollywood musicals and possessed more of the energy and stylistic quirks of French cinema. This much was evident in its visual trickery and disregard for verisimilitude. One second the four Beatles are sitting inside a train compartment, the next they are outside, running alongside it and trying to get back in. The decision to make it a film about one day in the life of The Beatles meant that it was possible to replicate the kind of excitement seen in the Maysles' documentary. What it also shared with that earlier film was the way it dropped the viewer right into the middle of a commotion, without any preamble, explanation or desire to try to familiarize the audience with what they were about to see. It helped to lend the film a sense of realism hitherto missing in rock film (the Maysles' earlier effort excepted). Some also saw in the film something else that made it more 'realistic': a continuity between the frequent use of discontinuous images and jump-cuts – its 'out-of-focus' visual puns – and John Lennon's recently published *In His Own Write*, a collection of variously surrealist, Goons-like wordplay and nonsense verse.[11]

The opening chaotic chase scene that makes up the title sequence, with the four Beatles pursued by a screaming mob

The Beatles won praise for their on-screen naturalism in
A Hard Day's Night, released in July 1964, a film that closely
mirrored their real life at the time, as seen in the earlier *What's
Happening!* (first screened on Granada TV, UK, on 12 February 1964,
under the title *Yeah! Yeah! Yeah!*). 'Ringo', wrote one reviewer,
'emerges as a born actor. He is like a silent comedian, speechless
and chronically underprivileged, a boy who is already ageless.'

to the sound of the theme song, was a moment of genius that
encapsulated the film and Beatlemania in a few minutes. The
Beatles always within grasp but also always just out of reach: this
was a metaphor for rock stardom, and for a form that itself was
made by fans who had moved from one position to the other.
There is even an apparently spontaneous *vérité* detail, worthy
of the Maysles, when George Harrison falls flat on his face and
Ringo Starr lands on top of him as the crowd makes up ground
behind them.

It is surprising to watch the film now, nearly sixty years later,
and realize that it never tried to explain who or what The Beatles
and Beatlemania were. But by the time *A Hard Day's Night* was
released in the summer of 1964, The Beatles were already lodged

in the wider public consciousness, in no small part due to the scenes of pure pandemonium that would break out wherever they appeared. So well known were they that a newspaper report could read, 'in case any readers have just come from Mars, the Beatles are the four long-haired musicians who sing rock and roll music.'[12] The bedlam that was the background to the rise of The Beatles supplied the film with a ready-made narrative device: the group hounded from one place to another. The life of a Beatle was exhausting.

The film provoked speculation on the phenomenon from expert authority figures. William Sargant, a London-based psychiatrist, suggested that those who followed The Beatles were entranced, the targets of modern-day voodoo doctors.[13] The esteemed Dr Sargant, in being drawn into his analyses, no doubt overlooked the fact that he, too, like the reporters who besiege The Beatles in *A Hard Day's Night*, was also already under the spell. 'Which one are you?' a reporter asks Harrison as the group mingles with the press, apparently unable to distinguish them beneath their famous mop-top hair. 'What do you call that hairstyle?' 'Albert,' Harrison replies.

These seemingly novel hairstyles were a source of fascination and soon copied by fans.[14] Wigs were manufactured and sold as wearable mementoes of the film, suitable for those who were not permitted to grow their hair out like The Beatles. One of the funniest storylines of *I Wanna Hold Your Hand* concerns the teenage fan Peter, who sports a carefully cultivated Beatle cut but, in the chaos of the crowds gathering outside *The Ed Sullivan Show*, has to stay one step ahead of anti-Beatles toughs who are keen to shear off his locks. If that isn't bad enough, he has to negotiate a deal with his father, who has tickets to the show but will only hand them over if he agrees to have his hair cut into a military-style crew cut. As the time of Sullivan's show draws closer, he eventually relents and enters an empty barber-shop with his father, its rows of vacant chairs turned towards him like instruments of torture. 'Alright, kid, how do you want it?' the barber asks. 'I want him to look like a Marine,' his father grunts.[15]

A *Hard Day's Night* was a huge hit, and it decisively broke out of the formulaic treatments of rock hitherto seen in main-stream movies while also, from a British perspective, allowing The Beatles to distance themselves from the more derivative aspects of homegrown rock 'n' roll. Some of the most indelible images from the film are the scenes of the four Beatles larking around in a park, temporarily free from the grabbing hands of others – scenes that more broadly hinted at the accelerated expe-rience of rock 'n' roll fame that would further intensify in the years ahead.

The Richest Vandals in the World

The Beatles kicked open the doors for a whole wave of British beat groups. Within a couple of years, many of them would find themselves if not ascending to Beatles levels of popularity, then reaching the silver screen. More curious than this fact, however, were the others who saw different opportunities in The Beatles' example. Two young British film-makers with big aspirations fell into this category: Kit Lambert and Chris Stamp, then both still in their twenties. Lambert, who at 29 was seven years older than Stamp, had been the uncredited second unit director on *The Guns of Navarone*, a British-American production that had been the highest-grossing film during the calendar year of 1961 (*West Side Story*, released late in 1961, would claim the title of biggest box-office success for a 1961 film, although its earnings were mostly taken in 1962). Both men were working their way up to becoming directors in the British studio system and knew that they would get there very slowly, performing a variety of roles – camera operator, assistant director and so on – in order to pay their dues. It seemed like a deathly slow progress.

Lambert and Stamp saw the speed with which the pop world was moving and figured that their ticket out of what could turn out to be a dead end working at Shepperton Studios would be to find a rock 'n' roll band, become their managers and make a film about how they made them a success. Richard Lester, director of *A Hard Day's Night*, was only 32, a good twenty or more years younger than most directors. It was a decision that changed their lives, but not entirely in the ways that they expected. The film they wanted to make would also, like Lester's Beatles film, be in tune with the kind of cinema they admired – the new *cinéma vérité* and the French New Wave. All they needed to do was find a rock 'n' roll band – something different and which no one had seen before – and then come up with a screenplay.

Since the North of England had already spawned The Beatles and the Merseybeat phenomenon, Lambert decided that the world was perhaps ready for something different and figured that London was the place where they would find their band. He took to the task as if he were still serving in the Royal Artillery, setting up a map of the city 'on to which he pinned markers to divide up different areas of the capital'. He and Stamp then set about familiarizing themselves with what was going on in the music scene. After their working day at the film studio was over, Lambert and Stamp 'would both head off to a different part of the city to investigate whatever group was playing'.[16] One night, after months of fruitless searching, Lambert spotted a mass of scooters outside the Railway Hotel in Harrow and Wealdstone. His curiosity took him inside to the back room, where a band called The High Numbers were playing.

He found himself amid a throng of people, most of them young men who were dancing to the band. They were mods. As the world would soon find out, the mods would be defined by their opposition to another group of unruly youngsters known as rockers. Rockers rode motorcycles, listened to 1950s rock 'n' roll and wore black leathers; mods rode Italian scooters, liked American R&B music and wore suits. By summer 1963, The High Numbers were playing to the 'huge mod enclaves' that were to be found at the Goldhawk Club in Shepherds Bush, and in venues in Harrow and in Watford.[17]

The High Numbers had established a residency at the Railway Hotel, drawing crowds that regularly exceeded the few hundred permitted under licensing laws. It was a space that had been designed to maximize the impact of the performance: the windows had been blacked out, the heating turned up and the regular lightbulbs replaced with pinks and reds. The dance floor and bar were a microcosm of the new world of 1960s London: 'mod girls with elfin hairdos and desert-booted boys in voguish striped T-shirts dance in their own private spaces, their staring eyes and clamped jaws suggesting a mid-week amphetamine jag.'[18] On that very first night in July 1964, Kit Lambert saw the band's guitarist, Pete Townshend, smash his guitar onstage at the climax of the show; the following week, with Stamp present, drummer Keith Moon trashed his drum kit. Who on earth destroyed the tools of their trade, they wondered. It was extraordinary. This was clearly the new thing that they had been looking for, and the pair began filming the group and their fans; soon after, they took over as the band's managers, all in line with their plan to make the whole enterprise the subject of their film, which had the working title 'High Numbers'.

As Townshend later recalled, the group were willing to consider anything that brought them attention, so why not go along with these two fools who thought they could become film stars? They had already been 'trying and failing to get a guitar smashing moment into the national newspapers'.[19] Townshend, in particular, began to think that their audience – the mods later portrayed in another Who film, 1979's *Quadrophenia* – and the entire scene they were part of was going to be something very short-lived. He started to think of it as something that would, or could, blow itself up. 'Before the Who got big', he told Barry Miles in 1967, he wanted the band to get 'bigger and bigger and bigger and bigger' until they had a number one record.[20] Then they could do something outrageous, like blow themselves up on TV. 'Well-presented destruction is what I call a joy to watch,' Townshend said a couple

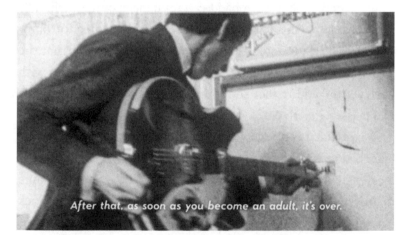

After that, as soon as you become an adult, it's over.

Pete Townshend of The Who during an appearance on German TV, when the words of co-manager Kit Lambert, speaking in German, were subtitled. He was explaining why The Who were the culmination of a series of post-war trends that gave birth to youth culture. *Lambert and Stamp* (dir. James D. Cooper, 2014).

of years later, after they had notched up a succession of Top Ten hits: 'I've always thought that high class, high powered auto-destructive art, glossy destruction, glossy pop destruction, was far far better than the terrible messy dirty disorganized destruction that other people were involved in.'[21] More than a year later, after The High Numbers had been renamed as The Who, the destructive sensibilities of this band would be transferred into the grooves of one of their early singles, 'My Generation'. This was a kind of rock 'n' roll containing more pure aggression than anything heard for years, a record made by nineteen- and twenty-year-olds and which ended in an orgy of noise and feedback. That in itself was an unprecedented move for a single ostensibly pitched at the charts – normally, a producer would fade out on something like that, but The Who made it the whole point. But it was real, in that it reflected the violence and dynamics of the onstage performance that Lambert and Stamp had caught on film – an aesthetic that in turn had been influenced by Townshend's art school guru Gustav Metzger, the self-styled pioneer of 'auto-destructive art'. In a 1961 manifesto, Metzger declared that the point of art should be to re-enact our cultural 'obsession with destruction' and reflect the 'pummelling to which individuals and masses are subjected' in industrial society. 'Auto-destructive art is art which contains within itself an agent,' Metzger wrote, 'which automatically leads to its destruction.'[22]

The dynamics that characterized The Who onstage became manifest as that agent of destruction. Some might say that rock was already destructive – just look at Jerry Lee Lewis tipping his piano off the end of a stage or setting it alight, or an angry Elvis smashing a guitar to pieces in *Jailhouse Rock*. But the key difference with The Who's Townshend was that he was part of an art-school-educated group of British musicians who would try to direct rock 'n' roll's destructive tendencies into something that was thought out and conceptualized. The Who came to be emblematic of the dissolution of boundaries that had separated popular culture, rock music and the other arts. As well as reflecting Metzger's ideas about destruction, a song's collapse into noise and feedback could be seen as the perfect complement to the dream of self-destruction that seemed to be willed in the very words of the song.

The stammering and stuttering of Roger Daltrey in 'My Generation' – hoping for death before decrepitude – was surely the most darkly ironic twist on rock 'n' roll's celebration of eternal youth. The destructive orgies practised by The Who saw rock venturing into new aesthetic terrain. In little time, they would achieve the fame bestowed by chart hits, with one writer in 1967 declaring them the 'richest vandals in the world'.[23]

At the core of the 2014 documentary *Lambert and Stamp* is the film that never was: 'High Numbers', the 40-minute documentary that they made in 1964 and which was subsequently thought to be lost. Snatches of it have surfaced over the years: there were images without sound in The Who documentary *The Kids are Alright* (1979), and later some with sound in Murray Lerner and Paul Crowder's *Amazing Journey: The Story of the Who* (2007). But it was not until 2014 that extensive excerpts from the film were seen and the story of its role in the making of The Who was told.

Aside from immortalizing the band then known as The High Numbers in magnificent performance footage, the other characteristic of the film is its fascination with the audience, as the camera moves through throngs of young men, dancing to the music but in a way more interested in themselves. It is a scene, Lambert later said, that has something of the 'witches' sabbath'

Lambert and Stamp (2014) re-uses original footage of London Mods
shot by Kit Lambert and Chris Stamp as part of their unfinished
film 'High Numbers' (filmed in 1964).

about it.[24] It is not hard to see what he meant. The mods are there
in vivid close-up, sometimes looking blank, other times staring
bug-eyed, caught in their amphetamine-fuelled ecstasy.

In the simplest of chronological terms, London in 1964 was
only eight years further down the road from *Rock Around the Clock*,
a film that had blazed an appropriately comet-like trail around
the globe, helping to set in train a series of events that would see
a couple of aspiring English film-makers become the real-life
counterparts of the kind of figures who discovered Bill Haley in
the fictionalized Hollywood account of the birth of rock 'n' roll.
While their film never saw the light of day in 1964, Lambert and
Stamp did prove one thing: that making it in rock 'n' roll could
be achieved much faster than making it in the film business.

Nice Boys Don't Play Rock 'n' Roll

By the summer of 1964, with The Beatles universally loved and quickly established as movie stars following the success of *A Hard Day's Night*, The Rolling Stones' youthful manager Andrew Loog Oldham – at twenty years old, younger than any of the group – thought that he needed to find some kind of film vehicle for his charges, one in which they could, like The Beatles, appear in a dramatic context. The key thing, though, would be to play them off against the image of The Beatles. As Mick Jagger later recalled, Oldham argued that the situation between the two groups might be best thought of as itself a movie scenario. The Beatles were obviously the good guys, so the Stones would have to be the bad guys.[25] As a result of press coverage of some of the Stones' adventures – not least their run-in with the law for 'urinating on a garage forecourt' – the group were already on their way to embodying the worst traits of a youth culture that, in the eyes of respectable society, had gone awry in no small part as a result of the influence of rock music.[26] An appearance on Australian TV in 1965, which was resurrected in 2012 for the Stones documentary *Crossfire Hurricane*, was prefaced by an introduction that accurately summed up the perception of The Rolling Stones at that point in time. 'I guess The Rolling Stones are not everyone's cup of tea, and that's the understatement of the year,' began a middle-aged figure:

> There are whole armies of parents who become homicidal just looking at them. Both onstage and off, the Stones don't exactly generate an aura of sweetness and light, and their carefully calculated air of 'blow you, Jack' has won them almost as many enemies as fans.[27]

With this kind of reaction, there was surely nothing unusual in their desire to get into the movies, especially since the existing career map of the typical rock or pop star, such as it was in those early days, seemed to suggest a detour into movies as a way of maintaining presence at a time when the only means of exposure was through record releases or concerts. Such had been the case with Presley, The Beatles and other British stars such as Cliff Richard and Tommy Steele. Oldham thought that a film would help the Stones emulate the success of The Beatles. But there was more: the importance of image to rock stardom made it clear that film could be exactly what was required to project the Stones even further into the limelight, especially once they had been established in the minds of the public as the villainous counterparts to the sainted Beatles. So, the young manager concluded, the right film could do wonders for the Stones' 'bad guy' image.

Oldham was initially obsessed with obtaining the film rights to Anthony Burgess's novel *A Clockwork Orange* (1962), the story of a roving gang of violent teenagers that was itself partly inspired by what Burgess had observed of the effect of rock 'n' roll on young people, as seen in the appearance of coffee bars and 'youths dressed very smartly in neo-Edwardian suits with heavy-soled boots and distinctive coiffures'.[28] As Burgess later wrote in his autobiography, these youngsters represented an expression of 'brutal disappointment with Britain's post-war decline'.[29] *A Clockwork Orange* stood out to Oldham as the perfect basis for a film adaptation that could not only provide the Stones with their first starring roles but help to cement their antihero status. Collectively, the Stones would play the notorious 'droogs', as the gang of violent friends refer to each other in the language of Burgess's book. It was a term that translated into something like 'friends in violence'.

Oldham's attempt to buy the film rights for the book failed. But once the disappointment was behind him, he began to look for alternatives, and it was soon being reported that the Stones would star in a film adaptation of a recent novel by Dave Wallis titled *Only Lovers Left Alive* (1964). The premise was not so dissimilar to the Burgess novel: teenagers take over a society that has descended into chaos, and the adult population subsequently diminishes rapidly through voluntary euthanasia at the horror of the world they now find themselves in. 'With the "oldies" dead,' the jacket copy stated,

> teenagers inherit the world, suddenly free to smash, loot and love as they like. Motorcycle gangs hold wild orgies in abandoned apartments and prowl through the shambles of disintegrating London in search of disappearing stocks of lipstick, gasoline and food, now the currency in a world of unspeakable violence.[30]

Oldham later told the *Daily Mirror* that the story was so perfect that the book 'could have been written for the Stones'.[31] But this idea, too, would eventually come to nothing, despite it being trailed in the press and talked up by Keith Richards, who spoke of looking forward to working with film-maker Nicholas Ray, director of the epochal teen classic *Rebel Without a Cause* (1955).

The failure to get the project off the ground was partly the result of the difficulties Oldham had in reconciling himself to the film business and its long-established practices, which made it appear decidedly sclerotic next to rock's battering-ram approach to getting things done. There are slightly divergent accounts of how the project fell apart. According to some reports, a script was developed by Ray in collaboration with British writers Keith

Waterhouse and Willis Hall, but the production was still unable to find the necessary cash to move ahead; other reports suggest that the members of the Stones 'lacked confidence in Ray'.[32] Whatever the real reason, the whole project collapsed, leaving the real-life movie-like baddies without a film to star in.[33]

The Stones film that did get made at this time, directed by Peter Whitehead and titled *Charlie Is My Darling*, achieved a kind of success – first, insofar as it was actually made, and second, in putting an end to Oldham's desire to turn the group into film stars. It was a low-budget documentary more in keeping with the Maysles brothers' *What's Happening!* than the outlaw counterpart to *A Hard Day's Night* that the Stones' manager had planned. Whitehead's film, though, was an interesting document in and of itself so that today, with the passage of time, it stands as one of the early classics of rock film.

It was not that easy to find someone in the London of 1965 who could make the kind of film that the Maysles had produced about The Beatles the year before, so when Oldham found out that Whitehead's short documentary about a gathering of American Beat poets at London's Royal Albert Hall – the film *Wholly Communion* (1965) – had been made using portable hand-held equipment, he quickly tracked him down and engaged him to film The Rolling Stones.

In *Wholly Communion*, Whitehead more or less did everything himself – he operated the camera as well as directing, producing and editing the film – and all very cheaply, on rented equipment and borrowed money.[34] Although he was working as a London-based newsreel cameraman for an Italian TV channel at the time, his role there – making short films on topical issues at some remove from possible interference – ended up giving him a lot of freedom to experiment, making him effectively a kind of independent film-maker.[35] In addition to his work for Italian audiences, he also ended up making 'clips', as the short pop music promos of the day were known, for shows like *Top of the Pops*, as a means of making some extra money.

For Oldham, the use of Whitehead would be a perfect solution in setting up a kind of real-life screen test for the Stones, and would be even more of a genius move if it produced results that he could show to help him raise the estimated £1 million he needed to revive *Only Lovers Left Alive* and finally move it into production.[36] And so, at a few days' notice, Oldham arranged for Whitehead to accompany The Rolling Stones on a short tour of Ireland, which he was to film however he saw fit; whatever material this produced would give Oldham more of an idea of what kind of screen presence the members of the band had.

Whitehead's *cinéma vérité* footage catches the Stones in various situations – writing songs in hotel rooms, travelling on trains and planes, running across railway tracks to escape fans and reporters, being mobbed onstage by teenage fans – and was later intercut with artfully slowed-down performances (filmed by Whitehead at the Albert Hall) that were set against the orchestral versions of their hits that Oldham had recently produced (as *The Rolling Stones Songbook* by The Andrew Oldham Orchestra). These elements, added after the fact, took the film away from the strict aesthetics of pure documentary and set it apart from the so-called direct cinema being developed in America through the work of the Maysles brothers and D. A. Pennebaker in the early 1960s. Even when it was first shown, viewers thought it had the feel of a document that captured a moment about to be lost to time, as if the scenes where the Stones muse about their own imminent obsolescence in some of the interview segments had been realized. What such interviews revealed about the group

Keith Richards (in shades and smoking cigarette) and Bill Wyman
(seated with cup of tea) besieged by fans at Heathrow Airport, 1965,
in Peter Whitehead's *Charlie Is My Darling* (1966).

was that, like many of their contemporaries, they had expected
their fame to be exceptionally short-lived.

Charlie Is My Darling reveals Brian Jones to be the most pessimistic of all the band members. Then again, it is impossible
not to look at this film with the full knowledge of what would
become of him. While Jagger mused on his good fortune at not
having to go back to the London School of Economics now that
'(I Can't Get No) Satisfaction' had made it to the top of the charts
in Britain and America, Jones gave the impression that he had
other, much more important plans. Making his own films, for
instance. There is a palpable sense of his being trapped already,
and it had only been a year since the Stones had achieved their
first chart success. 'I've never thought very far ahead at all,' he
told Whitehead. 'I've always been a little apprehensive about the

future.' The director later felt that the film caught a Jones who was already gone by then. 'For a young guy like that, a total narcissist, death was the trip anyway,' Whitehead told Oldham for his memoir of those years: 'He was in his prime, yet even then he was talking about the indeterminacy of everything, everything coming to an end. He could sense this rejection, this failure, this sinking into oblivion.'[37] That, in part, was because Jagger and Richards, having proved themselves as songwriters, had now taken control of the band that Jones had started – something borne out by Whitehead's footage of Jagger and Richards working on songs between gigs.

When he finally saw the film back in London, Oldham's reaction was immediate: on the evidence that was there for all to see, it seemed clear that the Stones were not going to make it as movie stars. The only natural presence of the lot of them, he felt, was drummer Charlie Watts, whose laid-back unflappability and utter lack of pretension set him apart from the rest. Jagger, by contrast, comes across as unsure of himself in the offstage interview segments, as if he didn't know whom he was playing to when the camera was on him. Richards, meanwhile, spends almost the entire time he is on screen either behind a guitar or hiding behind sunglasses. He had almost no interest in being filmed. Watts, on the other hand, was sure of who he was. He knew he was driven by motivations not shared by the other Stones. 'This is maybe where I differ from the rest,' he explained to Whitehead in the film, 'When I am at home, I can pick up a book and play a record. I have a wife, and that makes you a bit sort of cosy, in a way, I suppose. But I like it. I'm happiest at home.'

And so it was that the Stones' first screen effort was named after Charlie Watts, because of all the members, he – followed by the other ostensibly 'background' guy, Bill Wyman – was the least self-conscious of the band when the camera was on him. Watching the interviews as Whitehead edited the film, Oldham was struck by Watts's natural screen presence and imagined a scenario where he would be managing Watts and fielding offers from film producers looking for someone to replace Charles Bronson.[38]

More than two decades later, in another documentary, *25×5: The Continuing Adventures of The Rolling Stones* (1989) – released to mark the first 25 years of the band – Watts was still as keen as ever to get off the touring treadmill and head back home to his wife, and memorably described the experience of being in the Stones and reaching this anniversary as 'five years playing, and twenty years hanging around hotels and airports'.[39] Perhaps Oldham had missed something: a couple of years after *Charlie*, the Italian producer of Michelangelo Antonioni's *Blow-Up*, Carlo Ponti, came to the Stones with a script for a psychedelic sci-fi tale called 'Maxigasm', which he thought should star Jagger, Richards and Jones – those judged by Oldham to have no screen presence. As the deadpan Bill Wyman remarked, 'Charlie and I were obviously too straight for the project.'[40]

Charlie Is My Darling was shown briefly in 1966, but it soon vanished without a trace and would not see the light of day again until 2012, when it was released as a DVD. Despite being the first British rock 'n' roll road movie that was able to convey what the life of a band on the road was like, it would be eclipsed by others, not least Pennebaker's *Don't Look Back* (filmed before *Charlie* but not released until 1967). Having been paid £2,000 to deliver a film, Whitehead was powerless to do anything to keep his creation in the public mind as it became consumed in a decades-long dispute over the Stones' assets between Oldham and his replacement as the band's manager, Allen Klein.[41] When the film was shown again at some film festivals in 2004, Oldham felt that it captured the 1960s at a point of transition, just as the relative innocence of that black-and-white world was about to give way to a period that would be metaphorically splayed out in 'cinemascope and color wide-screen'.[42] And so it was. Within a year, the once gritty-sounding Stones, formerly a byword for the threat posed by rock music to society at large, would be singing 'We Love You' and releasing an album (in America) called *Flowers*, as if to cash in on the new mood that would be defined by terms like 'peace', 'love' and 'flower power'.

D. A. Pennebaker (middle) trains his camera on Bob Dylan during the singer's British tour of 1965, the source for what we see in *Don't Look Back* (released 1967).

3

ALTERED STATES

The 1960s revolutions in film-making that produced what would be described as a New Hollywood were inspired by the rise of a generation of writers, directors and producers who came of age in the 1950s. In important ways they would reveal themselves to be children of the rock 'n' roll era. As detailed in Peter Biskind's best-selling *Easy Riders, Raging Bulls* (1998, subtitled *How the Sex 'n' Drugs 'n' Rock 'n' Roll Generation Saved Hollywood*), they went on to bring some of rock's desire for self-invention into a Hollywood environment that was still controlled by people who had been at the helm since the 1920s and '30s.[1] As such, their rise, like the rise of rock, was one consequence of the massive post-war demographic shifts that were beginning to reveal their consequences in the 1960s. In many cases, they made movies that incorporated rock as an integral ingredient of a new kind of film-making.

As well as the broader cultural changes that would push film and rock into newer and more sympathetic contact in the 1960s, there were also significant innovations in equipment and technology that pushed film-makers towards rock as a subject particularly suited to their new aims and methods and which allowed them to overcome limitations that had previously restricted documentary film-making.[2] In America, the new trend in film documentary was known as direct cinema – what in Europe was more commonly referred to as *cinéma vérité* – and from its earliest days it formed a 'symbiotic relationship with rock'.[3] The key figures in forging the first wave of rock documentary films – D. A. Pennebaker, Albert and David Maysles and Richard Leacock – were all pioneers in this field; and their work was made possible in large part because of the self-built equipment they used, which was designed to allow them to get into much closer contact with their subjects.

Leacock and Robert Drew, who towards the end of the 1950s produced films for Time-Life, came up with 'a lightweight, portable camera with synchronized sound', which represented a major breakthrough and was able to work alongside other innovations, notably film stock suitable for low light conditions.[4] It completely replaced the need to have spotlights. The new cameras enabled smoother and more seamless filming, with 16 mm film 'loaded in magazines which could be replaced in seconds'.[5]

The other important development that set the work of these directors apart from previous rock movies was that they produced films that had no place for actors. Even the role of director had departed significantly from the conventional understanding of the term. It was the situations that they filmed that 'directed' what ended up in the can to be edited, rather than the conventional understanding of film-making as scripted direction. This made their methods particularly suitable to capturing a phenomenon that was becoming increasingly freewheeling, spinning out from the confines of 'entertainment' into the everyday. As such, there were 'no scripts, no sets, no lights, little or no narration and no interviews'.[6] The whole point of the approach was for the film-maker to be present with a camera and sound recording equipment, ready for whatever happened.

The new lightweight equipment released film-makers already working outside the mainstream even further from the kind of constraints that dominated movie-making. With these small, portable 16 mm cameras and mobile sound recording, there was little to prevent film-makers from following human subjects in daily situations wherever they led, and by doing so creating a more immediate, intimate and spontaneous kind of cinema. The fact that Pennebaker, Leacock and Albert Maysles had all worked on TV films for Robert Drew Associates between 1960 and 1962, and all wound up making multiple rock films, is no accident. Rock was not only what was topical and helping to accelerate social and cultural change; it was itself – beyond the walls of the recording studio and in the behind-the-scenes moments of life on the road – a kind of live-action 'happening' to match anything that was exciting the art world at the time under that description. Direct cinema had the potential to explode the entire context of rock into public view. Drew, the photographic editor at Time-Life, had established his production company to try to create a cinematic equivalent of the hugely influential and popular photojournalism he was involved with at *Life* magazine in the 1950s.[7]

The first film involving all of these figures was the documentary *Primary* (1960), which followed John F. Kennedy on the campaign trail as he sought the Democratic Party nomination for president. The film presented an entirely new fly-on-the-wall kind of experience that exploited the deadpan precision of the camera to produce 'highly revealing scenes' of the campaign, rendered as a fragment of its 'tedium and exhaustive repetition'.[8]

In 1962, Albert Maysles broke from Drew Associates and along with his sound recordist brother, David – who had been working as a Hollywood studio production assistant – set up Maysles Films. Their first joint effort, *Showman* (1963), was about the American film producer Joseph E. Levine, and their second was their 1964 Beatles film *What's Happening!* The latter demonstrated how adroit their methods were, with the completed film broadcast on British TV – under the title *Yeah! Yeah! Yeah!* – only five days after they had been contracted by Granada Television to film the band, who were then already midway across the Atlantic on their way to New York. *What's Happening!* would be the first 'fly-on-the-wall' rock film, and while it was probably seen by a huge TV audience on its initial broadcast, today it is rarely seen in its entirety (although snatches of it appear in numerous documentaries about The Beatles and that period).

THE ENGLAND that Bob Dylan arrived in for a tour that began at the end of April 1965 was not yet feeling the pull of the cultural forces that were welling up and which would make the second half of the 1960s, with its Paisley colours and psychedelic drugs, a quite distinct period. When we see Dylan arriving at Heathrow Airport in Pennebaker's *Don't Look Back*, he carries with him the aura of an exotic visitor; his perma-shades and frizzed-out hair had visibly transformed him from the image cultivated in his early folky days into a kind of embodiment of the Beat aesthetic, which seemed, at least, to be more of an influence on his recent work than his musical predecessors were. *Don't Look Back*, of course, exists in glorious black-and-white, but, looked at another way, Dylan was already in advance of the colour explosion of the psychedelic era. In songs like 'A Hard Rain's A-Gonna Fall' (1963), 'My Back Pages' (1964) and his recent 'Subterranean Homesick Blues' (1965), the images were stacked up and then peeled away like the colours and shapes of a kaleidoscope chasing new patterns.

But Dylan's status as the shaper of a new consciousness aside, he was also, on a more mundane level, simply the latest pop star to be chased by fans. Many of them, as we see in *Don't Look Back*, were young women keen to find out more details of his private life, such as whether or not he had any brothers or sisters. In that respect there is much that could be said regarding what Pennebaker's film reveals about the nature of rock culture at the time and what else – aside from his music – helped to make Dylan a pivotal figure in the understanding of the 1960s.

Pennebaker presented Dylan in a way that would initially make it hard to sell the film. It was too dark – in the sense of not being well lit – so that it seemed to have more in common with the kind of pornographic movies that were screened in out-of-the-way places: dark rooms in backstage areas of theatres, the interiors of cars and trains, hotel rooms full of so many people it was hard to figure out what was going on. In short, anything that offered the context for what was seen onstage and heard on records. Nobody had any idea what would come of the filming; no inkling of how it would reflect the personas of its various participants back to the public. When Dylan arrived to view a screening back in New York, it was with a notepad. He intended to make notes on how he thought the film could be tweaked or improved to show him in the best possible light, but soon gave up when he realized that there was no way of polishing this material.

This was a behind-the-scenes look not just at Dylan but at the whole operation. The negotiating style of his manager, Albert Grossman – don't give an inch and always ask for more – is there in the famous scene where he and British showbusiness hustler Tito Burns play off the BBC against Granada Television to secure more money for a Dylan appearance. Pennebaker recalled that sometime after the film was released, he was having lunch with Grossman in New York when one of Grossman's old friends approached their table and commented at how amazed they were to have seen him in *Don't Look Back*, acting 'like some sort of bandit from the swamps'.[9]

As with the Maysles' *What's Happening!*, we learn through context what the subject is, rather than through the vision of the film-maker – no biographical details or location information are given; no names are attached to many of the memorable characters who drop in and out of the film, without explanation – people such as 'the High Sheriff's lady', as one backstage guest (a local dignitary) in Newcastle introduces herself, appearing on screen like a fantastic caricature of a bygone age, greeting Dylan and his road manager Bob Neuwirth with an invitation: 'If you come back again,' she says in the poshest of tones, 'I'd love to have you both, you and your friend, at the mansion house.' As a slightly embarrassed Dylan looks on awkwardly, Neuwirth, cigarette dangling from his mouth, presents her with one of Dylan's many harmonicas, saying, 'This is for you.'

More often than not, however, *Don't Look Back* shows Dylan and his entourage coming up against a cast of squares representing the old ways, who often don't know what to make of them. In one of the movie's now iconic scenes, a hotel manager arrives at Dylan's room to ask for the noise to be kept down, only to find himself face-to-face with Grossman:

> HOTEL MANAGER: Who's in charge?
>
> GROSSMAN: In charge of what?
>
> HOTEL MANAGER: Who is in charge of this room?
>
> GROSSMAN: What do you mean 'Who's in charge of this room?' It's rented to Bob Dylan. What do you mean, who's in charge of it?
>
> HOTEL MANAGER: Are you Bob Dylan's manager?

GROSSMAN: Yes, I'm Bob Dylan's manager, but I'm not in charge of his room.

HOTEL MANAGER: No, you're in charge of Bob Dylan?

GROSSMAN: No, I'm not in charge of Bob Dylan.

HOTEL MANAGER: We've had complaints about the noise – above, below.

GROSSMAN: Oh, that's unfortunate. We'll try to hold it down.

HOTEL MANAGER: And if it isn't organized in five minutes, I will ask you to leave.

GROSSMAN: Why don't you get a constable – would you please?

HOTEL MANAGER: I will.

GROSSMAN: Please do that. There's been no noise in this room, and you're one of the dumbest assholes and the most stupid persons I've ever spoken to in my life. If we were someplace else I'd punch you in the goddam nose – you stupid nut.

Don't Look Back also shows us some of the consequences of fame that would force Dylan to retreat from public view a few years later. Back in the USA, when he had appeared at the Newport Folk Festival, his arrival onstage with an electric band did not go down too well with those who viewed him as an artist working more in the folk tradition. And while there was no band here on this tour, he still finds himself besieged by fans, journalists and other musicians who continue to think of him as primarily a word artist, a poet, as if the words on 'Subterranean Homesick Blues' could be heard any other way than with *that* sound, which is to say this was not merely about words or 'poetry' but a new kind of rock, a rowdy blues-infused rock 'n' roll *combined with* those words. In one scene, a journalist corners Dylan and says, 'do you even think your young fans understand a *word* of what you are singing?' This sense of Dylan as a man with a message is there, too, when we see and overhear a journalist in a phone booth calling in his review copy:

> he is not so much singing as sermonizing . . . colon . . . his tragedy perhaps is that the audience is preoccupied with the song . . . paragraph . . . so the bearded boys and lank-haired girls all eyeshadow and undertaker make-up applaud the songs and miss perhaps the sermon . . . they are there . . . colon . . . with it . . . comma . . .

Exploding Plastic Inevitable

Back in America, rock was beginning to take a turn into aesthetic decadence with The Velvet Underground, whose debut album, *The Velvet Underground & Nico* (1967), was to be found inside a cover featuring a mysterious banana and signed with the words 'Andy Warhol'. The Velvet Underground pushed rock 'n' roll into a new kind of space, one of media environments that chimed with the theories of Marshall McLuhan. Some even believed that the result – particularly the multimedia performances that the band gave in 1966 – offered up something that might be powerful enough, and substantial enough, to compete with longer-established forms such as the novel and cinema.

One of Warhol's motivations for becoming involved with The Velvet Underground was the idea that they could be a vehicle for helping to expose the new work he was doing in film. Using his films in a rock 'n' roll context, in the view of his film-making associate Paul Morrissey, would also be a way of bringing in money.[10] In fact, Warhol was making so many films – 'two or three full-length films a week' – that even their meagre budgets of \$3,000 to \$4,000 were starting to mount up.[11] By the time he released *Chelsea Girls* in late 1966, it was said he had already made 150 films, whose number included a silent film of the Empire State Building titled *Empire*, which lasted just over eight hours, and the five-hour-plus *Sleep* – a film of someone sleeping.[12] 'I like boring things,' Warhol told the *New York Times*.[13] But boring was expensive: the cost of film stock and processing was draining his finances, and as a method it would always lead Warhol to shoot more rather than less footage. He just filmed reels and reels of whatever grabbed his attention at any given moment.

Warhol's patronage secured The Velvet Underground a record deal with MGM Records – the music arm of Metro-Goldwyn-Mayer, one of the oldest Hollywood movie studios – and enabled the group to garner plenty of early press attention in America, with most of the critics shocked or bamboozled at what they presented. One early review observed that this was a music that 'actually vibrates with menace, cynicism and perversion'.[14] When they were not making extended ventures into what most listeners thought was pure noise, there was the occasional soft, more downbeat song, which were sung by the former fashion model Nico, possessed of a voice that was akin to the sound of a 'memento mori'.[15] Nico herself had some film connections, having played a small part in Federico Fellini's *La Dolce Vita* (1960) as a result of her fame as a fashion model. She also had a musical past that pre-dated her working with The Velvet Underground.

In 1965, after she had become fed up with modelling for TV adverts, Nico developed her interest in singing and wound up in London, where The Rolling Stones' manager Andrew Loog Oldham signed her to his Immediate Records label. She made one single, the lilting 'I'm Not Sayin'', which was a good record but not a hit – though at another time it might have been; it featured the talents of Brian Jones of the Stones as well as Jimmy Page, later of Led Zeppelin but then a session musician and house producer for Oldham's label. Nico's pop career never took off, but while in London she met Warhol's close associate Gerard Malanga, who suggested that if she was ever in New York she should call Andy at The Factory.

Later that year, when Warhol and Morrissey finally met Nico in New York, newly arrived from London, they thought that she had a physical presence – tall, blonde and strong-looking – that would work with The Velvet Underground. 'She looked like she could have made the trip over right at the front of a Viking ship,' Warhol noted.[16] As unconventional as Nico's voice was, this was an era when things were opening up, and what might have seemed uninteresting three or four years earlier could now be just the right thing for the times. Art, film, fashion and rock were finding new forms of association, and Nico seemed to be right in that mix at the intersection of these previously separate worlds. She handed a copy of 'I'm Not Sayin'' to Warhol as well as another demo that featured her singing the Dylan song 'I'll Keep It with Mine', which she claimed had been written especially for her after they met by chance in Paris in 1964. Dylan, it seems, recognized her from *La Dolce Vita*.[17]

With Warhol no longer painting, his income had begun to dry up, and the new forays into movies had not yet resulted in any success or money. It was then that he developed the idea for his *Exploding Plastic Inevitable*: the multimedia sensory assault of The Velvet Underground and Nico playing live accompanied by his own films, lighting and dancers. In 1966 they toured, and it was a success; the film-maker Ronald Nameth shot a week's worth of

A frame from Ron Nameth's record of Warhol's *Exploding Plastic Inevitable*, with Gerard Malanga dancing as part of The Velvet Underground's multimedia performance.

performances of these shows to create what would be described as his 'dazzling kinaesthetic masterpiece'.[18] In *Exploding Plastic Inevitable*, form and content became one as the vision on screen made it seem that the film itself had 'been exploded and reassembled in a jumble of shards'.[19]

Nameth's work aside, film was to be integral to the performances of The Velvet Underground in ways that went beyond its use as a means of documentation. Warhol's films were integrated into the group's total performance for the first time at a performance on the occasion of a dinner for the New York Society for Clinical Psychiatry, which took place in the plush ballroom of Delmonico's hotel in New York. 'Why are they exposing us to these nuts?' one psychiatrist asked a reporter there to witness the event, as Warhol and his assistants moved among the diners with hand-held cameras, guerrilla style, 'using the psychiatrists' as unwitting players in a forthcoming film.[20] As The Velvet Underground took to the stage, Warhol ran a projector showing one of his films, *Vinyl*. As that played on the screen it was superimposed with another movie from a projector run by Morrissey, showing close-up shots of Nico singing 'I'll Keep It with Mine'. 'Looking ghostly in the flickering movie lights, Nico on stage picked up the song from Nico on screen and the band joined in behind her,' playing on until they got to the dirge-like 'Venus in Furs', when they were joined onstage by Malanga and Edie Sedgwick 'gyrating in a free form dance pattern'.[21] The whole ensemble was now playing in front of two movies, *Vinyl* and *The Velvet Underground and Nico: A Symphony of Sound* (the latter containing footage of a Velvet Underground rehearsal being broken up by the NYPD), both running silently next to each other.[22]

New Decadents

The mingling of rock music with art, fashion and film was also increasingly to be seen in London. The emergence of The Who in 1964, bringing mod culture and fashions overground with them, was in large measure due to the fact that they had been chosen by the young and ambitious film-makers Kit Lambert and Chris Stamp to be the subject of a documentary that they – in exile from the strictures of the British film industry, as we have already seen – would direct, thereby finally making it as film directors. Two years later, in an April 1966 cover story for America's *Time* magazine, London was being been trumpeted as the new capital of everything hip. The magazine's guide of how to be 'swinging', with its advice on 'what to read, what to wear, where to be seen', was greeted with derision by some in London as a facile attempt to latch on to a quite complex phenomenon without getting beyond the superficiality of images of Carnaby Street and mod fashions.[23]

What was heralded as a new 'pop' or 'mod' culture was real enough, however, and at its core seemed to be London's burgeoning population of young people – one-third of the city's population was estimated to be aged between 15 and 34 – who helped to fuel the music scene and the people around it.[24] The other players in the city's cultural life – 'playwrights and photographers, rock stars and fashion models, actors and directors' – began to move in and out of the once separate domains that they had existed in, bringing into closer relationship the strands of an emerging cultural renaissance.[25] The results of this, as Mark Harris notes, had 'a worldwide impact on fashion, photography and art' and, soon enough, on the film world too.[26] For the editors at *Time*, London was seen to represent 'a new type of civilisation' that expressed itself through pop culture.[27]

One of the biggest cinema hits of 1966–7 was Antonioni's *Blow-Up*, which was initially seen as a kind of counterpart to this new London. That impression was perhaps due in part to the fact that it was the vision of an outsider, its Italian director. In the *Observer* newspaper, in fact, the film was dismissed as 'a precious film version of *Time* magazine's celebrated clanger about Swinging London'.[28] It was, indeed, the screen vision of a culturally unique time and place. Today, moreover, it takes on a different relationship to the world it represented, a place defined by the collision of once separate and distinct cultural spheres, which we see come together through the figure of Thomas (played by David Hemmings), a fashion photographer in search of some kind of meaning but caught in the superficiality of what would be described as Swinging London.

Bored with the daily procession of models and fashion shoots, Thomas seeks out more fulfilling subjects that show another London, one stranger and more real than what fashion and pop culture had thrown up. In fact, the latter had assumed such power over the cultural life of the city that all that seemed to matter was the next new thing. It was, in the words of one writer and cultural observer, Edward Lucie-Smith, the pursuit of impermanence for its own sake – even the creators of these 'advertisements, posters, pop songs, Carnaby Street clothes . . . don't expect them to last', he wrote. 'The product itself must be sacrificed to preserving the apparatus which produces products. Obsolescence keeps the machines turning.'[29]

In his forays into the London beyond this pop world, *Blow-Up*'s Thomas moves from the instantly mythologized Swinging London to the overlooked, rather grittier world of doss houses and landscapes seemingly given over to endless reconstruction, as seen in the film's images of a city whose rubble-strewn fringes gave way to new modernist towers.

Back in the pop world, Thomas stumbles into a rock 'n' roll club, in a scene that would unwittingly document something of the state of flux that – in its tireless quest for the new – had propelled rock music into an almost avant-garde concern with formal destruction, something initially pioneered by The Who and their high-concept, equipment-smashing song endings that seemed to cause the recognizable song form fall in on itself. On a set that was built to recreate a The Ricky Tick Club (relocated in the movie from Windsor to central London), Thomas enters through a door plastered with flyers and adverts, one of which declares:

HERE LIES BOB DYLAN: PASSED AWAY
ROYAL ALBERT HALL, 27 MAY 1966

The date was significant as the occasion of Dylan's recently completed 'electric' tour, when audiences seemed to be shocked on a nightly basis by a sight and sound that they were either unwilling to accept or unable to comprehend: their folk hero, Bob Dylan, coming across like a rock 'n' roll beatnik (as opposed to the folk beatnik seen the year before in *Don't Look Back*) and surrounded by what fans seen in another Dylan film, Martin Scorsese's *No Direction Home* (2005), dismissed as a 'pop group'. Here were young men positioned behind electric guitars, drums and other instruments, being carried away by the whirligig of an organ and guitar that was barely rooted in place by the drummer's beat. It was, for many, symbolic of Dylan's death as an artist. As Thomas enters the club in *Blow-Up*, the sound that he is confronted with is, to all intents and purposes, a continuation of the kind of racket with which Dylan had attacked his audiences. Here, however, the audience is portrayed as jaded, apathetic and beyond shock. Though they are subjected to wave after wave of the next new thing, it seems to wash over them.

Onstage are The Yardbirds, chugging through an anxious, pilled-up rendition of 'Train Kept A-Rollin'' (or 'Stroll On', as it was renamed in the film) that seems to encapsulate their own accelerated journey through Chicago-style R&B to psychedelic pop to something like a prototype heavy metal. The twin guitars of Jeff Beck and Jimmy Page mould a sound that alternates between the pummelling of a riff that hits like a heavy blow and twisting, jagged leads that pierce the air. It all seems like a carefully sculpted chaos, the guitarists at once competing against and complementing each other. It was a new twist on the

David Hemmings as fashion photographer Thomas in
Michelangelo Antonioni's *Blow-Up* (1966) stumbles into a
performance by The Yardbirds in front of an unresponsive audience.

disorientating effect that had been achieved on their earlier studio
version of the song, where the twin recorded voices of Keith Relf
working against, rather than in harmony with, each other ramped
up the sense of anxiety.

As Thomas stands in the audience, looking on, Beck's ampli-
fier begins to cut out, and he thumps it with the body of his
guitar. After another few half-hearted knocks fail to solve the
problem, he takes off his guitar and slams it onto the floor, dig-
ging into its hollow body with the heel of his shoe and then
breaking it up into useless fragments. In front of him, the zombie
audience momentarily come to life when he throws the broken
instrument towards them, seeming suddenly like pack animals
bearing down on their prey. Thomas emerges from the scuffles
with a piece of the guitar and runs out into the street, only to
casually dispose of it once he is no longer being chased. The
scene, like the rest of the film, contains its own elements of

staged exaggeration – The Yardbirds' performance had in fact been repeated numerous times over a number of days, with Beck refusing to use his own valuable guitars in the scene and instead smashing his way through a succession of cheap stand-ins. Yet for all that this was a staged destruction, it nonetheless projected an essential truth in foreseeing something about rock music and the glee with which it blew up its own boundaries as it raced into the more hallucinogenic second half of the 1960s.

The Yardbirds had also not been Antonioni's first choice to play this part. The two other contenders were The Who and The Velvet Underground. The latter's debut album had not yet been released, but their association with Warhol and the fact that they were signed to MGM – the company behind *Blow-Up* – brought them to the director's attention.

Elsewhere in London at around the same time, through events promoted by the London Free School and performances at places like the UFO Club, a similar breaking down of the rock performance as a predictable event was going on. At concerts

Jeff Beck of The Yardbirds smashes his guitar to pieces in *Blow-Up*.

put on by the London Free School, members of the audience were seen rolling naked in a large heap of jelly that had been plopped onto the floor. Pink Floyd were doing something similar to The Yardbirds, with drawn-out, loosely structured songs, and often appeared as shadowy figures beneath the wild lighting effects that made it look like they were laboratory specimens under microscope slides that had been blown up to supersize. Some of this Pink Floyd can be seen and heard in Peter Whitehead's *Tonite Let's All Make Love in London* (shot during 1966 and early 1967), a film that could be seen to be another take on the already mythologized idea of Swinging London. Whitehead tried to encompass the various aspects of 'pop' London: music, film, art, literature and fashion. The voices of Michael Caine, David Hockney, Edna O'Brien, Mick Jagger (lifted from the previous year's *Charlie Is*

Peter Whitehead, here with Keith Richards and Mick Jagger, was an early pioneer of the promo clip. In addition to his films *Charlie Is My Darling* (1966) and *Tonite Let's All Make Love in London* (1967), he made clips for BBC's *Top of the Pops*.

My Darling), Andrew Loog Oldham and Julie Christie provide a series of cues and counterpoints that cut up Whitehead's own impressions of London in 1966–7 as a place of accelerated change.

Sometimes this is evident in his use of music: 'Out of Time' by Chris Farlowe, set to images of people dancing, here sounds like it is aimed at the remains of the old world, illustrated elsewhere by Buckingham Palace guardsmen and other tourist icons of pre-1960s England. At other times it is heard in the words of people like Alan Aldridge – who had designed the sleeve of The Who's *A Quick One* album (1966) and was then the art director for Penguin Books – who told Whitehead that what he was interested in was 'absolute ephemera. I do it today and forget about it ... by midnight.' What defined the pop sensibility, Aldridge said, was that it was 'for the minute. And it's for the minute I absolutely do the job, and it's forgotten. I sometimes even forget to look at it printed.'

The use of Pink Floyd in *Tonite Let's All Make Love in London* occurs specifically in the impressionistic sequences of the film that appear at the beginning and end: the beginning with its blurring, indistinct colours of London facades and traffic, and the end with images shot at The 14 Hour Technicolour Dream, an event that they had headlined at Alexandra Palace in April 1967. The more overtly psychedelic feel of the film at these edges – with its arbitrary cuts, variation of speed and frames cut from the film to achieve a stuttering effect that disrupts a sense of continuity – was in tune with the broader sensibility of the time and came just before one of the defining moments of the decade: the so-called Summer of Love. There could not have been any more representative soundtrack to this period than Pink Floyd, whose Syd Barrett was one of rock's earliest explorers of the psychedelic, as well as one of its most notable casualties.

What the Floyd and The Yardbirds had in common was that they represented rock's turn towards more nuanced modes of artistic expression – a splintering of the form that symbolized rock's movement towards a kind of decadence. It would be a consequence of pushing the idea of the rock musician as artist to an extent hitherto unseen. The pursuit of discordant sounds, apocalyptic lyrical themes, irony and world-weariness – so that the music became a source of images centred on destruction, death, social decay and excess – as well as the projection of the artistic self as its own work of art, had been absent in both the first phase of rock 'n' roll in the 1950s and in pop music more generally.

The real counterpart to *Blow-Up*'s iconic guitar-smashing scene was brought to life on American TV in 1967 when, on the eve of their performance at the Monterey Pop Festival, The Who appeared on the *Smothers Brothers* variety show performing 'My Generation'. At the end of the song, as it cascades into noise and chaos, Pete Townshend launched a twirling guitar into the air, before thudding it against the floor and stabbing its neck into his amplifiers, eventually breaking it apart on the studio floor. Keith Moon had placed some stage explosives in his bass drum to set off as Townshend was doing his thing, but when the explosion went off it knocked him off the drum riser. Waving the smoke aside with an outstretched arm and a cheap acoustic guitar slung over his shoulder, Tom Smothers walked onto the set. Townshend, looking like a guilty schoolboy, immediately took the guitar, fell to his knees and sacrificed that too, bringing auto-destructive art to the land of American television.

California Kaleidoscopes

What had been taking place in London was a prelude to one of the watershed events in 1960s youth culture, which arrived with the Summer of Love. On 25 June 1967, The Beatles had taken part in the first worldwide satellite broadcast, titled *Our World*, when they appeared in a recording studio alongside producer George Martin as one of the representatives of the British contribution to a day-long schedule of global programming. At their feet was a gathering of famous friends to watch as they performed a world premiere of a new song that would be squarely in tune with the new era, 'All You Need Is Love'.

The place where things had really started to stir into a more overtly psychedelic form was San Francisco. On 14 January that year, the first of several 'Gathering of the Tribes' events took place on a warm winter's day with the media in full attendance. The Human Be-In, as it was called, would give the world beyond California a first glimpse of hippies in 'full regalia'.[30] The hippies were the 'strange new counterculturalists' whose presence would grow over the coming year.[31]

The Human Be-In aimed to herald a revolution of consciousness and set an example to America of how, as a country, it might reform itself along the lines of this new counterculture and organize life in new and more peaceful ways; its only enemy would be the old ways, the way things were.[32] The events of that January day – which saw 20,000–30,000 people gather in Golden Gate Park – received extensive national media coverage, with all the major news magazines and television networks registering the rise of this counterculture 'with varying degrees of befuddlement'.[33] What followed in its wake was a flood of young people from all over America heading to California: college kids,

Scenes from the Human Be-In, a key event in the emergence of 1960s counterculture, held at Golden Gate Park, San Francisco, in 1967, seen here in Jack O'Connell's *Revolution* (1967). The crammed stage holds the equipment of the Grateful Dead, who performed after the crowd was addressed by Timothy Leary and Allen Ginsberg.

creatives, runaway teenagers, dropouts and various other misfits, including the then unknown Charles Manson, freshly out of prison.

At the heart of San Francisco's counterculture were a handful of rock bands that found themselves in the city's Haight-Ashbury district, taking advantage of its relative affordability. They took over old Victorian houses and turned them into sprawling, free-flowing communal residences. Such ways of living embodied one aspect of the hippie rejection of bourgeois morality. The hippies promoted free love and hallucinogenic experiences and sought a new kind of spiritualism that could offer an antidote to consumerism. They also hated the political system and sought to develop a mode of existence that would avoid being sucked into it. In the eyes of the dominant culture, it was an expression of naive idealism; a 'Children's Crusade'.[34] In early 1967, local TV station KPIX visited the rising stars of the music scene, the Grateful Dead, in their Haight-Ashbury commune, where the band's lead singer, Jerry Garcia, summed up the new philosophy as an attempt to move 'the whole human race ahead a step': 'We're not thinking about any kind of power . . . we're not thinking about revolution or war, or any of that. That's not what we want. Nobody wants to get hurt, and nobody wants to hurt anybody. We would all like to be able to live an uncluttered life.'[35] The music scene that grew up around this hippie ethos remained relatively insulated for a time, with San Francisco almost an island cut off from the more business-orientated music scene in Los Angeles, never mind its disconnection from what was going on elsewhere in the USA or in Britain. And while the music scene existed amid a proliferation of other forms of creativity, there was a 'peculiar absence of artistic commerce' that set the city apart from places like London or New York.[36] When The Velvet Underground visited San Francisco in 1966 the encounter ended in mutual loathing, with local promoter Bill Graham (originally from the Bronx himself) referring to the visitors as 'disgusting germs from New York' and the group's guitarist Sterling Morrison complaining that San Francisco had stolen Warhol's idea of rock music as the centrepiece of a new multimedia art that also employed film, lights and other projected effects to simulate mind-altering experiences.[37]

Monterey Pop, shot in June 1967 by direct cinema pioneers Albert Maysles, Richard Leacock and D. A. Pennebaker (who acted as director), captured some of the main players in the West Coast rock scene, whose twin poles were Los Angeles and the emerging San Francisco Bay Area. But the two scenes had so little in

common that there was really no 'West Coast scene' if that
meant California as a whole. Los Angeles was a long-established
focal point of the music industry, and whatever scene existed
there had grown up in an environment that had been created by
the record companies, studios and commercial imperatives – and
the long history of producing pop music – that pre-dated rock
'n' roll. Its rock scene, for the most part, existed alongside an
entertainment milieu rather than an underground one. The rock
scene in San Francisco was something else altogether, its roots
in an emerging culture of 'beatniks and crash pads, poets and
painters, [and] every kind of drug imaginable'.[38]

The Grateful Dead, in fact, had gained some renown for their
performances at the Acid Test parties organized in the Bay Area
by Ken Kesey and the Merry Pranksters in late 1965, where LSD
was passed out to anyone who was willing to show up. There they
met people like Allen Ginsberg and Neal Cassady (the inspiration for Dean Moriarty in Jack Kerouac's *On the Road*), as well as
Kesey and his Pranksters, and developed their loose, free-form
kind of rock music. 'The Grateful Dead did not play in sets,' Tom
Wolfe wrote of the Acid Tests in his novel *The Electric Kool-Aid
Acid Test* (1968):

> No eight numbers to a set, then a twenty-five-minute
> break, and so on, four or five sets and then the close-out.
> The Dead might play one number for five minutes or
> thirty minutes. Who kept time? . . . The Dead could get
> as stoned as anyone else. The . . . non-attuned would
> look about and here would be all manner of heads,
> including those running the show, the Pranksters,
> stroked out against the walls like slices of Jello.[39]

More than a year before the Summer of Love, the LSD phenomenon was drawing the interest of the media, with major magazines and periodicals running investigative articles. For a few dollars a dose, *Life* magazine reported, one could experience a ten-hour 'trip' and – if you were lucky – be delivered into a 'a world of beatific serenity and shimmering insight', but at other times into states of 'frenzy and terror'.[40] Whatever the outcome, LSD was life-changing, as *Life* concluded: 'the person who has taken this remarkable drug never sees life quite the same way again.'[41] Roger Corman's LSD film *The Trip* (1967), set around the rock scene of LA's Sunset Strip, attempted to illustrate the experience and sensations of an acid trip with visual effects and tricks that had been put together by Dennis Jakob, 'a notorious Nietzschean wild man' and UCLA film school friend of The Doors' Jim Morrison.[42] The LSD trip is represented by a rapid montage of shifting shapes and colours, overpowering sensations that send a hallucinating Peter Fonda staggering out onto the street only to find that he has wandered into a world that seems to exist under strobe lighting, his jittery body against a streetscape of saturated colour.

At the Monterey Pop Festival, the two scenes, LA and San Francisco, met each other on neutral territory – though Monterey was close enough to San Francisco that some in the Bay Area rock scene considered it their backyard – under the gaze of Pennebaker's film crew, their numbers added to by the inclusion of a number of artists from elsewhere. Of the San Francisco-based bands, only Jefferson Airplane were a known quantity outside the scene – they were riding high in the Top Ten with 'Somebody to Love' as the festival got under way. The other leading bands from the scene had only released their debuts a few months earlier (Grateful Dead, Moby Grape, Country Joe & The Fish), with the rest doing so after the festival, later in 1967 or '68 (Big Brother & The Holding Company, Quicksilver Messenger Service).

A snatch of the locally famous Big Brother & The Holding Company, fronted by Janis Joplin, filmed in spring 1967, is seen in Richard Lester's *Petulia* (1968), the tale of a San Francisco socialite (played by Julie Christie). They appear amid the opulence of an upmarket hotel, 'all sparkling cut-glass chandeliers and plush, blood-red carpeting', as the entertainment at a fundraiser, where they play to a crowd of disinterested onlookers dressed in ballgowns and tuxedos.[43] The Grateful Dead also pop up in the movie, first as hippies hanging around on the street and later in a nightclub scene, performing their song 'Viola Lee Blues' with the full-blown visual experience of liquid projections and strobe lights that would become associated with the period and seemed to have been devised, as *Vogue* magazine reported, as 'sensorial assaults' intended to simulate 'a trip into the realm

San Francisco's Haight-Ashbury hippy scene was detailed prominently in Richard Lester's *Petulia* (1968), which also featured appearances by the Janis Joplin-led Big Brother & The Holding Company, performing at a charity ball. The movie was filmed in spring 1967, in the lead up to the 'Summer of Love'.

Petulia also had minor roles for Grateful Dead band members (Jerry Garcia, left, and Bob Weir) as street people.

of expanded consciousness'.[44] Similar scenes reflecting the same kind of kaleidoscopic experience are seen in Jack O'Connell's *Revolution* (1968), a quasi-documentary filmed during 1967 that also includes images from the Human Be-In.

At the Monterey Pop Festival there was no love lost between the main Los Angeles-based festival organizers – music business mogul Lou Adler and John Phillips of the Mamas & the Papas – and the representatives of San Francisco's more organic music scene. The Grateful Dead in particular were being as difficult as they possibly could with the promoters and were soon being referred to by Adler and Phillips as the 'Ungrateful Dead'.[45] The sense of hostility towards Los Angeles and everything it stood for had been around for a while. 'As early as 1965,' Barney Hoskyns wrote, 'San Francisco hippies were routinely dismissing LA as a plastic dystopia, the polar opposite of everything Haight-Ashbury stood for.'[46]

When it was originally released in 1968, *Monterey Pop* should have featured all of those San Francisco groups alongside the

Scene from Jack O'Connell's *Revolution* (1967), shot in San Francisco.

Mamas & the Papas, Buffalo Springfield, The Byrds and Canned Heat from Los Angeles; perhaps not in total harmony, but at least as the symbolic affirmation of California's rise as the new capital of rock in the late 1960s. But only three of them made it into the movie: Jefferson Airplane, Big Brother and Country Joe & The Fish. The rest of the film was filled out with performances by Ravi Shankar, Simon & Garfunkel, Eric Burdon and his new Animals, The Who, The Jimi Hendrix Experience and Otis Redding, a few months before he perished in a plane crash. The reason for the omission of those San Francisco bands was that they refused to sign over the rights to recordings of their performances (although clips of all from the footage shot by Pennebaker and his crew would surface over the years).[47] As the film's director, Pennebaker might have theoretically been in a position to try to convince these groups that it would be to everyone's benefit if they were in the movie, but in addition to the fact that most of these bands were unknown beyond the Bay Area at the time, he didn't really care about them. 'I was the most ignorant person there,' he later said. This event was so alien to his interests – despite him having gained some recognition for *Don't Look Back* – that he might as well have been a visitor from another planet who had turned up with a camera.[48]

It is a notion perhaps borne out by the film's use of Scott McKenzie's 'San Francisco (Be Sure to Wear Flowers in Your Hair)' over the opening titles. The song, written and produced by the festival's two LA architects, Phillips and Adler, was intended as a kind of theme for the festival – it was a Top Ten hit before the cameras started rolling – and a way of drumming up publicity for the festival. It was total anathema to the San Francisco bands, who saw it as another typical Tinseltown product, 'like an instruction booklet for tourists'.[49]

Despite such evident tensions, for many the festival and the subsequent film would be remembered for their cultural

Jimi Hendrix in *Monterey Pop* (1968). The mostly unknown (in America) Hendrix painted his guitar the day before the performance and famously set it alight at the end of his show.

significance as one of the high points of the decade. For Eric Burdon, who is featured in the film performing a suitably psychedelic take on The Rolling Stones' 'Paint It Black', it was the sole communal event of the times that came off, 'a harmonic convergence of the hippie era'.[50] These were people who had been liberated from the stultifying 'self-consciousness' that had kept previous generations of Americans uptight.[51] The new generation glimpsed in *Monterey Pop* not only grew from roots in rock music and Beat culture but was nourished by a trenchant opposition to the war in Vietnam. San Francisco was a supply base for the war, and it was there that the ethos of peace and love blossomed most strongly. 'All that shiny hair, orangeade, beautiful hands, shades, watermelon, shoeless feet in tights, flowers', wrote Renata Adler in a *New York Times* review, couldn't conceal the 'serious young faces' that, before the war in Vietnam, 'we didn't seem to have'.[52]

Ravi Shankar in ecstasy, *Monterey Pop.*

The performance highlights of the film – Jefferson Airplane and Big Brother aside – were the acts from outside California: The Jimi Hendrix Experience, Otis Redding, Hugh Masekela and the spellbinding ragas of Ravi Shankar. Of all these figures, *Monterey Pop* arguably did most for Hendrix, whose ritual guitar sacrifice might have been designed to upstage The Who, who ended their set, as ever, by smashing everything up like vandals. Hendrix dedicated his act of destruction to the crowd, as an act of love, spraying a specially painted Fender guitar with lighter fuel before setting it alight. The film would help make Hendrix, who was as unknown in America as some of the San Francisco groups who asked to be left out of it, one of the biggest rock stars of the rest of the decade. His first single in the USA, 'Purple Haze', was only released there the day after the festival closed. Arriving from England to be introduced by Rolling Stone Brian Jones, 'dressed in the latest Carnaby Street clothing' and surrounded by British managers, musicians and hangers-on with British accents, almost everyone assumed Hendrix was one of them.[53]

John Milius's script for Coppola's *Apocalypse Now* (1979) was written to the sound of The Doors and Wagner. His idea was to tell a story of the Vietnam War as a clash between an ancient Eastern culture and an invading Californian hippy culture, exemplified by the sound of The Doors' kaleidoscopic song 'The End'.

4

MAKING MOVIES

When Iggy Pop first saw The Doors onstage in 1967, he was transfixed by the sight of Jim Morrison, his head topped by shiny black hair that seemed so long it might as well have reached down to his crotch. 'He looked like Hedy Lamarr in *Samson and Delilah*,' Iggy thought, except for the fact that Morrison was careering around as if drunk and antagonizing the audience.[1] When the *New York Times* reported on a Doors show that same year, the newspaper's correspondent could see how, with Morrison up front, this was a group that would have as much claim on the hearts of teenyboppers as The Monkees did; but, at the same time, there was also something very different going on. Morrison, he wrote, gave every impression of being someone doomed by fate, 'someone who knows he is too beautiful to ever enjoy true love', and he and The Doors represented a vision 'packaged in sex' and with the implicit motto of 'Nirvana now'.[2]

The Doors' sound and the sentiments expressed in many of Morrison's lyrics often pushed them into the kind of terrain where visions of transcendence and darker, more forbidden desires could be explored than one might have found in much of the rest of the pop charts. Curiously, the description that the journalist had used to sum up The Doors, 'Nirvana now', was also a slogan that could be heard on the tongues of many. Hippies had begun to sport it on lapel badges, which would be the precise point of origin for the film that gave new life to The Doors almost a decade after Morrison's death – *Apocalypse Now*.

The Doors, founded by former UCLA film graduates Morrison and keyboardist Ray Manzarek, rode on the hallucinogenic promise of the era. Morrison named the group after Aldous Huxley's *The Doors of Perception* (1954), an account of the author's experiences taking the psychedelic drug mescaline, and it would become clear over his short career that the injunction that made up the title of their first hit – 'Break on Through' (1967) – was taken to some kind of conclusion in his own pursuit of transcendence through, among other things, self-destruction. The music of The Doors also swam against the peace and love tide more commonly associated with 1960s California – mainly due to the prominence of the San Francisco scene – representing, rather, something like the dark undertow of the era. That much was clear in the 16 mm film clip that Elektra Records produced in 1967 for The Doors' single 'The Unknown Soldier'. It was a strange choice for a single, given its heavy anti-war sentiment and the sense of doom conveyed by Morrison as he barks out some of the words like a drill instructor to the sound of martial drumming and disorientating fairground organ. No one was going to be dancing in the clubs to this sound.

The film was equally unpalatable when it came to the mainstream outlets where it might have been shown. The four Doors members walk along Venice Beach carrying musical instruments – a sitar and tablas – and arrive under a pier, where Morrison is tied to a post with ropes. Newsreel images of the Vietnam War are intercut with flashes of executions, hippies and machine gun fire, and Morrison, looking like a bum who has been found sleeping on the beach, starring as a condemned man. Towards the end of the song, Morrison is executed, his limp body held up by the ropes as blood spills from his mouth, before 'Unknown Soldier' switches in its final verse to the sound of celebration at the war's end. There is no miming or acting out of the song in the conventional way one might expect of a clip made to accompany a tune vying for a place in the charts.[3]

When the single was itself banned across the country because of its anti-war lyrical content, it was obvious that TV stations would refuse to show the clip. So The Doors started to use it in their shows as a prelude to their arrival onstage. If they did not show the film, then Morrison and the other members of the band acted out the execution, with the singer collapsing on the floor as Manzarek on organ and John Densmore and drums signalled the gruesome finale. This 'acted out' version is captured in a Granada TV special, *The Doors Are Open*, shot in 1968 at London's Roundhouse, which the film-makers then intercut with scenes of military graves. The sound of The Doors would be the perfect complement to Francis Ford Coppola's *Apocalypse Now*, a movie released in 1979 but to all intents and purposes one that originated in the late 1960s.

Apocalypse Now was, in the words of its screenwriter, John Milius (who completed the first script in 1969), about a 'rock 'n' roll war'.[4] More specifically, he thought about it as the clash of two cultures: one embodied by the Californian hippie and psychedelic rock culture – carried overseas by the young soldiers – and what he saw as the ancient, pre-communist culture of Vietnam that the invaders were set on destroying. In the opening moments of the film when Captain Willard (Martin Sheen), a Green Beret and sometime CIA assassin, wakes from a hallucinatory dream after consuming too much cognac the night before, it is to the sound of The Doors. Their kaleidoscopic sex and death epic 'The End' invades his mind and provides the soundtrack to his nightmarish visions, its sound wrapping itself around Coppola's highly aestheticized images of the hellish scenes of helicopters dropping napalm. When we hear the music and see the images, it is as if the two were made to go together. The use of The Doors' songs, along with other rock music, was also intended to convey the idea of the rock 'n' roll war. Milius thought that these soldiers – many of them teenagers – were carrying around a headful of rock music, making it unlike any other previous war. He wrote the screenplay while listening to a non-stop diet of Wagner and The Doors' first album (the source of 'The End'), and both feature prominently in the film.[5] The music sits alongside the more literary sources for *Apocalypse Now* – Joseph Conrad's novella *Heart of Darkness* (1899) and Michael Herr's reporting of the war, published in *Esquire* magazine in 1969 – as the element that lodges it in its time and expands the range of Coppola's cinematic palette.

Herr's two-part article 'Khesanh' (a reference to the most remote u.s. Army outpost in South Vietnam) had been used by Milius when he was doing research for the script and would later supply the voiceover narrative for the Willard character.[6] Herr's account of life among the American forces contained its own interesting allusion to the way that rock music had seeped into the war. The rock music that he carried with him in his mind caused him to experience near-hallucinogenic reactions to what he was witnessing. Stuck in a strange landscape, with 'death and mystery' hidden in the hills that surrounded him, he watched as men and helicopters moved in and out of the army base; at the same time, he saw the scene 'from the vantage of the hills', the scene merging with the words of a song going around in his head. It was a new record by The Beatles, whose words now took on an 'incredibly sinister' meaning: '"The Magical Mystery Tour is waiting to take you away," it promised, "Coming to take

Apocalypse Now. As The Rolling Stones' '(I Can't Get No) Satisfaction' blares out
of a portable radio, Clean (Laurence Fishburne) dances on board the patrol
craft. The voice of Willard (Martin Sheen) narrates the details of his mission
to terminate Colonel Kurtz (Marlon Brando), a wayward officer who had
submitted a report on the situation in Vietnam blaming rock 'n' roll for helping
to degrade the quality of the American fighting force.

you away, dying to take you away . . .". That was a song about
Khesanh: we knew it then, and it still seems so.'[7] There are other
strange coincidences in how *Apocalypse Now* and The Doors were
related to each other: Morrison's and Manzarek's time at UCLA
overlapped with Coppola's own film studies there. More bizarre
is the fact that Morrison's father, George S. Morrison, a U.S. Navy
admiral, was the officer in command of the ship at the centre of
the Gulf of Tonkin incident in 1964 – the best candidate, if there
could have been one, for the singular event that effectively accelerated the Vietnam War into the kind of situation that *Apocalypse
Now* depicted. In an earlier version of the screenplay there was
another scene built around the sound of The Doors, in which
the character of Colonel Kurtz (played by Marlon Brando in the
film) prepares to meet an attack from North Vietnamese forces
by blasting out The Doors through huge loudspeakers as the
enemy advances.[8] He discusses the plan with Willard, who warns
him of an attack, but Kurtz is unfazed:

WILLARD: You're gonna get hit tonight, bad – a whole regiment of NVA regulars . . .
KURTZ: . . . We'll have ourselves a helluva airstrike tonight, a lightshow. How do you like The Doors: 'C'mon baby, light my fire . . .'.
Willard shrugs.
KURTZ: Do you?
WILLARD: Yeah, I like it . . .
KURTZ: I love it.
WILLARD: You've gone crazy.[9]

It sounds like a scene that might have raised the phantasmagoric dimensions of the film to even greater intensity, but while Coppola is said to have filmed Brando teaching the extras who were playing Kurtz's private army the words to 'Light My Fire' in their own language, nothing of the scene remains in the later versions of the film.[10]

FOLLOWING ANTONIONI to London in search of a rock band was Jean-Luc Godard, the pre-eminent figure of French New Wave cinema, who came for The Rolling Stones. If the Stones, as Andrew Loog Oldham suspected, were never going to cut it as film stars in the Beatles mould, they could at least find other ways of trading on their image as the bad guys of rock 'n' roll. Godard's original plan, in the words of Bill Wyman, had been for the Stones to 'act as a kind of backdrop to the story of a girl who arrived in London and freaked out'.[11] By chance, he ended up filming the complete evolution of the song that would be used as the film's title.

Sympathy for the Devil (aka *One Plus One*, 1968) draws a link between artistic creativity – represented by the Stones working on a record in the studio – and political violence. Godard took scenes of The Rolling Stones' *Beggars Banquet* sessions as they painstakingly construct a song, 'Sympathy for the Devil', from nothing, and set them alongside dramatic scenes of political revolutionaries, drawing a parallel between the work of art and the work that is required to build a revolutionary consciousness.

By 1968, the time allotted for studio work for established artists like the Stones seemed to have expanded infinitely from what it had been just a couple of years earlier. It was another instance of the stretching of the form that was more readily seen onstage when songs were transformed into the stepping-off point for extended musical workouts. But in other respects, studio time existed in radical contrast to the temporality of on-stage performance: in many ways the two had no relation to each other, and Godard understood that he was observing a pro-cess and not a performance. This was an entirely different way of seeing rock 'n' roll: not as the thing that in the end became a commodity for sale, but rather as the product of a situation aris-ing from the interaction between a number of people. Godard's camera – carrying the viewer with it as it sweeps across the cavernous room at London's Olympic Studios – brings us into the middle of something uncertain and confusing. We see mem-bers of the band scattered about the studio behind large sound baffles, put there by engineers to separate out each element of the music as it is recorded so it can be edited into a 'performance' later. Some of the band members wear headphones to monitor more closely the sound they are creating, considering adjust-ments as they go. It all seems to take a tremendous amount of time. Mick Jagger and Keith Richards confer and then play along with earlier takes of the track on the playback, repeating the same groove, building it up layer upon recorded layer. They slowly tease out the song, willing it to take its own shape. With the endless stopping and starting, it is many hours before 'Sympathy for the Devil' emerges. The laborious process produces one of the most durable artefacts of the Stones' six-decade-long career. The presence of Godard might have had a rather different outcome on the fate of that song had Bill Wyman and producer Jimmy Miller not been there to rescue the tapes after an all-night session when the heat from the film crew's lighting equipment set fire to the studio ceiling. Having retrieved the tapes, they ran for safety and watched as three fire crews went inside to tackle the blaze. 'Guitars, amplifiers, a Hammond organ and photographic equipment were all soaked,' Wyman recalled. 'After the firemen had finished, Jimmy Miller and I returned the undamaged tapes to the studio's tape vault and we left for home.'[12]

Godard, Philip Norman writes, had intended the film to end with scenes from the making of the song, showing that the Stones

Scenes from Jean-Luc Godard's *Sympathy for the Devil* (or *One Plus One*, 1968).

had still not resolved their ideas into the finished form, but that was not the way it turned out.[13] When the movie was completed, the producers found it difficult to make sense of the fictional episodes that were centred around Black Power revolutionaries engaged in acts of violence. The *International Times*, the leading British counterculture publication of the day, described the film as 'a collage with no fixed plot'.[14] Wondering how they were going to get 'bums on cinema seats', the producers decided – without Godard's knowledge – to recut his film to give more weight to the Stones' recording session, ending the film with the resolution Godard did not intend: the completed song.[15] Godard was so furious that when the film was premiered at the London Film Festival he 'threw a punch at one of the producers in the cinema foyer'.[16]

Marty Goes to Woodstock

The rock festival concert film reached its apex early on with *Woodstock* (1970), Michael Wadleigh's film of the now legendary three-day celebration of 'peace and music' held at a farm in Bethel in upstate New York in August 1969. No other film could quite match its scope or ambition, or compare in terms of bearing witness to an event of such significance. In its wake came many pale and uninspired copies that flickered over cinema screens in the following years as producers tried to emulate the massive and unexpected commercial success of the film, which was an epic in more than one sense.

The film seemed to have little relation to the rock music documentaries that had come before, and in that regard it was perhaps more influenced by Wadleigh's own background as a film student at New York University (NYU), where he met and worked with Martin Scorsese (who was a year ahead of him), acting as director of photography on the latter's first feature, *Who's That Knocking at My Door* (1967).[17] Wadleigh also worked as cinematographer on a small film called *David Holzman's Diary*, written and directed by Jim McBride (later to direct the 1980s Jerry Lee Lewis biopic *Great Balls of Fire!*), another fellow NYU film student. *David Holzman's Diary*, a pseudo-documentary story of a film-maker who begins to film his day-to-day life, had itself been inspired by the work of the likes of the Maysles brothers and Pennebaker, whose fly-on-the-wall approach could be seen as a means of offering the promise of revelation while at the same time enabling, through the appearance of realism, an approach that allowed for the subtle manipulation of the truth.

Another key moment in film that was influential among Wadleigh's film student contemporaries was Abraham Zapruder's 26-second home movie of the John F. Kennedy assassination. Even on the basis of the frames published in *Life* magazine – all that was publicly seen of the footage for years – it was clear that Zapruder, in virtue of being in the right place with the camera rolling, had produced the most compelling and authentic piece of *cinéma vérité* ever filmed. The message was clear: you had to be where the action was. 'The name "Zapruder" became a way of describing a certain kind of phenomenon,' Wadleigh said. 'If you had a very high quotient of amateurism in your technique, but the *content* was just superb – if what you were filming was absolutely riveting and captivating and couldn't be topped – why that was like one hundred per cent on the Zapruder Curve.'[18]

But *Woodstock* couldn't have been more different from the deadly slice of real life that Zapruder shot. The subject here was an event that would contain much that the film producers could plan in advance within the broader context of all the other unknowns of the situation; and, being spread over three days rather than mere seconds, the end result was not just going to offer itself up ready-made. It would have to very much be constructed after the event through painstaking editing.

Looking over what had been filmed would prove to be a Herculean effort. The volume of film was so substantial that you could pick your preferred unit of measurement to highlight the scale of the task: it was variously described as '70 miles of raw footage', '35,000 feet of film', '120 hours of film' and so on. The crux of the task now was to view it all and then sculpt it into a movie – one that Warner Bros. could send out to theatres. But perhaps, in other respects, the basic principle of the enterprise was still in keeping with the documentary essence of a Zapruder: you point a camera at something interesting, hope for the best, and work out what to make from it all later.

Filming such a sprawling and chaotic event also created innumerable problems for the production itself. Not only were these the expected technical glitches and logistical failures – which included running out of film, a camera crew communications system failing before it could be used and performers reluctant to be filmed – but the eventual challenge of dealing with and making a coherent movie out of those many miles of celluloid. In reducing more than one hundred hours of footage to a three-hour movie, *Woodstock* would become proof of the well-worn adage about necessity being the mother of invention. It would be recognized as 'one of the most notable models of the craft of editing since the Steenbeck editing table was invented', highlighted especially in the innovative use of a split screen that almost magically allowed 'another hour or two of footage to be squeezed in' to those three hours without distorting the basic structure and organization of the film.[19]

Woodstock's innovative use of a two- and three-way split screen
was devised as a way to get the most out of the vast amount of
footage that had been shot. Above left is the stage under construction,
and right, the arrival of the pilgrims at the festival site.

There was also the more specific and complicated issue of
how to deal with so many musical performances shot without a
synchronized soundtrack. Wadleigh and his editors – including
Martin Scorsese and Thelma Schoonmaker, who had also met at
NYU – spent months examining the performances as filmed on
multiple cameras, each capturing the same moment from different viewpoints. It was a nightmare trying to find onstage cues
that would allow them to match all of this material to audio
tracks that had been captured separately on tape. Most films are
made using 'slates' that indicate the point at which action begins
and contain vital information that gives an editor reference
points for identifying visual and sound sources so that they can
sync up the footage with an external soundtrack. With *Woodstock*
there was none of that. Instead, each reel had to be forensically
examined – made more difficult by the fact that many of the
performances were filmed in near darkness – to find the cues
that would allow the correct soundtrack to be matched to the
images. Sometimes it could not be made to work. Scorsese, for
example, took on what became an impossible task: trying to

match up audio to the footage of the Grateful Dead. The light was so bad that he was unable to find sync points, and eventually he gave up.[20] The Grateful Dead are not often recalled as one of the acts that played at the festival, and this is precisely because they are not in the film.

Back at the actual event, Wadleigh had needed a crew of seventy people to produce all this material, which covered not only the musical performances but the ways the event took shape and inevitably spilled out into the life of the surrounding community. Twelve of the crewmembers were shooting film. Some shot the action onstage, while others were sent out around the site to look for interesting material that might give a flavour of the festival as it developed. For three days, most of the crew were

Director Michael Wadleigh (shirtless at right), editor Thelma Schoonmaker, cinematographer Richard Pearce and assistant director Martin Scorsese (background, in glasses) working on *Woodstock*.

stuck on the site – that field in Bethel – just like everyone else who was there, and subject to the same deprivations. After the performances ended each day there was nothing else they could do but find a place to settle down for the night, so most of them slept backstage or underneath the stage. Scorsese may have been something of a rock aficionado, but that was back in the city. Wearing a white dress shirt and cufflinks, he seemed far from in tune with the style and attitude favoured by the peace and love generation, and arrived on the site seemingly unaware of where he was or what he had got himself involved in. The city-sized gathering and battlefield-like conditions came as a total culture shock to him and underlined the fact that – as one of his fellow cameramen recalled – it was only about 'the second or third time' he had even been out in the countryside.[21] 'At one point Marty tried to take a nap in a pup tent under the stage' but ended up bringing the whole thing down on top of himself: 'He had claustrophobia and was screaming for somebody to help him. But he wasn't Martin Scorsese yet, he was just some schmuck from Little Italy.'[22]

If the setting all sounds suitably messy – and a sign of the battles to come with everything from the elements to the unsanitary conditions – Wadleigh had a plan in mind for how the sprawling chaos of such an unpredictable event in such a place could be made into a film that would do much more than just present a series of musical performances. In fact, some of the most memorable parts of the film have nothing to do with the music. The rainstorm that halted the festival for several hours after Joe Cocker's almost show-stopping performance – enough to match the near-biblical scale of the gathering – became part of the film's record of how so many people could stick it out under such conditions. It also fed into the projection of the event and subsequent film as evidence that this was a crowd of people who were, in some bizarre and perhaps even misguided sense, interested as much in the idea of getting back in touch with nature, in communion with countless thousands of others, as they were in witnessing a rock 'n' roll show.

Before the film crew had even arrived in Bethel, Wadleigh was thinking that it could be a kind of contemporary retelling of *The Canterbury Tales*: in this case, the record of a mass pilgrimage to worship at the countercultural feet of Grace Slick, Joe Cocker, the Grateful Dead and Jimi Hendrix, the stage a modern equivalent of a cathedral.[23] Viewers of this film would be able to get some insight into what lay behind some of the individual trips that people made in order to bring this huge mass of humanity together in one place; the efforts of site workers, such as the sanitation workers who cleaned out the portable toilets; and also the effect the festival had on those who lived near the site. Wadleigh visited the town of Woodstock in advance, seeking advice from sometime residents and counterculture figures Allen Ginsberg and Hugh Romney (aka Wavy Gravy, as he would appear in *Woodstock*). Both were veterans of the West Coast Acid Tests and the Human Be-In of 1967, and they encouraged Wadleigh to think of the event in consciousness-expanding terms, as a trip 'back to the garden'. Wadleigh took this on board and started to describe his project to others as a film about 'a journey out of cities, which were complex and dirty and problematic, back to a pureness of nature'.[24]

The filming and editing of the musical performances was considered by many who viewed the film on its first release in 1970 as daring and innovative. *Film Quarterly* noted that 'the use of the split screen, of continually varying screen size, and the stunning, complex editing, sets up a visual rhythm which nicely enhances the music.'[25] For the film's audience, it was the closest many had ever got to the performers; and it was the most effort that had ever been put into editing to present the experience of performance on film, with cameras at times seemingly floating inches from the faces and instruments of the performers, revealing little details that made the viewing experience wholly different from the in-person one, where most people would have witnessed the acts at some distance. These were all things that only enhanced the film as a unique cinematic artefact: the sandaled feet of Richie Havens, like an ecstatic desert mystic who had wandered onstage, are seen frantically stomping out his rhythm; Joe Cocker, his battered star-spangled boots showing the wear that the sheer physicality of the effort it took to produce the voice heard when he threw back his head and opened his mouth; and the bare feet of Janis Joplin, arriving onstage as if from some relaxed gathering backstage.

An improvising Richie Havens was persuaded to open proceedings at the Woodstock festival, delivering one of the most unforgettable performances to be found in *Woodstock*.

DURING THE editing of the film, Scorsese – who eventually became the most well-known of all those who were part of its crew – was still trying to figure out how he was going to establish himself as a director who might get to make a movie with as much appeal as *Woodstock*. But he was often left to do firefighting jobs on other movies, such as another effort that has since vanished into oblivion, *Medicine Ball Caravan* (1971, directed by François Reichenbach). It was a project that had come about solely due to the success of *Woodstock*. Trying to strike lightning in more or less the same place twice, Warner Bros. didn't wait for the next big countercultural event to happen but instead conjured one up by 'dropping a million or so dollars on a bunch of hippie rockers to drive across the country in a caravan of buses, giving free concerts and generally doing their thing, while a crew filmed their antics'.[26] The result – after Scorsese had been brought in to re-edit it – was a box-office flop. After being brought in to work on some montage sequences in Robert Abel's *Elvis on Tour* (1972), Scorsese had had enough of rock 'n' roll (or so it seemed), later declaring that he didn't want to 'spend the rest of my life editing pop documentaries'.[27] How little did he know that more than four decades later he would still be doing it.

Film Music Film

In the decade after its release, the spirit of *Scorpio Rising* seemed to be most evident in the celebrated opening sequence and titles of Scorsese's *Mean Streets* (1973), where the Phil Spector sound of the Siren-like teenaged Ronettes' hit 'Be My Baby' lures the restless Charlie (Harvey Keitel) into his slumbers, carrying the viewer into a mind reeling back through the images of a life and establishing a backdrop in 8 mm memories for the tale about to unfold. 'Be My Baby' was a song that for Scorsese captured that moment in time: 'You can't beat that. I mean, that's 1963 or 1962 in New York . . . We used to hear that late at night. There was always a social club stuck in the back of some building and that song was always playing, echoing in the streets.'[28] But the part the song plays in this scene is more than just as a soundtrack. The scene in which Charlie wakes up, looks in the mirror and then puts his head back down on the pillow was composed of three cuts, the idea for which came to Scorsese from the three drum beats at the beginning of the Ronettes' song.[29] In its use of a so-called 'drop-needle' music soundtrack (that is, music taken straight from records), *Mean Streets* further developed Scorsese's understanding that rock 'n' roll, as much as other movies he had seen or anything else, held the key to 'the zeitgeist'.[30] Music had always left a strong impression on him, 'creating images' in his head that took him to another place, suggesting how they 'might be used in certain pictures'.[31] Often he would have the music that was to be used on the soundtrack blaring from speakers on set as the actors prepared to shoot their scenes – as well as making for a heightened atmosphere, it would give Scorsese ideas about how to compose shots for the camera.[32]

Scorsese's use of rock soundtracks was genuinely pioneering, and he had been among the first to really work with the possibilities of music that came straight from the records rather than being made for a particular film. *Who's That Knocking at My Door*, which premiered in 1967 but was not given a theatrical release until 1970, came with a soundtrack of 1950s and '60s records. As well as featuring more recent rock like 'The End' by The Doors, the Scorsese style immortalized in more successful movies later in his career was already on show here in the slow-motion tracking shots, cuts and fades that bring the characters closer to us. When we see J. R. (played by Harvey Keitel) hanging out with his neighbourhood friends, passing around handguns in between drinks, their silent laughter and interactions move with the Latin groove of Ray Barretto's 'El Watusi' (1962). For Scorsese, the music was not meant to be a mere tool of nostalgia – as it would be in other movies – but something that could be worked in with such precision that it would almost be playing a part of its own, with even the vocals of a song sometimes 'hitting between certain lines of dialogue'.[33]

In the wake of *A Hard Day's Night*, which delivered the film's American distributors, United Artists, unexpected riches not only through the tickets they sold but by virtue of the sales of a soundtrack that they ended up with the rights to (The Beatles' normal U.S. releases were on Capitol Records), the floodgates opened. It was a film that made rock more palatable to some in Hollywood for purely business reasons, but more crucially the music also appealed to other film-makers of Scorsese's generation, who soon saw this post-*Scorpio Rising* way of using music in film – applying it to visual content totally separate from the song and performer – as a new facet of film-making.

The most mainstream and successful of these movies was *The Graduate* (1967), directed by 35-year-old Mike Nichols and using the recordings of Simon & Garfunkel. The film follows the passionless affair between Benjamin Braddock (Dustin Hoffman), a college graduate recently returned home, and the wife of his father's business partner, Mrs Robinson (Anne Bancroft). *The Graduate*'s significance in rock's relationship with film is found in the way that the songs of Simon & Garfunkel – 'The Sound of Silence' in particular – become a key to making sense of its depiction of a character drifting aimlessly between youth and adulthood. The fact that the music ended up being used in such a way can be traced to Nichols's unexpected introduction to their music.

After rising each morning, Nichols found himself listening over and over to two Simon & Garfunkel albums that he had received as a gift. *Sounds of Silence* and *Parsley, Sage, Rosemary and Thyme* (both released in 1966) had nothing to do with his work; they were just what he happened to be listening to at the time. He would then go to the studio and shoot the scenes for the movie as it had been scripted. Gradually, however, the music seemed to take over his thoughts about the film and how Benjamin could be portrayed on screen. Before long, he was 'cutting sequences in his head' to songs like 'Scarborough Fair' and 'The Sound of Silence'.[34]

When Simon & Garfunkel had originally cut 'The Sound of Silence' in 1964 it had been a version that contained only voices and acoustic guitars. When it was released as a single, it flopped. A couple of years later, unbeknown to them, it was remade by their producer Tom Wilson, who added electric guitar, bass and drums to the original recording to try to capitalize on the folk-rock sounds of The Byrds and Bob Dylan that had taken over the airwaves. It changed how the song was heard, and the addition of the new reverb-laden instrumentation made it 'spooky and spectral, as if listeners were walking into a long, darkened tunnel'.[35] Right from the beginning of *The Graduate*, that version of the record establishes the same kind of mood when Benjamin is seen arriving back home from college. Wearing the look of someone who doesn't know where he is going, Benjamin moves impassively through an airport terminal building, carried along by a moving walkway as the entirety of 'The Sound of Silence' plays over the titles. Never before had a Hollywood movie so

Benjamin (Dustin Hoffman) reflects on what he has done after abducting bride-to-be Elaine (Katherine Ross) – the daughter of his lover – in *The Graduate* (1967). This was the first major film to be constructed around rock music; in this case the songs of Simon & Garfunkel represented the thoughts and feelings that Ben was unable to express.

masterfully identified rock music as a dramatic component that could provide the key to the inner life of a character and their fears and emotions. But by 1967, for many people rock was what really gave voice to their feelings. Nichols's idea was to make Simon & Garfunkel the inner voice of the often silent Benjamin.

'The Sound of Silence', although conceived and recorded years before the film, couldn't have fitted the film's subject any better: the song's lyrical imagery reflects the late adolescent and early adult confrontation with meaninglessness in its images of people driven towards a shallow existence of materialism and 'neon' superficiality. Together with the remarkable, passionate vocal interplay of Art Garfunkel and Paul Simon, the record was a time capsule of suppressed emotion at the point of exploding, and it captured a sense of generational angst and alienation. In the movie, the song swells up at those moments when Benjamin seems to be silently, blankly perturbed by the situation he finds himself in. 'Every time you would hear us,' Simon later said, 'it would be as if Benjamin was speaking.'[36]

The song is heard at key points in the film. One particularly notable use occurs when Benjamin floats in the pool of the family home after his first night spent with Mrs Robinson, where it enables Nichols to choreograph a tricky visual montage. With the California sun beating down on his already browned body, Benjamin stirs and drags himself out of the family pool, putting on a shirt. As he walks towards the house we see – in a background blur – that his parents are barbecuing by the side of the pool, but a split second later, when he walks through the door to enter the house, he is back in the hotel room where he conducts his affair with Mrs Robinson. There, as he lies down on the bed, she unbuttons the shirt he has just put on and runs her hands over his body. Benjamin looks on blankly as Mrs Robinson gets dressed. He rises to slam closed a door through which his parents are seen sitting silently in their kitchen. The musical sequence reaches a conclusion with Ben re-entering the pool. The song, with its mournful sentiments, followed by a brief snatch of another Simon & Garfunkel song about doomed romance, 'April Come She Will', helps to condense the image of Ben already trapped in an ill-fated affair that will not resolve his anxieties about the future course of his life. The musical sequence reaches a conclusion with Ben re-entering the pool. As he hoists himself onto his waterbed, he lands once again on top of Mrs Robinson in the hotel bed, only to be jerked back to reality by the voice of his agitated father. 'Ben, what are you doing?' 'Well, I would say that I'm just drifting,' he replies. 'It's very comfortable just to drift here.' The whole sequence – the music and the mood it establishes, and its discontinuity of time and place – takes us into the mind of Benjamin, who is by this time feeling trapped in the affair, going around in circles, his life turning back in on itself when he should be moving forward into the time of adult responsibilities.

As Paul Simon later remarked, it would be closer to the truth of the matter to say that Nichols rewrote and reconstructed what had been scripted around these recordings, rather than merely using the music for soundtrack.[37] While the use of recorded rock music that had already existed in its own right would become increasingly common in the decades ahead, it would be far more the case that the music was added an afterthought, slapped on to the movie to help enhance its commercial appeal (as would be the case by the early 1980s, when rock soundtracks arguably began to ruin films). For many directors who had come of age as part of the rock generation, the music was absolutely fundamental to their work. It was essential, even, to how they looked at the world in some cases. Wim Wenders, another pioneer of the pre-recorded rock soundtrack in films like *Alice in the Cities* (1974) and *Kings of the Road* (1976) – where it was heard in naturalistic settings, on radios and jukeboxes – once claimed that for him, rock was often the starting point for the films he made, so much had it become lodged in his subconscious as a source of images and even stories. 'I think rock 'n' roll has been my most important influence,' he once said, 'more than any pictures or stories.'[38]

Robert Altman similarly made use of existing recordings – in this case, from singer-songwriter Leonard Cohen – in the construction of his movie *McCabe and Mrs Miller* (1971). Unusually, the music would not be used within a contemporary setting, as was the case with *The Graduate*, but in a western. Altman had been familiar with Cohen's 1967 debut album, *The Songs of Leonard Cohen*, at the time it was released, but had forgotten about the record until after he shot his movie, when it occurred to him that he could use some of the songs as a temporary fix during editing by allowing him to establish a specific rhythm in certain scenes. Altman later claimed that it had worked because the songs must have unconsciously influenced how he was thinking of the film to such an extent that when he began shooting the scenes, he fitted them to the songs 'as if they were written for the film'.[39]

It was never the intention at that point that the music would appear in the finished film, but three songs – 'The Stranger Song', 'Winter Lady' and 'Sisters of Mercy' – remained in the film after Altman managed to obtain permission to use them. But that was not the end of the influence of Cohen's album on *McCabe and Mrs Miller*: other sequences were 'created with other songs in mind, to the point where images from the songs can be said to permeate the film'.[40] From the opening scenes, Cohen's 'Stranger Song' 'establishes the character of John McCabe' – played by Warren Beatty – and its words are reflected in Altman's images. 'Winter Lady', meanwhile, was Mrs Miller's (Julie Christie) theme.[41]

One of the most well-known uses of rock music in film at the time was in *Easy Rider* (1969), Dennis Hopper's tale of two bikers – Billy (played by Hopper) and Wyatt (aka 'Captain America', played by Peter Fonda) – as they travel across America from Los Angeles to New Orleans. 'The characters here are gentle, disarmed crusaders,' wrote Peter Conrad, 'who set out to find remedies for the discontent of the 1950s.'[42] In rock 'n' roll, the promise of liberation is contained in the voices and music of self-created people, and as the 1960s progressed it travelled much further than it had before from the artists to those who listened to it, for whom this sense of self-invention and personal emotional liberation would sum up an ethos, a way of life, whose ultimate values were to be found in transcending the bounds of time and place. For *Easy*

Rider, Hopper sought out music that would reflect what was going on in the minds of the characters. 'It wasn't necessary to have anybody playing it, it wasn't necessary to have it coming from a jukebox or radio,' averred a *Billboard* report on this new phenomenon they called 'Filmrock': 'The music was in Captain America's head as it was in the audience's head.'[43]

One of the film's most iconic moments, establishing the outlaw quality of the two central characters, occurs right at the beginning. Billy, wearing 'suede and flapping fringes', is a modern-day cowboy, while Wyatt/Captain America, the 'Stars and Stripes emblazoned on his leather jacket and crash helmet', appears to be some kind of 'explorer of uncharted psychic spaces'.[44] After we see them loading up their motorcycles and getting ready to take to the road, Captain America takes a long look at his wristwatch, a symbol of how society could control people by conditioning their perception of time. In a gesture that

Phil Spector (right, in orange-tinted glasses) as Connection in *Easy Rider*, a small cameo that reflected the increasing interaction between the film and rock worlds of the period.

signals there is no going back, the watch is removed and tossed into the dirt by the side of the road. As the engines of the two motorcycles fire up, carrying the two men down a long stretch of road into the distance, Steppenwolf's anthem for a life of carefree and boundless motorized exploration, 'Born to be Wild' (1968), explodes out of the screen with a force that was enough to pin back viewers in their cinema seats. The film's famous ending, a random act of violence that sees a hillbilly in a pickup truck take aim with a shotgun, first at Billy, who is blown off his motorcycle, and then moments later – and unexpectedly – at Captain America who suffers the same fate, bringing the film to an abrupt and shocking close. Watching this in Germany, the 25-year-old Wim Wenders felt that *Easy Rider* represented how people like him were seen by the older generation. He left the screening in a daze, feeling as if he himself was playing a part in a film at that moment. It was the shock of self-recognition, the realization that it could have been him up there:

> I stood outside and realized that I really look like the characters in the film, that I like the music of Jimi Hendrix, that I don't get served in a lot of bars around here, and that I have been locked up in jail for *nothing*. There will come a time when people will shoot here, too, I thought.[45]

Easy Rider was in a league of its own, becoming one of the highest-grossing films of the era. This was due in part to its soundtrack (itself a million-seller), which captured the spirit of the times and provided another means for audiences to identify with the film in addition to the settings, the characters and their ways of talking and acting. 'Films like *The Graduate* and *Easy Rider*', concluded an analysis published in *Billboard* in 1970, 'have indicated a new and valid method in which songs with lyrics instead of scoring can be employed.'[46] *Billboard*, as the leading trade publication of the music business, was signalling the commercial opportunities that lay ahead and delivered a conclusion that sounded almost like an instruction to Hollywood, if it still needed it: 'It is no longer necessary for anybody to be pictured singing whatever the song is. The audience does not require it.'[47]

The Last Waltz

The impact of Wadleigh's *Woodstock* in 1970 was immediate and far-reaching for those who became known through their appearance in the film. But for others, including 1960s icons such as the Grateful Dead, Creedence Clearwater Revival and Ravi Shankar, not being included in the film – whatever the reasons for this were – ended up making their performances that day slip somewhat out of the public memory of the event. One other act who never made it into the film – their manager, Albert Grossman, would not allow it – was The Band.

Music from Big Pink, The Band's 1968 debut, seemed in places to hark back to a time before rock 'n' roll existed, and as such it might have been thought to be in tune with the 'back to the garden' ethos that had framed the Woodstock festival when it was conceived as a retreat from the modern industrial world. The Band even lived in the town of Woodstock, like refugees from that world. Still, they were not exactly in the right place at the right time when they took to the stage on the third day of the event, Sunday 17 August 1969. Following the blistering finale of 'I'm Going Home' by Ten Years After, which even Hendrix later said he wouldn't have liked to have followed, the intimacy of The Band's low-key, old-fashioned songs was not entirely designed to please an audience of hundreds of thousands who had been sitting in mud for countless hours.[48]

Eventually, however, they would find the film-maker who was able to turn one of their performances into something that could come alive on the big screen. Scorsese, a veteran of the Woodstock festival and movie, returned again to music as a subject with *The Last Waltz*, his film of The Band's final concert, held on Thanksgiving day in 1976. Released in 1978, it was a kind of anti-*Woodstock* statement, cinematically speaking – a vision of rock music at the height of its 1970s reign that signalled the end of an era not only for The Band but for a certain kind of rock music that had grown out of the 1960s and events like Woodstock.

The Last Waltz was much touted at the time of its release, garnering probably more critical acclaim than any rock film then or since. There can be no doubt that this was due in part to what Scorsese was able to bring to the film in the way of professionalism. By 1976, following the successes of *Mean Streets* and *Taxi Driver*, he was already being heralded as one of the leading forces in American cinema, and his decision to shoot a rock film struck many as being far from the wisest choice for someone in his position to make. On hearing of Scorsese's involvement in the film, which had to be planned and executed under conditions of heightened secrecy because of his contractual obligations elsewhere, many acquaintances and film industry insiders thought that it must be a joke, as 'only hacks were supposed to do rock-concert films'.[49] In fact, some attributed his seduction by the project at a time when he was trying to finish a studio film – *New York, New York* – as evidence that his own suspected drug use had seen him seduced by the 'sex, drugs and rock 'n' roll' lifestyle that The Band knew only too well and which they would discuss in the interview segments of the finished film.[50]

In contrast to the era of rock documentary that began with direct cinema and reached a high point with *Woodstock* – an era defined by the use of 8 mm and 16 mm stock and films that sought to be more or less witness documents – Scorsese decided to shoot in 35 mm, and meticulously planned the shooting of the concert with a two-hundred-page document that contained detailed instructions for every one of the seven cameras that would be covering the stage. In fact, 'every line in every song was scripted' so that the cameras 'could focus closely on the person who was singing it'.[51]

A cast of 1960s rock luminaries appeared as special guests at the farewell concert (Bob Dylan, Joni Mitchell, Neil Young, Van Morrison and more), joined by San Francisco poets such as Lawrence Ferlinghetti and Michael McClure and blues veteran Muddy Waters. The various musical performers all rehearsed their short sets with The Band, who had to learn dozens of new songs and arrangements for the one-off show in a short space of time. For some of the group, notably drummer and founder member Levon Helm, the filming was an unwelcome intrusion on top of the already fraught atmosphere surrounding the event. 'It was more or less shoved down our throats,' he said of the idea to turn the concert into a movie. The other members of The Band suspected it was guitarist Robbie Robertson's idea of a ticket to a future career in Hollywood.[52] But they went along with it. Helm's attitude was to just get the whole unpalatable affair over with: 'do it, puke, get out.'[53]

Onstage, the Band that we see in *The Last Waltz* show no sign of the tensions that were at play behind the scenes in the run-up to the concert. After what Robertson described in the film as

Rick Danko (left), Levon Helm (behind drums) and Robbie
Robertson (right) in front of a specially assembled horn section
during the filming of Martin Scorsese's *The Last Waltz* (1978).

sixteen years on the road (it was more accurate to say sixteen
years together), they were able to fall into a natural musical sympathy with each other. Whether they were playing their own
songs – with 'Ophelia' (Helm on vocals) and 'The Shape I'm In'
(sung by Richard Manuel) particularly indelible performances
– or supporting guests such as Dr John, Ronnie Hawkins or
Muddy Waters, the film as a document offered proof of what the
many years on the road had made of them: a group of exceptional
musical talents capable of transcending the rock idiom to become
something that was truly and timelessly American (which considering all but Helm were Canadian is interesting in itself).

For the staging of the actual concert, which was planned in
advance of the film, promoter Bill Graham had decorated the

stage of his fading Winterland Ballroom with props borrowed from the San Francisco Opera's production of *La Traviata*. It suggested an ambience of elegant classicism that unwittingly also reflected an idea of rock as itself having reached its 'classic', high modernist peak. There were also huge chandeliers dangling above the stage that came from the props department of 20th Century Fox and were probably last seen in *Gone with the Wind*.[54]

As a film, *The Last Waltz* became celebrated for its cinematographic merits. These can be seen in the way that the cameras at times give a sense of floating on air in a kind of balletic interaction with the musicians, gliding behind The Band just as they lift one another into a singular harmonious entity. In the attention paid to editing and the coverage of the action onstage to the almost total exclusion of the audience, it was a film that raised itself above the usual standards of rock performance documentation, which was often chaotic. In fact, so closely planned was every shot that it was clear that Van Morrison's exit from the stage at the finale of the song 'Caravan' – a purple-suited, platformed-shoed figure high-kicking like a chorus line dancer, his face an image of ecstasy – was not orchestrated. It might have been the only moment in the film that Scorsese had not detailed in the shooting script.

Scorsese's interview segments with the members of The Band in *The Last Waltz* were filmed two years later and would be revealing of the quickly changing times, the air crackling with the unresolved tension of the disputes that drove the group to split at the end of that 1976 Winterland concert.

Nic Roeg's *Glastonbury Fayre* (1972) captured the people and performers at one of the last of an era of mass events that began with Monterey Pop Festival in 1967.

5
THE AFTERMATH

'I had imagined this journey as a quest,' says Stefan, the idealistic dreamer of Barbet Schroeder's 1969 film *More*, as he sets out on a quest for new and life-affirming experiences – ones that will take him to an early death. 'I wanted to burn all the bridges, all the formulas. And if I got burned, that was okay, too.'[1]

The hippie dream was, in part, the dream of rebirth or self-creation, but the waking aftermath was something of a downer. In *More*, Stefan (played by Klaus Grünberg) takes off in pursuit of the sun and winds up in Ibiza, the 'white island' that became a magnet for hippies in the 1960s. There, the beautiful but destructive Estelle (Mimsy Farmer) introduces him to heroin. Their lives gradually implode as a blinding and relentless sun beats down on the pair, who spend their time strung out or sprawled naked over coastal rocks. The downbeat and often ambient music that Pink Floyd provided for the film sets the mood for a tale that becomes a metaphor for the waning of the Summer of Love's euphoric promise. Schroeder, in fact, chose Pink Floyd in order to provide music that he thought his characters would listen to. It was music to serve not as background but rather in the manner that Wim Wenders was developing a cinema that portrayed lives intertwined with the sound of rock: it would come out of radios, or be heard playing through loudspeakers in a room that was the centrepiece of a particular scene.[2]

Barbet Shroeder's *More* (1969), with its Pink Floyd soundtrack, told a story of an unfulfilled desire for greater and more intense experiences born of the hippie ethos of freedom from all burdens. Estelle (left) teaches Stefan how to roll a joint on an album cover.

Like the students seen in Antonioni's near contemporary film *Zabriskie Point* (1970), Stefan and Estelle were like most of the Woodstock generation, the children of a culture that seemed to demand that the revolution of youth be not only for the moment but forever. It was an impulse that had soon arrived at a point of personal and countercultural exhaustion. Characters such as

Stefan and Estelle represented extensions of rock culture and its spread into new ways of living that marked 1969 as a very different time from 1967. They represent the other side of the optimism of the late 1960s, the demise of which, with more specific reference to rock music and culture, is usually located in the events recorded in the film of The Rolling Stones' 1969 American tour, *Gimme Shelter*, directed by Albert and David Maysles and Charlotte Zwerin (released in December 1970).[3]

Gimme Shelter culminates in a free concert at the end of the Stones' tour that was originally intended to be held in San Francisco's Golden Gate Park – the site of 1967's Human Be-In – but, in a sign of how lacking in foresight the whole idea was, the organizers only found a venue two days before the event. That was Altamont Speedway, a site some 100 kilometres from San Francisco. Though hastily planned, some began to refer to the event as a West Coast Woodstock.[4] As the cameras followed the Stones disembarking from a helicopter, someone emerged from a throng of fans and punched Mick Jagger in the face. If the free concert idea already contained enough problems to doom it, the nadir came when some Hells Angels – providing ad hoc 'security' in exchange for crates of beer – started to beat up people in the audience, cutting their way through the massed crowd using lead-weighted pool cues. In *Gimme Shelter*, the first signs that all is not going well come early in the day, when Jefferson Airplane grind to a halt mid-song. Paul Kantner of the band grabs a microphone. 'I'd like to mention that the Hells Angels just smashed Marty Balin in the face and knocked him out for a bit,' adding sarcastically as he looked towards the Angels, 'I'd like to thank you for that.' A Hells Angel grabs another microphone and starts arguing with Kantner.

Still, the music would resume under the realization that there was no way out and that stopping now might make things even worse. The bands continued as the light fell – The Flying Burrito Brothers, Crosby, Stills, Nash & Young (who do not feature in the film) and finally The Rolling Stones. During the Stones' set, the cameras would occasionally turn from the action onstage and register the aftermath of yet another skirmish in the darkness where the audience stretched a long way back and out of sight. Large spaces kept opening up in the crowd within sight of the stage as people ran from Hells Angels swinging their pool cues. The violence culminated with the killing of the eighteen-year-old Meredith Hunter, the shocking act captured on film as a swarm of Hells Angels descended on him. Viewing the performance scenes that follow – the band onstage unaware of what has just happened – the viewer's gaze is continually drawn to the side and front of the stage, where Hells Angels loitered menacingly, swigging booze, and to worried faces in the audience, pushed tight near the front, looking up at a clearly terrified Jagger, who tries to dance his way out of the nightmare. Towards the end of the film, when we see the Stones scrambling aboard a packed helicopter that looks like it will not be able to get off the ground, it is like a scene from a war movie.

If *Gimme Shelter* represented the last of the 1960s *cinéma vérité* creations that the Maysles brothers had pioneered, it gave the impression of being much less a film about a rock 'n' roll band on the road and much more about a change in the cultural weather. The way it was served up to the public was not to everyone's liking. The film-makers, some said, had failed to spell out the lessons to be learned from the dangerous countercultural dreams revolving around the idea of a self-organizing utopia. But the Maysles insisted that they were being true to the principles of direct cinema in leaving it for the viewer to draw their own conclusions, resisting the 'burdensome expectations' that their film would provide answers and point the finger of blame.[5]

The historical proximity of Altamont to Woodstock, the event that it is usually contrasted with, with both coming in the last months of that eventful decade, make it easy to see the moment captured in *Gimme Shelter* as a terminal point for the counter-culture. *Woodstock*, the scenes of which showed hundreds of thousands gathering peacefully to listen to three days of music, amazed viewers whose own lives were far removed from those that appeared on screen. As itself a high point of the hippie era, the festival and subsequent film might have been slightly mis-leading in its depiction of America at the end of the 1960s. It was an era of peace, love and war as much as it was one of peace and love. The year before, American cities were rocked by race riots following the assassinations of Martin Luther King Jr in April and, in July, of Robert F. Kennedy, who was running for the office of president and was assassinated in the closing days of his cam-paign. Indeed, an image of the 1960s approaching the dark end that Altamont represented is also at the core of another film – one less known and remembered – *Songs of America* (1969), a Simon & Garfunkel TV special that proved to be too dark and pessimistic for the network that had originally commissioned it.[6]

Simon & Garfunkel were popular enough that they had been able to wangle full creative control of the film from the NBC network. The upside for NBC was that their stars would take the project more seriously, put more of themselves into it. But the flipside was that the network would have no control over the film, and no idea what awaited them when they sat down to preview it.[7] To direct the special, the duo enlisted the young actor Charles Grodin, who had recently filmed a role in Mike Nichols's *Catch-22* (1970), which also starred Art Garfunkel. *Songs of America* opens with sweeping images of often desolate American landscapes – roads, shacks, garbage, images of urban poverty – and a sense of racial and political tension in the air. In a car, we see Paul Simon talking about Beethoven's forthcoming 200th anniversary in 1970. 'Somebody else's 200th birthday is coming up,' Garfunkel says, 'America.' Simon, wearing a sorrowful look, replies, 'You think it's gonna make it?'

When the television executives saw the film's scenes of the iconic 1960s figures who had been slain by assassins – the Kennedys and Martin Luther King – and the Robert F. Kennedy funeral train watched by mourners, all accompanied by the sound of 'Bridge Over Troubled Water', they realized that they were not getting nice pictures of the two stars singing on camera. Shocked at the bleak picture they had been presented with, they asked for it to be re-edited and toned down. When it was clear that this was not going to happen, they had no hesitation in dropping the film and giving it to Simon & Garfunkel to do whatever they wanted with it – it would not be broadcast on NBC. *Songs of America* would eventually be picked up by the rival CBS network and shown in November 1969.[8]

Hippies and Revivalists

In the immediate aftermath of *Woodstock*'s huge success there were films made of rock festivals in Toronto (Pennebaker's *Sweet Toronto*, featuring John Lennon and the Plastic Ono Band, Chuck Berry and others) and the Isle of Wight (Murray Lerner's *Message to Love*, featuring Hendrix, The Who and Leonard Cohen, which remained unreleased for more than two decades), and other less celebrated events in the Netherlands (*Stamping Ground*, 1971) and New York (*The Day the Music Died*, a release in 1977, the subject of which was a chaotic 1970 festival), which spawned even lesser-seen movies. Often these were events featuring largely the same acts that had come to worldwide attention through *Monterey Pop* and *Woodstock*. These films might be seen as examples of how the twin businesses of music and film continued to try to keep pace with the audience, cashing in on a formula that seemed to give the people what they wanted.

Few of the films that were made of such events were able to capture a pivotal cultural moment to rival Wadleigh's *Woodstock*. The one that did manage it was Lerner's *Message to Love*, a film that took 25 years to see the light of day, only being released in 1996. Its subject is the Isle of Wight Festival, held in late August 1970 and attended by an estimated 600,000 people, a scale that put it on the same kind of footing as Woodstock. With some of the same 1960s icons present – Joan Baez, Hendrix, John Sebastian, The Who and Sly & The Family Stone – it has frequently been described as the last of the mass countercultural festivals that would achieve the scale of Woodstock. But for all its similarities to Woodstock, the Isle of Wight Festival seemed to lack the peace and love vibes and 'take care of yourself' announcements that had emanated from the stage in upstate New York that summer's day only a year earlier.

From its opening montage, the film quickly establishes a context for a different kind of experience: police helmets atop marching bodies, a corrugated steel fence encircling the field full of people, banknotes spilling onto the ground in a tent behind the stage and being counted out, and – to top it off – the master of ceremonies and festival organizer, Rikki Farr, screaming at the audience that they were selfish pigs who could go to hell. As the viewer becomes accustomed to the idea that things are not quite obeying the exhortations for peace and love, the sound of John Lennon and Yoko Ono's 'Give Peace a Chance' wafts unconvincingly from the festival sound system and over the heads of the audience – this, after the crowd had been harangued from the stage once more by Rikki Farr. Near the beginning of Kris Kristofferson's performance, the hostility coming from the audience was washing over the stage, and the singer – who would end up soon being cast in a succession of movies as a kind of laid-back tough guy – looked over at his band and said, 'I think they're gonna shoot us,' before abruptly downing instruments and walking off.

The sense of a collapsing counterculture had already been aired by this time – *Rolling Stone* magazine had delivered just such a verdict on the Altamont festival in its 21 January 1971 cover story, 'Let It Bleed' – and here on this little island off the edge of England was an event that merely reinforced the idea. Writing in the *Observer* newspaper, rock critic Tony Palmer noted that the festival 'provided the most sordid, pathetic and comical voyeuristic trip of our time', an impression eagerly taken up by a media that could not wait for it to fail and for these hippies to disappear.[9]

Lerner's movie – perhaps one of the real gems of rock film – was 'gleaned from 175 hours of film shot by nine crews who spent more than a month on the festival site'.[10] The eventual release of the film in 1996 has been followed in the years since by single-performance films culled from the same footage: The Who, Jimi Hendrix, Leonard Cohen and Jethro Tull. But *Message to Love*, as a festival film, is about something bigger and more interesting than the musical performances. And while many of the performances are today regarded as some of the most significant of the artists' careers – the festival was Hendrix's last performance, taking place twelve days before he died, and Jim

Morrison would perform only a handful of times after this before he, too, died, in 1971 – the music onstage as seen in *Message to Love* is often overtaken and overwhelmed by the revelation of how chaotic it all was; how much it really seemed to underline that the spirit of 1967 had almost evaporated.

Lerner skilfully uses a handful of witnesses and onlookers – one is tempted to say, ready-made 'characters' – from in and around the festival, who periodically pop up on screen to place what was going on into the perspective of that moment in 1970. No doubt the film was put together with the hindsight of more than two decades having passed, but these figures act to deflate the sense of the 1960s rock stars as latter-day gods and inject a large measure of humour into the picture of an event that to all intents and purposes – marked as it was by endless days stuck in a field with no easy way off the island – seemed about as much fun as a season in hell.

The most scabrous character is identified on screen as 'The Commander', apparently a member of the public whom we assume is an ex-policeman or ex-army officer. But there is also 'The Agent', the good-humoured Bert Block, an American promoter and former 1930s bandleader who was working as part of the festival production. These two older figures function as commentators on the loopy countercultural mores that are running up against reality at the festival. The ruddy-faced Commander – whom we only ever see speaking to camera with an unlit pipe dangling from his mouth – recognizes the power of this rock music, sees in it something capable of hypnotizing a group of people and leading the young to places they would be better off not going to. 'You see, the whole thing,' he declares, 'if you have kids running about naked, fucking in the bushes ... I don't know that's particularly good for the body politic.' His words segue straight into the bizarre sight of Tiny Tim – a vaudevillian music hall invader sent from the pre-counterculture world that The Commander would approve of – singing 'There'll Always Be an England' through a megaphone. His performance is to the obvious delight of the audience, who seem for a moment to wave and cheer in harmony.

The Commander's concern for public morality was shared by the authorities as well: to discourage nude bathing on the site, Tony Palmer reported in *The Observer*, the police, with the aid of the Royal Air Force, 'dropped smoke bombs into the midst of the bathers . . . many thought it was cs gas, and panic spread'.[11]

The two-faced attitudes of some of the performers are laid bare by Lerner. As the organizers are seen backstage counting cash, appeals are made from the stage for money from those who have managed to gatecrash the site – or else the bands won't play. Just then, Tiny Tim appears again, overheard telling a journalist that he thinks it should be a free festival. Bert the Agent conspiratorially reveals to Lerner that Tiny Tim had refused to go on moments earlier unless he was paid immediately in cash. 'He can't sing with his ukulele without the money,' he says. 'He doesn't *tune up* without the money, Murray, y'understand?' Out on the fringes of the site, Lerner's crew are observing the corrugated iron fence, which has been daubed with swastikas and is guarded by an exceptionally thin line of security guards with barking dogs. The massing crowd simply run right through and trample it down.

The artists onstage, as one of those lingering outside the barriers says, are nothing more than 'plastic gods' who are only interested in money. Lerner asks this long-haired figure – it transpires that he is a former advertising man from New York – what he thinks should be in the film. The audience, he says, implying it is they who made the event, not the people onstage. 'You should put an empty field at the beginning,' he says to the camera, 'and then an empty field at the end.' He and the others would be the real stars of it all, 'invisible gypsies' who would clean it all up and leave the field as it was. At the end of film, much like the end of *Woodstock*, a scattering of tiny figures can be seen. Looking like matchstick people in the vast field, they try to tidy up, but the site is totally strewn with rubbish, looking as if a dozen tornados have just blown through.

Some of the newer acts who appear in the film, like Emerson, Lake & Palmer, were able to exhibit a kind of showmanship and musical dynamics executed at high volume that fitted the moment and disarmed the audience. Keith Emerson, bare-chested under a glitter jacket that dazzled under the stage lights, stabbed his Hammond organ with kitchen knives to obtain a deafening sustained chord, rocking the huge instrument back

Keith Emerson gets physical with his Hammond organ during Emerson, Lake & Palmer's performance at the 1970 Isle of Wight Festival, as seen in Murray Lerner's *Message to Love*.

and forth and spinning it around on one of the corners of its base as these new progressive rockers blazed through their heavy rendition of Aaron Copeland's 'America', a hit for Emerson's previous band the Nice in 1968 that had become something of an anti-Vietnam war anthem, and probably the only number in this, their debut public performance, that the audience would have been familiar with. In other circumstances it might have been enough to upstage the one act that had always possessed the kind of visceral musical attack that here met its perfect audience: The Who. Now, at the last of the great countercultural gatherings, these veterans of the first, Monterey Pop, and also the most famous, Woodstock, were chosen by Lerner to close out the film.

In keeping with their performances at those events, there would be no appeals for calm or attempts to ingratiate themselves with the audience. In fact, to see them in the movies that represented these great events – *Monterey Pop*, *Woodstock* and *Message to Love* – is to see how unlike that era they were. It is almost as if The Who crashed right through the 1960s in tune with the Isle of Wight audience who had crashed through the barriers, which is to say heading towards a future that was of their own making but yet to reveal itself fully. The evidence of *Message to Love* is that The Who were the most astonishing sculptors of noise that rock had so far produced. It is something that was also reflected in their album of the same year, *Live at Leeds*. The calibrated violence and form-stretching of 'Young Man Blues', characterized in large part by Townshend's remarkable control of volume and dynamics, revealed a band that was capable of transcending the limits that studio recording placed on their music as much as anyone in that era when rock was transformed into something that often seemed to be far from its origins. But when the song ends with Roger Daltrey screaming that what the young had left today was 'sweet fuck all', we are also right back there at those beginnings.

Other performers seen in *Message of Love* – including Joan Baez and Joni Mitchell (who sang her song 'Woodstock') – are seen as lost figures, in the blink of an eye now hopelessly out of tune with the charged atmosphere but still singing of hippie verities that were being smashed to bits all around. The film casts a jaundiced eye back on some of the artists, the organizers and audience – most of whom don't really come out of it looking that good – which allows *Message to Love* to reveal rock and its countercultural offspring crashing up against the barrier of its own unrealizable expectations.

Probably the last document to record the quasi-spiritual quest that the counterculture had come to represent was *Glastonbury Fayre* (1972), Nicolas Roeg's documentary about the 1971 Glastonbury festival, which took place in Pilton, Somerset, a short distance from the Arthurian vale of Avalon. It was, one report noted, 'one of the weirdest events ever staged in modern Britain'.[12] Into the fields arrived not only a sprinkling of homegrown rock adventurers such as Arthur Brown, Fairport Convention, Terry Reid and Family, but American singer-songwriter Melanie, who would ring in the summer solstice during her set. Along with them came not only the long-haired hippies but Christian missionaries, Krishnaites, dogs, old ladies dressed for the village fete, Hells Angels and a thirteen-year-old Indian guru who appeared onstage to celebrate peace and love and declare that he had found a replacement for money, if only they would listen to him.

For centuries, nearby Glastonbury Tor had been a site of religious worship, and the locals had long been accustomed to strange pilgrims arriving in the nearby town. By the early 1960s, the tor was of renewed interest to archaeologists, who surveyed the mound in search of the remains of King Arthur's Camelot. As the hippie era dawned, it became like a magnet to a new generation of spiritual seekers. 'Hippies, poets, mystics, weirdos and sundry unclassifiables have hitchhiked and tramped into the town from all over,' *The Guardian* had written a year earlier, looking for 'vibrations'.[13]

Andrew Kerr, the festival organizer, thought he could take advantage of this era when people gathered in large, remote fields to listen to rock music. He arranged for the festival's new Pyramid Stage to be sited on a ley line that was said to connect Glastonbury to Stonehenge, that other site of pagan spirituality in southwest England. Roeg's film shows those there to be just as interested in this aspect of the gathering, and freaking out at the chanting and drumming taking place among the audience members, as they were in the music onstage, as some of the acts seem to go through the motions without stirring much of a response. One performance that seemed to rupture the hippie atmosphere was that of Arthur Brown, known for the song 'Fire', a hit for The Crazy World of Arthur Brown in 1968. Brown had gained notoriety for wearing flaming headgear and setting out to shock. Here he was flanked by a band who looked like extras from a horror movie, his guitarist appearing like an unhinged Andy Pandy who might have fitted into shock-rocker Marilyn Manson's band several decades later.

The sparse crowd and freak-out behaviour seen in *Glastonbury Fayre* leaves the strong impression that there, in 1971, only the most committed of spiritual seekers were still willing to endure the trials of the rock festival pilgrimage: the mud, the insanitary conditions, being fed like some medieval marching army temporarily encamped in a giant field. A mere 12,000 people attended the festival, and it has the air of the aftermath about it (there would not be another Glastonbury festival until the end of the 1970s). The aftermath of that aftermath, however, can be seen in two other contrasting concert films from around the same time: *Pink Floyd: Live at Pompeii* (1972) and *The London Rock and Roll Show* (1973).

Live at Pompeii, while representing a performance in a public setting, cannot really be described as a concert movie. With no audience present, the kind of soundscapes that had come to characterize the post-Syd Barrett, pre-*Dark Side of the Moon* period floated free in the ancient surroundings of Pompeii. It is a performance that seems to be in keeping with the other film-related soundtrack music the band were making in the late 1960s and early 1970s and which was coming to characterize their work more generally.[14] Some of the sounds and textures on their 1968 album *A Saucerful of Secrets* could aptly have been described as cinematic music. As well as the soundtrack to Barbet Schroeder's *More* (and later his *La Vallée*, 1972), they had provided music for Antonioni's *Zabriskie Point*, working closely with the director

Roger Waters (left) and David Gilmour play not to the masses but to Roman ruins, in *Pink Floyd: Live at Pompeii* (1972).

147

A scene from *Pink Floyd: Live at Pompeii* (1972).

during the making of the film. It led them to save up their film music leftovers for future use as they informally adopted a 'policy of recycling anything remotely useful'.[15]

In *Live at Pompeii*, the sound of the spacey 'Echoes' cuts away from the band performing in the setting of the 2,000-year-old amphitheatre to images of the band members traipsing over a steaming Mount Vesuvius looking like 'four Kings Road hippies transplanted to a prehistoric landscape'.[16] The fact that there is no audience to witness the performance seems significant in light of later accusations that Pink Floyd and other 1960s survivors had grown too distant from their origins and their audience. The film also perhaps signalled the fact that *Woodstock*-style documentaries, presenting rock as part of a wider cultural phenomenon, had somewhat run their course.[17] 'The music and the silence and the empty amphitheatre would mean as much' to cinemagoers, said director Adrian Maben, as watching a filmed performance that was also about – and had cameras trained on – 'a crowd of thousands'. It was, in other words, a different kind of event.[18]

The London Rock and Roll Show (1973), directed by Peter Clifton, was the first of a number of mid-1970s throwbacks to the pre-counterculture rock era. A straight performance film of a day-long concert held at Wembley Stadium in London in 1972, it featured 1950s luminaries such as Little Richard, Chuck Berry, Jerry Lee Lewis and Bo Diddley sharing the stage with some more contemporary acts (MC5, Gary Glitter) for an audience of ageing Teddy Boys, for whom the 1960s might have felt like a bad dream. When one 1950s icon, Little Richard, 'attacked his piano and screamed about Black Power', it was, if nothing else, a reminder of the fact that the here and now was not the one that these fans yearning for yesteryear hoped to find.[19] As the film's roving cameras survey the events beyond the stage, the then little-known figure of Malcolm McLaren is visible – purveyor of records and clothes to the Teddy Boys of England from his King's Road boutique Let It Rock, not yet notorious but already the subject of a *Rolling Stone* feature on his part in the burgeoning rock 'n' roll revival.[20]

It is unclear if the generally lacklustre performances that are featured in this film played a role in McLaren soon ditching his Teddy Boy obsession, setting in chain the events that would lead to the Sex Pistols forming with his encouragement almost exactly three years later. As seen in another concert film of 1973, *Let the Good Times Roll* – which employed the split-screen techniques of *Woodstock* to generate a sense of excitement – there was no shortage of interest from concert audiences in these stars of the 1950s. But Chuck Berry's 'My Ding-A-Ling' aside – a big novelty hit of in 1972 – they weren't bothering the charts or really appealing to kids. In fact, there seemed to be a distinct lack of fraternity around as the various figures who might have claimed the mantle of King of Rock 'n' Roll squabbled. 'I haven't seen any hit records by Little

Richard lately,' Jerry Lee Lewis declared. The only crown that Lewis deserved, Richard retorted, was 'King of Stupidity . . . I don't see how he has the nerve to put on the shoes that I threw away.'[21]

Backward Glances

There were few lasting signs until the early 1970s that rock 'n' roll would do anything but continue its tendency to blaze a trail into an uncertain future. Certainly, there were exceptions: in the period before The Beatles hit America in early 1964, there were indications that the lack of action in rock – by then absorbed at the mass level into the controlled entertainment industry – was leading still young but maturing listeners back to their love for the music of the mid-1950s. And songs like 'In the Still of the Night' by The Five Satins (1956) and 'Earth Angel' by the Penguins (1954) had reappeared in the American charts in the early 1960s.[22] The fact was that by 1960, so-called 'oldies' comprised a real – but temporary – trend, especially with listeners approaching their mid-twenties.[23] Like the pre-Beatles 1960s, the early to mid-1970s seemed to mark a similar period in which a fixation with the recent past became a stronger and more long-lasting cultural force.

But it was not always clear what was motivating it, or if such backward glances could have any real merit beyond the desire to once again exploit a known commercial quantity. When Bob Dylan's film about his 1966 tour of the UK and Ireland, *Eat the Document*, was released in late 1972, Vincent Canby of the *New York Times* thought that now, getting on for a decade later, it looked like a document 'left behind from the Pleistocene age of rock'.[24] That was a recognition of how fast things had changed, not only in the world of rock but in the wider world. The optimism of the JFK era through which Dylan rose had given way to the Vietnam War and Richard Nixon in the White House. 'Times, attitudes, and interests changed,' Canby noted. 'This Dylan hysteria, recollected in tranquillity, seems distant indeed.'[25] Dylan was 31 years old in 1972, at least half a decade beyond the point in life when it was presumed an interest in rock 'n' roll would expire. He was, in other words, already an old man by rock standards.

But it was not just Dylan who seemed to be looking back. Don McLean's 'American Pie', a massive hit in late 1971, presented what was effectively a cultural history of rock 'n' roll sung as an epitaph. Elton John's 'Crocodile Rock' of late 1972 looked back at rock 'n' roll as the sound of a carefree world. The British singles charts were populated by glam variants of 1950s rock. Alvin Stardust sounded like an exaggerated Gene Vincent and wore a carefully constructed look of rock 'n' roll rebellion. An advert for the British film *Stardust* (1974), about the rise and decadent demise of a fictional rock star within little more than a ten-year period, posited the idea that rock had travelled some way from its golden days and, in these days of concept albums, had lost touch with its audience. 'Remember the '60s?' the posters exclaimed: 'Remember when things weren't just great, they were groovy!'

In that film, David Essex plays Jim MacLaine, now distanced from his origins by stardom and likewise isolated from his audience and the things that had made him famous in the first place (his origins having been told in the previous year's *That'll Be the Day*). Such films were made in part because there was a ready-made audience for this kind of looking back. As much as records from bygone eras could have a powerful, almost narcotic effect that drew the listener back in time, cinema could embody something more: something like a simulacrum of that past with all its vivid and audiovisual power. It was clear that there had been enough of the necessary distance between the present and rock's early days to make the nostalgia work – all that was required was someone or something that could bring the past vividly back to life on screen in a way that transcended all previous attempts. That film would not be *Stardust*, or its predecessor of the previous year, *That'll Be the Day*, but George Lucas's *American Graffiti* (1973), which was not about musicians or performers but rather used the music to carry its audience back to a time and place when the first rock era was coming to a close.

American Graffiti is a dreamlike vision of the USA in 1962, frozen in a crepuscular, neon-lit moment. The film hardly has a story and instead is little more than a collection of vignettes of a late summer's night in 1962. Teenagers cruise around town in hot-rodded cars with gleaming polished surfaces that catch the reflected streetlights, weaving in and out of places where waitresses on roller skates emerge from neon-lit diners, serving milkshakes while Bill Haley's 'Rock Around the Clock' and the sound of the mysterious DJ Wolfman Jack are heard booming out of some car. The film gets close to the essence of rock 'n' roll as a kind of temporality or time in life, one that the kids in 1962 would have no sense of outlasting in that particular moment.

It achieves this by both stressing the significance of this life after dark to what it felt to be free in Modesto, California, in 1962 – director George Lucas's world – and by positing the complex, tenuous relationship that the characters' lifeworld has with their sense of the future and the world beyond. Some scenes are so perfect that we suspect that it is surely Lucas's dream of his own past, or a past he wished he had lived. When we see the hot rod contender, John Milner (played by Paul Le Mat), he is exiting a

Neon, chrome and light: the surfaces of *American Graffiti* (1973) lull the viewer into a dreamlike past.

local garage after a tune-up and on his way for the big showdown against an out-of-town cruiser (played by Harrison Ford). The car and the forecourt furniture are so luminous against the deep night that he soon vanishes into that it is like stumbling into someone's dream.

If it was a dream that Lucas himself had nurtured, it soon becomes clear that we are looking into a time and place that would soon be changed forever. What lay in wait – and what the audience who saw this film in 1973 had already experienced – was the 1960s: the Kennedy and King assassinations, Vietnam,

The Beatles and the British Invasion, drugs and hippies, Woodstock, and a new kind of rock 'n' roll that by the time of the film's release often revolved around themes of violence and alienation, paranoia and excess.[26] In the 1962 of *American Graffiti* there are only fleeting glimpses of change ahead, and indeed only the brightest of the characters understand that things can never really stay the way they are, despite the all-encompassing experience of the endless summer night. If there is anything that comes close to a central focal point in the sprawling film, it is the figure of Curt (Richard Dreyfuss), who is caught between the desire to stay here in this place and an equally powerful need to move away and start a new life. For much of the night he scours the streets looking for a ghostly female presence driving around town – was she real or did he imagine her? – who had mouthed the words 'I love you' at him as she waited at a set of traffic lights.

Curt is destined to escape once he realizes that the mystery woman is a trap. His friend Milner, slightly older, has never had an inkling of moving on to anything different. Milner senses that things are no longer what they were and observes to one of the younger nightbirds that it used to take hours to run the circuit of the town. Now? Not so much. The changes he notices come through the music on the radio. 'I don't like that surfing shit,' he says to a passenger in his car who is playing around with the radio. 'Rock 'n' roll's been going downhill since Buddy Holly died.' In fact, Milner displays the signs of someone realizing his place in the flow of time and the inevitable intimations of mortality that surround him in this small town. He ends up – not for the first time, we suspect – walking round a junkyard, looking at the wrecked cars he had once raced and cruised with on nights like this.

American Graffiti became one of the primary examples used to illustrate what the cultural theorist Fredric Jameson described as a postmodern aesthetics of nostalgia that established a new way of projecting a kind of 'mesmerizing lost reality' into screen life.[27] This is a past that is approached not through the accuracy of facts but rather through 'stylistic connotation' that achieves 'pastness' by its 'glossy qualities'.[28] Looks and fashions equate to the essence of the time period. The film established a trend that continued in a succession of later films with allusions to such a rock 'n' roll past, including the likes of *Back to the Future* (Robert Zemeckis, 1985), *Peggy Sue Got Married* (Francis Ford Coppola, 1986) and *Hairspray* (John Waters, 1988).

IN NOT *Fade Away*, a movie directed by David Chase (better known as creator-director of *The Sopranos*) that opens in 1963, the cultural world of New Jersey teenager Douglas (John Magaro) is sustained by rock 'n' roll: records, unattainable guitars behind glass windows, Bo Diddley and The Rolling Stones on the family TV screen. He peruses album sleeves and takes in the images and notes that are often found on the back, which open up the music further into other imaginative realms, suggesting a future of unlimited possibilities. Rock 'n' roll created the so-called generation gap because it became the property of the swelling population of baby boomers that Doug belongs to, catapulted into the kind of economic independence and social freedoms their parents never knew.

Doug's embrace of rock 'n' roll as more than mere music sets him at odds with his father, Pat (James Gandolfini), who sees in the way his son dresses and wears his hair a world heading in the wrong direction. Pat smirks at the sound of Dean Martin's voice, coming from the living room TV, thanking his guests The Rolling Stones for doing a turn on his show. 'Aren't they wonderful,' Martin says, eyes rolling heavenwards to the sound of studio audience laughter. 'That was The Rolling Stones, who are now heading back to London to have a hair-pulling contest with The Beatles.' *Not Fade Away*, like many post-*American Graffiti* movies, makes use of soundtrack music to locate the characters in time and place. In the wake of the British Invasion in 1963, Doug forms a band with other local teenagers. They make some demos and audition for famed producer Jerry Ragovoy (Brad Garrett), but never make it.

As the sounds of Bo Diddley and the Stones give way to the Small Faces, The Yardbirds, Moby Grape and references to Jimi Hendrix and the *Tibetan Book of the Dead* – the inspiration for The Beatles' psychedelic masterpiece 'Tomorrow Never Knows' – we are aware that this is a journey through the 1960s. Just as rock music would, by the end of the decade, find fertile ground in California, so Doug in 1969 finds himself in Los Angeles. At a party in the Hollywood Hills, he thinks he spots Charlie Watts of the Stones. Doug tries to get his group back together again, but his bandmate and friend since childhood Wells says it's not on the cards: 'You ever read the *Tibetan Book of the Dead*? There is no past. No future, either. Just the now, so you don't need to be hung up about whether you're in the band, or some other band, or no band at all.' As the film draws to a close, Doug has left the Hollywood house party behind and finds himself standing at the corner of Hollywood and Vine, the iconic shape of the Capitol Records Building – the 'stack o' records' building – lit up in the night sky. A beaten-up car full of sinister-looking Manson Family types tries to pick him up, but he waves them away. He stares into the window of a music store, just as if he were back in New

John Magaro as Douglas in the backwards-and-forwards-looking
1960s-set film *Not Fade Away* (2012), which ends with a car
driving around Los Angeles in 1969 blaring out the yet-to-exist
Sex Pistols – the sound of a radio broadcast from the future.

Jersey in 1963 looking at guitars and saxophones and other rock
'n' roll totems. But the magic seems to have worn off. Lighting
up a cigarette, he looks into the sky as a car approaches, carrying the sound of a voice that says, 'Radio Magic KFKJ, the music
of tomorrow' over a sound that anyone watching the film now
would recognize as the Sex Pistols playing a ragged live version

of Jonathan Richman's 'Roadrunner' – a sound that was still half a decade from being made in 1969. As the car disappears off into the distance, a quizzical Doug tries to hitch a lift in the same direction.

If that on its own didn't disrupt the film's sense of time and place, then the final scene, in which Doug's younger sister Molly suddenly appears out of nowhere in the middle of the empty Hollywood road that carried away the car playing the music of tomorrow, surely does. 'I had to write this term paper,' she says, looking straight into the camera, at us: 'And I made it about how America has given the world two inventions of enormous power. One is nuclear weapons. The other is rock and roll. It's a question, I wrote, of which one is going to win in the end.' As she dances down the middle of the road to the sound of the Sex Pistols, the end titles roll over images of a pre-Beatles band performing on TV circa 1962. They too seem to be dancing in time to the same sound of the future. Moving backwards and forwards in time, *Not Fade Away* gently mocks the easily digestible nostalgia of rock films that recreate and idealize the past. Its message seems to be that if rock remains true to its original spirit, then it is – as a phenomenon itself – a kind of endless recycling and reinventing anew of what had gone before.

6

THE NEW PEOPLE

After scoring a hit in 1969 with 'Space Oddity', David Bowie, who had been on the fringes of the London rock scene since the mid-1960s, when he still went by the name of David Jones, seemed to vanish back into obscurity just as unexpectedly as he had appeared. Although he came through on the tail of the same London R&B boom that had propelled others like The Rolling Stones and The Yardbirds into the limelight, he also had markedly different influences and an unusual background as a performer. Immediately prior to achieving this first hit, Bowie had been performing songs as part of a touring mime revue under the direction of Lindsay Kemp. In a 1968 piece in London's *Times* newspaper, a reviewer noted that Kemp's *Pierrot in Turquoise* featured 'wistful popular songs' from a new singer called David Bowie.[1] Elsewhere at around the same time, he garnered notices as a mime who performed on concert bills with people like Marc Bolan and his pre-glam rock incarnation of Tyrannosaurus Rex.

But it was during this period that Bowie first recognized the possibilities of a more theatrical approach, developing ideas about how rock and theatre might be combined.[2] A trickle of singles and albums failed to make any real impression until 1972, when he scored hits with the albums *Hunky Dory*, released in December 1971, and *The Rise and Fall of Ziggy Stardust and the Spiders from Mars*, released in June.

On the cover of the first of these albums, *Hunky Dory*, a blonde, long-haired Bowie took on the appearance of 'a female star of the silent cinema days'.[3] In little more than a year, he would become one of the biggest stars of the British music scene, his rise closely related to a very calculated strategy of constructing a 'star' persona that he could inhabit almost as if he were an actor. Aside from its implicit reference to the invented names often bestowed on performers by Svengali-like managers since rock's early days, 'Ziggy Stardust' presented what seemed like the first thoroughgoing attempt by a rock performer to invent themselves into stardom by assuming the role of a fictional figure who in that fiction was a star.

As well as his theatre connections, Bowie had made a few small appearances on film, including a fleeting appearance in the British film *The Virgin Soldiers* (1969). In a blink-or-you'll-miss-it moment, he seems to move in and out of shot as if on wheels in the background of a bar-room scene, something he would almost replicate decades later with a fleeting, 'passing through a room' appearance in David Lynch's *Twin Peaks: Fire Walk with Me* (1992). By 1972, though, Bowie had quickly been recognized by observers of the rock world as not only a unique figure but an unusual songwriter who drew on traditions that pre-dated rock. Some thought, almost accusingly, that he was a mere dabbler who was not authentically invested: he was 'basically an actor', Richard Williams wrote disapprovingly in 1972. 'When he and his lead guitarist, Mick Ronson, flash in and out of perfectly stylized poses, you know they're kidding.'[4]

Bowie's ambitions expanded as quickly as his fame increased. From out of nowhere, he had achieved such an elevated status in the music world that he was able to confer, through a kind of patronage unknown to any of his peers since The Beatles, equal success on the likes of Lou Reed (whose *Transformer* album of late 1972 he co-produced), Mott the Hoople (whose single 'All the Young Dudes' he wrote and produced) – both of whom rose from cult status to the top of the charts – and Iggy and The Stooges (whose seminal 1973 album *Raw Power* he 'sprinkled his magic fairy dust' on).[5] It had been a meteoric rise since the point at which Bowie had hatched the idea for Ziggy Stardust, and, little more than a year after he had first conquered the charts as Ziggy, he decided that the ideal time to retire the act would be in London that July, at the final concert of his 1973 tour. It was this concert that D. A. Pennebaker filmed as *Ziggy Stardust and the Spiders from Mars*.

As had been the case with *Monterey Pop*, Pennebaker knew next to nothing about his subject, even initially thinking that he was going to London to film Marc Bolan, whom he had some awareness of.[6] He arrived in London a couple of days after the offer to film the concert was put to him, just in time to catch the penultimate show of the tour that evening. It was soon apparent that there could be problems with lighting in the Hammersmith Odeon, with its cinema-like unreflective surfaces of dark carpets, darkly painted walls and upholstered seats. Although the film was intended as little more than something that Bowie's record company could use to demonstrate the laserdisc technology they were developing, the film did eventually receive a belated cinematic release in 1983, when some viewers thought it was 'a poorly lit, hastily shot, haphazard and grainy film' that, in truth, was something like the film equivalent of a bootleg record.[7]

Most of the film does indeed languish in a deep murkiness. Pennebaker, for his part, thought that he and his assistants had made sufficient adjustments to the stage lighting to do the job. One of the main characteristics of the film would emerge as a consequence of these limitations, with Pennebaker – adhering to the direct cinema ethos of the situation being what really directed the film – finding a novel solution. On the afternoon of the final concert, Pennebaker and his crew mingled with the fans who were already gathering outside the Hammersmith Odeon. He had signs made and put up on walls and lampposts around the venue requesting that fans bring flash-bulb cameras to the concert that evening and instructing them to take as many pictures as possible during the concert. 'This', he said, 'illuminated the audience a little more and gave them a constant presence in the film.'[8]

In those illuminated flashes that Pennebaker called for, the audience is glimpsed in various stages of ecstasy – heaving and writhing and sobbing, with hands thrusting out to try to touch the object of their devotion. In the sequence midway through the

Bowie fans emerge from the darkness briefly in
Ziggy Stardust and the Spiders from Mars (1982).

David Bowie performs 'My Death' in D. A. Pennebaker's
Ziggy Stardust and the Spiders from Mars, the 1973 London
concert at which he killed off the Ziggy Stardust character.

film when Bowie performs Jacques Brel's 'My Death', Pennebaker's
improvised lighting solution produces a sense of how this
invented star, Ziggy Stardust, seemed so thoroughly to have
become emblematic of something more than a passion for the
music. The song underlined the transformation he was about to
make into another, different David Bowie. When the announce-
ment was made from the stage that this was the 'last show ever',
the audience let out a collective and spontaneous cry. The symbolic killing of Ziggy Stardust would later inspire Todd Haynes's
fantastical and fictionalized version of the people and events that
culminated in that final concert, *Velvet Goldmine* (1998), a kind
of rock detective story in which a fan-turned-investigative-
reporter (played by Christian Bale) who witnessed the final
concert by the Bowie-like glam rock star Brian Slade, tracks down

the Iggy Pop-like Curt Wild (Ewan McGregor) and others in a quest to find out what became of the vanished star, now believed to be dead.

Given the theatrical nature of Bowie's career up to that point and the ability to reinvent himself that he had already demonstrated, it seemed only a matter of time before he would follow what was becoming a time-honoured path from music into film. In fact, he was by then already floating to anyone who would listen 'endless ideas for movie versions of his albums'.[9] In 1975 he established a production company to make films and called it Bewlay Bros. (after his song 'The Bewlay Brothers').[10] 'I've done nine screenplays over the past year,' he told one interviewer, explaining that it helped to deal with the boredom of life on the road.[11] Partly as a way of exerting pressure on his American record company to do more to promote his music there, Bowie's manager, Tony Defries, let it be known that his client was now considering film roles. One of those that had been mentioned was a possible role in an adaptation of Robert A. Heinlein's 1961 science fiction novel *Stranger in a Strange Land*, a story about a Martian who comes to Earth.[12]

But it was not to be. He did, however, get to star in a film where he played a visitor from another planet, Nicolas Roeg's *The Man Who Fell to Earth* (1976). Roeg knew relatively little about Bowie before he saw him in a film titled 'Cracked Actor' that was made in 1975 by Alan Yentob for the BBC documentary strand *Omnibus*. Roeg and his producers had been looking for someone unusual to play the part of Thomas Newton, an alien who travels to Earth to find a way of transporting its water back to his own dying planet. The actor they sought had to be human in terms of physical appearance but at the same needed to appear just a bit different – enough to convey an essential strangeness, as if the alien visitor had been copied from a kind of blueprint of how to build a human. When Roeg saw 'Cracked Actor' he was convinced that this was the man for the role. Yentob's portrait captured an already 'spaced-out', detached and alien-like Bowie, then nearing the end of a period living in Los Angeles, a place that he felt no affinity for and that saw him lapse into severe cocaine addiction. The David Bowie revealed in 'Cracked Actor' was a shapeshifter already moving into his next phase, able to transition between personae that he temporarily identified with before throwing off like a suit of clothes. Bowie was, in fact, a kind of actor playing a succession of parts. But that did not mean he could act in film the way professional actors did, playing someone outside their experience, someone they *are not*.

For *The Man Who Fell to Earth*, Roeg made use of Bowie's Englishness, believing that it would enhance the sense of foreignness of an alien who lands in America.[13] Little else was changed in terms of how he looked. The red-orange hair with a blonde streak that Newton sports in the film was just the way Bowie already looked. Alongside his rake-thin physicality, it made for a look that was unusual already – he was a perfect and ready-made 'alien'. Another aspect of the Newton character played into Bowie's rock-star image (just as it had, vice versa, worked its way into the film character), and that was the fact that over the span of time the movie covers – some quarter of a century – all the characters, except for Newton, age visibly. In keeping with the Peter Pan-like nature of everlasting youth that sustained rock culture in so many ways and for so long – not least by the idea of the endlessly self-inventing rock star – Newton is only worn down psychologically, not physically, by life on Earth.

Roeg developed a fascination with singers – he had already used Mick Jagger in *Performance* in 1971, and he cast Art Garfunkel

David Bowie as Newton in *The Man Who Fell to Earth* (1976).

in 1980's *Bad Timing* – believing that the appeal of rock stars as actors was that they were often people who never seemed to reach a fixed point amid their own ceaseless reinventions. 'They don't know who they are yet,' he explained.[14] That, in fact, may be one of the most acute insights into rock stardom, and a clue as to why these performers only occasionally succeed as film actors. Rock stars, who essentially always 'play themselves', are always remaking themselves in light of experience and in the service of self-directed creative impulses. Their real 'role' might be thought of in terms of a constant process of reinvention within a milieu in which remaining static for too long can be professionally suicidal. David Bowie, however, simply shifted through the various personae of his career and stayed . . . David Bowie.

Following the *Man Who Fell to Earth* shoot, Bowie resumed his musical career, entering one of his most productive periods, during which he released the albums *Low* and *Heroes* (both 1977) and produced Iggy Pop's albums *The Idiot* and *Lust for Life* (also both 1977). In April 1977, the two appeared together in the unlikely setting of Dinah Shore's TV show – by then called *Dinah!* – where the audience would have been more used to watching segments about cooking or homewares. But there on the sofa were David Bowie and Iggy Pop, promoting the *Lust for Life* album. As Dinah struggled to get the two men to explain their music, asking Iggy what it was like to crawl on broken glass, she fumbled around for the right description for what it was that Iggy did. 'Is it punk rock?' she muttered, 'I mean, explain it to me.' 'My understanding of punk rock,' Bowie cut in, 'is it's something that's happened in England, really, in the last couple of years.'

Disturbances at the Ground

'Actually, we're not into music,' Steve Jones, the nonchalant twenty-year-old Sex Pistol told the *New Musical Express* after a show at London's Marquee Club in early February 1976. 'We're into chaos.'[15] During their 'moronic' tune 'Pretty Vacant', Neil Spencer reported, he had already sensed this as he watched a chair sail 'gracefully through the air, skidding across the stage'. The group never blinked an eye; they just kept on playing. Perhaps this was because it had been thrown by singer Johnny Rotten, who had sauntered offstage to get a look at his band from the audience point of view and was now causing a ruckus.[16]

Two days later, Derek Jarman – then a little-known maker of short art films – found himself in a crowd gathered in front of this same band. Jarman danced, twisting himself around the floor with a hand-held Super 8 camera pointing towards the band, immortalizing their youthful faces and other Bresson-like images, such as the close-up of a band member's shoe surrounded by the detritus of a party. The grainy, silent footage brilliantly captured the four Sex Pistols as if they were performing beneath the gaze of strobe lights. It would be the first film of the soon-to-be-infamous Pistols, although it was as much about Jarman's experience of an event as it was about a band in performance. In fact, in both this point-of-view aspect and in its grainy 8 mm amateurism, the film matched the aesthetics of the so-called punk rock that the Pistols would soon bring to national attention: it aimed to abolish the distance between audience and band, fans and stars. Anyone could be a star, it declared.

From the perspective of the present, more than four decades after the fact, one might see this little artefact as reflecting the kind of 'being there', Zapruder-style authenticity that had been a hallmark of rock film since the early 1960s. The lack of sharpness and definition and the absence of framing produce a result that chimes with how we think of the memory of things past: that is to say, not as the source of crystal-clear and sharp images that can be magically brought into the mind's eye but as something a bit hazy, blurred and indistinct. For such reasons, the film has the aura of the genuine. It is the witness document of a birth moment.

Jarman was not the first film-maker to take an interest in the Sex Pistols. Julien Temple, then a student at the National Film and Television School, chanced upon them not long after they first started rehearsing with a new singer, John Lydon – not yet renamed as 'Rotten' – in the late summer of 1975. He recalled 'an *Alice in Wonderland* moment' when he found himself drawn to the sound coming from an empty warehouse in London's abandoned docklands. 'I heard a Small Faces song coming from a building, wafting on the wind with the newspapers,' Temple said:

> I followed it up some creaking stairs, came to the top,
> put my head through and there was this band rehearsing.
> I got a jolt of something very different to anything I had
> come across before. The band were smashing up the song,
> singing 'I want you to know that I hate you' instead of
> 'love you'.[17]

Temple began an association with the Sex Pistols in early 1976, and in 1977 he put together a short feature that contained material he had re-filmed from videotaped TV appearances, titled *Sex Pistols Number 1*, which would then be shown before

A frame from the earliest film of the Sex Pistols, shot by
Derek Jarman in February 1976. Low-grade film would forever
become associated with the punk era. It was an instance of the
medium accurately matching the aesthetics of its subject.

the Sex Pistols took to the stage at their live shows. The film established the rise of the Pistols in the near mythical terms of the outraged tabloid headlines that would make them household names in a country where hardly anyone over twenty had even heard a second of their music.

The film understood the Sex Pistols as something more than the music – as something that had inherent visual qualities that had to be brought to the screen to achieve its maximum potential. The rise and fall of the Sex Pistols, it turned out, would be inextricably linked to their representation and appearance on screen, not least their notorious introduction to the nation resulting from a last-minute appearance on Thames Television's early evening magazine programme *Today*. The host, Bill Grundy, later claimed to have been totally oblivious to what was about to unfold when the Pistols and their entourage of oddly dressed fans walked onto the set, thinking that he would 'introduce yet another quite ghastly pop group' and then get the hell out.[18]

The Pistols and the small group of fans that seemed to accompany them – labelled 'the Bromley Contingent' in music press reports – were drunk by the time they sat down in front of the cameras. 'They are punk rockers,' Grundy said, addressing the mothers, fathers and children sitting in the living rooms of Greater London and the Home Counties, the areas where the show went out to. 'The new craze, they tell me. Their heroes? Not the nice clean Rolling Stones.' Looking at the Pistols and their entourage, Grundy added: 'You see, they're as drunk as I am.'

As the camera drew back from a close-up of Grundy it revealed the group seated in front of a handful of fans who stood behind them. One of them, Siouxsie Sioux, pouted for the camera, catching the attention of Grundy. She said to him, 'I always wanted to meet you.' 'Really,' he replied, 'we'll meet afterwards, shall we?'

It was the spark that provoked a torrent of profanity from the Pistols' Steve Jones, the likes of which had never been heard before on television. As he reached the conclusion of a tirade directed at Grundy that ended with the immortal line, 'what a fucking rotter', the presenter could only say to the camera, 'Well that's it for tonight . . . I'll be seeing you soon,' addressing the viewers, before looking towards the Pistols and adding, 'I hope I'm not seeing you again.' In the words of Steve Severin – co-founder of Siouxsie and The Banshees, who was also standing there behind the Pistols – seeing this moment being replayed endlessly throughout the years on TV cultural histories of the era had turned it into something he found it hard to believe he was present at: it was like watching 'the moon landing or Kennedy being shot'.[19]

If there was one thing that characterized punk and set it apart from what immediately preceded it, it was the importance that audience participation in the entire phenomenon began to assume. The earliest and most well-known document of the London punk scene of 1976–7 is Don Letts's *The Punk Rock Movie* (an 8 mm film that was later blown up to 16 mm for screenings), much of which focuses on the people who came to witness these new punk groups at venues like The Roxy in London.[20] Letts was not a film-maker in any meaningful sense of the term, but – drinking in the can-do spirit of the times – he found himself in the right place at the right time with a cheap camera in hand. Not knowing a thing about how to make films did not worry him; he simply pointed the device at whatever grabbed his attention, 'pressed the trigger' and learned by doing.[21]

Letts had been acquainted with the main figures in this developing London scene since 1973, when he got to know the Pistols' manager Malcolm McLaren and his partner Vivienne

Don Letts in the DJ booth at The Roxy in 1977, where
he also filmed much of *Punk Rock Movie* that same year.

Westwood through their King's Road boutique, then in the process of morphing from its former 1950s-themed identity as Let It
Rock into Too Fast to Live, Too Young to Die (before assuming
a more confrontational identity as SEX), which they infamously
styled as the only place to obtain 'fetish wear for the office and
the street'.[22] For Letts, McLaren – a former art school student
whose unfinished graduation project was a film about life on
London's Oxford Street – would become an early influence, and
embodied a desire to see art as something that rose up from
unlikely places and might be found in the coincidence of time,
place and circumstance in ways that could not be predicted.
McLaren showed Letts that there was 'a tradition and a lineage'
behind the things he was doing – his boutique, the interest in
rock 'n' roll and art – and that it didn't just come out of nowhere:
'it had a continuity and he made me understand that if you were
brave enough and you had an idea you could be part of this thing
. . . and this is before punk.'[23]

Soon, Letts would be fronting Acme Attractions, a competitor to McLaren's boutique, pulling in many of the same youngsters and selling such things as 'electric blue zoot-suits and jukeboxes' while blaring reggae all day long.[24] The ambience he helped to create inside the space of the shop was enough to lead Andy Czezowski, who did the accounts for Acme, to hire him as the DJ for the new punk venue he was opening in a disused gay club in Covent Garden. It would be called The Roxy. It was the perfect venue for the punks to play to their still small audience.

The Roxy was, like punk at the time, not for everyone. As one witness remembers it, it was a 'really seedy place, with filthy toilets and rickety old stairs leading to a cement basement where the bands played'.[25] Encouraged by the amateur efforts of the fearless punk bands who played when he was not DJing, Letts began to film them – The Clash, Siouxsie and The Banshees, The Slits and others – and the strange creatures who made up their audience, who were sometimes more interesting than the people who made it onto the stage. *Punk Rock Movie* – which like the

Siouxsie and the Banshees perform at
The Roxy in Don Letts's *Punk Rock Movie*.

Pistols' Grundy incident would later achieve recognition through its reappearance as source material in later documentaries – included images of The Roxy's denizens shooting up in the toilets and posing on the dance floor. Letts was also able to get away with this because everyone assumed that it was just Don, the guy who played the records and sold weed, shooting some home movies. 'It ain't no *Ten Commandments*, that's for sure,' Letts told *Sounds* magazine in 1977.[26] 'It has about the same effect as going to an early Pistols, Clash or Slits gig. It's not clean or processed or technicolourized, it's just as it was. In fact, it's *punk* quality.'[27]

For some, such as writer Barry Miles, Letts's *Punk Rock Movie* would not be the best film about British punk. That, he suggested, was Derek Jarman's 'highly romanticised' film *Jubilee* – dismissed by punk's main protagonists – in which the 'sensibility of the time' lent itself to a fable in which punk-era London was projected four hundred years into the future to provide an allegory of social collapse.[28] *Jubilee*'s punks are characterized by the nihilistic violence of a gang of young women led by Mad (Toyah Willcox) and Amyl Nitrate (Jordan), who roam the streets to a punk rock soundtrack, leaving a wave of destruction and dead police in their wake.

Letts's footage, along with work by Temple and others, and complemented with new interviews with the era's main protagonists, was later seen in arguably the best more-or-less-traditional documentary about the rise and fall of punk: the BBC *Arena* film titled *Punk and the Pistols* (directed by Paul Tickell). Broadcast in 1995, the film's exploration of how punk began as a disturbance that came up from below was intercut with scenes and dialogue from *Quatermass and the Pit* (originally broadcast as a live TV serial in 1958–9), in which a spacecraft is discovered beneath the streets of London and alien beings escape into the surrounding area. Its dialogue and images of faces stunned by the realization that the discovery has come too late, that they are already among us, is brilliantly deployed in *Punk and the Pistols* as an allegory for punk's own sudden, shocking appearance in the Britain of 1976. 'Imps . . . demons . . . and foul noises sent by the devil . . . did appear,' Professor Quatermass says, running his finger over a prophetic medieval text, suddenly joining the dots. 'In 1762 a well was being dug, in 1927 a new Tube extension, and now – do you see? – they are all disturbances of the ground.'

New York and No Wave Cinema

The less sensational rise of New York punk was one of several intertwined storylines in the HBO drama series *Vinyl* (2016), created by Martin Scorsese, Mick Jagger, Rich Cohen and Terence Winter. The story centred on the figure of Richie Finestra (Bobby Cannavale), the head of a fictional record label named American Century. In the feature-length pilot episode, directed by Scorsese, we find ourselves back in 1973, with the music scene in New York City seemingly at an all-time low. It is the transition period between the 1970s rock of Led Zeppelin – we see Richie try and fail to sign the band to American Century – and the coming of punk, disco and hip-hop, a transition that plays out over a further nine one-hour episodes as Richie searches for the next big thing to save his ailing record company.

The point of departure for the story is a dramatic recreation of a New York Dolls performance in a dilapidated quarter of New York in 1973. Sitting in his car on an apparently abandoned street, Richie has just met with his dealer and is snorting coke, unaware of anything around him that might be a cause for concern. All of a sudden, people are running everywhere; their feet thud and pound onto the back of his car and over the roof. Shaking himself back to reality, he gets out of the car and follows the crowd, who are disappearing into a building on the other side of the road. Inside is the Mercer Arts Center, a space that has been hosting local rock 'n' roll bands for a couple of years. In real life, the Mercer would become 'the center of New York's underground music scene'.[29]

Onstage, in front of a wild crowd, are the New York Dolls, a band that Richie's label had already missed out on. As they whizz through their set amid scenes of near chaos before an audience of what was in reality a 'substantial and previously subterranean following for their band of trash-rock', we see that the building is beginning to creak.[30] The floor and walls shift and the beams holding up the ceiling groan, with dust raining down on people's heads. The sense of what is going on is lost in the tumult of the moment, and the Dolls continue to play – not noticing people making for the exit – until finally the ceiling falls in, burying anyone who never managed to heed the warning signs and get out. After a moment of stillness, Richie eventually rises from the rubble and stumbles out onto the street to find himself a man born anew, convinced once again of the power of rock 'n' roll. As the story of Richie unfolds in *Vinyl*, he goes on to sign up a punk band called the Nasty Bits, whose demo tape has found it into the hands of his secretary, Jamie (Juno Temple).

The Nasty Bits would be a stand-in for the New York punk bands who did appear in the same landscape in the mid-1970s, although in *Vinyl* their English singer, Kip Stevens (played by James Jagger), possesses a Johnny Rotten-esque demeanour. As an exercise in carefully crafted nostalgia, *Vinyl* blends the real with the fictional, and sometimes with only the slightest adjustment to the facts: the New York Dolls did play at the Mercer Arts Center, and the building did collapse (in summer 1973), although the series used some artistic licence in placing the New York Dolls inside it at the time. In fact, it was a band called the Magic Tramps who were playing when the Broadway Central Hotel fell into the Mercer from above.[31]

The image of the ruined building that Richie stumbles out of nonetheless provides a fitting scene of New York City at the time, when even President Gerald Ford had told the bankrupt city it could go to hell. As with London and The Roxy that became a backdrop for Letts's *Punk Rock Movie* – hidden within the semi-abandoned Covent Garden – punk in New York would sprout largely unnoticed at first in the Bowery district, at the club called CBGB. In the words of Debbie Harry, who honed her act with Blondie there, CBGB was a 'dive bar on the ground floor of one of the many flophouses' in the area.[32] The emergence of this unlikely setting as a focal point for a new musical explosion came at the tail end of the period when the bankrupt city was being abandoned as people moved out in large numbers to the suburbs, leaving places so deserted that, in the words of journalist Legs McNeil, 'you really got this feeling that the parents had left and you could take over and do whatever you want.'[33]

At the end of 1975, McNeil and a friend, John Holmstrom, started a magazine that they called *Punk*, and threw up adverts for it wherever they could. But the idea that they would invent this new scene was still a kind of private fancy. Chris Stein of Blondie recalled seeing the posters around the Bowery – 'Punk is Coming! Punk is Coming!' they screamed. 'Here comes another shitty group with an even shittier name,' he thought, 'but when we went out to the newsstand one day there was this new comic rock mag that everyone loved immediately.'[34]

The earliest footage to come to light of the New York bands that would soon be championed by *Punk* magazine – Ramones, Talking Heads, Television, Blondie and others – was filmed at CBGB in 1975 and 1976. Richard Hell of Television (and later Richard Hell & The Voidoids) was one of the most striking-looking people to be found around the place. Styling himself as something of a departure from the previous era associated with the New York Dolls, he sported an original hairstyle that was described at various times as being inspired either by a photo from 1871 of a seventeen-year-old Arthur Rimbaud or by Jean-Pierre Léaud's hair in François Truffaut's film *The 400 Blows* (1959).

In Amos Poe and Ivan Král's *The Blank Generation*, a 16 mm film of the CBGB scene named after one of his songs, Hell is a jittery presence. Adverts for screenings of Poe and Král's film that

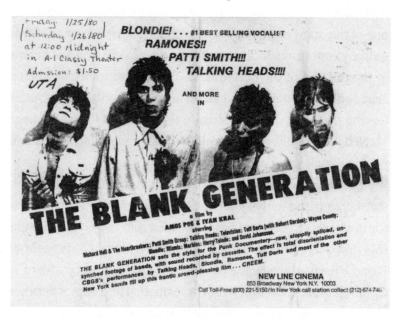

A flyer for Poe and Kral's *The Blank Generation* (1976),
featuring an image of the Heartbreakers with Richard Hell (centre left)
and Johnny Thunders (centre right).

Patti Smith in *The Blank Generation*.

ran in *Creem* magazine declared that this was punk documentary as it was supposed to be. The ad outlined some of the film's punk virtues: 'raw, sloppily spliced, un-synched footage of bands with sound recorded by cassette. The effect is total disorientation.' The film still possesses novelty in its 'candid camera' style footage of the emerging figures of the scene in unlikely situations – pushing cars, climbing up fire escapes and so on.[35]

Where the cross-dressing New York Dolls represented a challenge for mainstream audiences unwilling to accept a band with such a provocative look (they were once arrested in the American South and charged with female impersonation), they still represented the continuation – even if in an ironic sense – of the idea of the rock star as a glamorous figure. Their songs dealt in the kind of street-level subject-matter patented by Lou Reed, but they still looked somewhat incongruously 'dolled-up' like extras from one of Andy Warhol's 'superstar' films. Richard Hell songs like 'Blank Generation', meanwhile, were not only cut through with 'alienation and disgust and anger' but matched by a look and demeanour that was resoundingly anti-glamorous.[36]

The band that Hell (real name Richard Myers) had first started playing at CBGB with, Television, rejected anything that smacked of glamour and didn't want to be associated with encouraging star worship. 'One thing I wanted to bring back to rock 'n' roll,' Hell said, 'was the knowledge that you invent yourself. That's why I changed my name, why I did all the clothing style things, haircut, everything.'[37] The image of danger that punk represented could be seen in an image by Roberta Bayley that was used in early adverts for Television and later for showings of *The Blank Generation*. The members of the band, wearing white shirts spattered with fake blood, illustrate the memorable and enticing slogan, 'Catch them while they're still alive.'

The punk aesthetic is also present in the way that *The Blank Generation* disrupts the conventional practices of documentation that earlier figures such as Pennebaker and the Maysles brothers had worked so hard to perfect. For a start, the sound and images are not in sync. The syncing of sound and images shot on the run was one of the great breakthroughs of direct cinema's practitioners, but Poe and Král were simply unable to do that. They filmed *The Blank Generation* with cheap equipment and later added the music soundtrack, which itself had been recorded on a cheap twenty-dollar cassette machine. It is a feature that nonetheless made the film a document in tune with the times: 'a cinematic analogue to the primitivism of the music'.[38]

Out of the environment that developed around CBGB and the Bowery came not only a new music scene but a new film culture that drew for its talent pool on many of the punk and new wave musicians who lived around the Lower East Side of the city. For the musicians and film-makers, CBGB became a place where paths crossed and ideas were exchanged.[39] The 'anyone can do it' amateurism of the scene was a direct influence on aspiring film-makers like Jim Jarmusch and Amos Poe, who would use amateur actors such as Debbie Harry in starring roles for super-low-budget productions. Jarmusch realized from observing bands like Television, Ramones, Blondie and Talking Heads that it was not necessary to be 'a virtuoso musician to form a rock band'.[40] The same principle could be applied to film.

Following *The Blank Generation*, Poe would do just that, going on to make many underground films that not only demonstrated a devotion to the very punk idea of 'discovering cinema by doing' but worked to bring the two elements of the scene further together.[41] Poe's films would often be set around the same places where the music lived – CBGB, the Mudd Club, the Lower East Side – and often focused on the music scene. Ivan Král already had a more formal relationship with the music scene, as a member of Patti Smith's early group, and he had also played bass guitar with Blondie. But Poe used Debbie Harry in films such as *Unmade Beds* (1976), a film made for $4,000 in which she acts out the role of Jacques Demy's Lola singing a sultry number a cappella. Harry's looks drew interesting movie star comparisons: she was a 'punk Garbo' and 'the Marilyn Monroe of punk rock', in some descriptions.[42] Adopted as an infant, she was capable of encouraging the idea that Monroe might have been her real mother, describing it as a 'secret fantasy' when she was growing up and people told her she looked like a movie star.[43] But she did not care for the 'punk' label, describing it, with a great deal of insight, as more of a 'time signature' than anything specifically musical: 'Punk to us is a time in New York, a time in the world. Acid is before; glitter is before; R 'n' B is before, and now it's punk. But it's all rock-and-roll straight down the line.'[44]

It would not be long before Nicolas Roeg was trying to cast her in a film adaptation of *Flash Gordon* that he was working on

Debbie Harry in Amos Poe's *The Foreigner* (1978), one of a number
of roles she played in small budget, pre-fame independent films connected
to the No Wave art/film/music scene of the mid- to late 1970s.

(he later abandoned the project).[45] But she and Blondie were
soon being asked to write and sing the title song to the mainstream Paul Schrader-directed *American Gigolo* (1980), which
became 'Call Me', a number-one hit for the band both in the USA
and the UK.

Taking a cue from the fact that the music scene had initially
developed completely outside the music business and made no
concessions to commercial viability, Poe was more interested
in film as art than in any conventional Hollywood conception
of cinema. The primitive nature of *The Blank Generation* – its
jumpy, iconic black-and-white snapshots of Patti Smith, Debbie
Harry and Richard Hell – might be said to reflect the formative influence that the Kennedy assassination footage had on
him as a teenager; particularly in what it revealed, through *Life*

magazine's detailed presentation of frames from the Zapruder film, of the relationship between frames and narrative. *Life* had famously dissected the Zapruder footage in search of clues to the murder, and that kind of forensic interest in the visual, breaking down the continuity of film into its components, was something that made a big impression on Poe. 'The idea that frames followed frames, that there was a sequence, and that sequence contained narrative' suggested the storytelling possibilities of cutting up and mixing what he shot, and reconstructing it in the editing.[46] Alongside the Zapruder footage and films such as *A Hard Day's Night* and late 1960s American films like *Bonnie and Clyde* and *The Graduate*, Poe's main inspiration was found in the films of the French New Wave.

Just as Jean-Luc Godard had seen himself as making 'American' movies in France, Poe decided that what he would do was the converse: make French-style, Godard-like movies in America.[47] In 1976, it was an idea that seemed 'like a bit of a joke', but it provided the impetus for films that were in tune with the 'tenor of the times'.[48] While Poe never really broke through to a wider audience, the talent pool that seemed to sprout spontaneously from the streets included people such as future directors Susan Seidelman, Jim Jarmusch and actor-director Steve Buscemi.[49] Jarmusch's breakthrough feature, *Stranger Than Paradise* (1984), developed as a collaboration with John Lurie, leader and saxophonist for the Lower East Side band The Lounge Lizards. Many of these figures would show up on the public-access cable show *TV Party*, presented by music journalist Glenn O'Brien and Chris Stein of Blondie (with Amos Poe, among others, running the cameras).[50] Of all the figures to come out of the CBGB scene, one candidate for film stardom might have been Richard Hell, whose look and style became one of the templates for punk fashion. But after appearing in Seidelman's low-budget film *Smithereens* in 1982 – playing a former punk rocker and ladies' man who maintains his iconic hairdo with dabs of beer – his next role was a much smaller part in Seidelman's breakthrough mainstream film, the Madonna star-vehicle *Desperately Seeking Susan* (1985), in which he got to play the sleeping – or possibly dead – boyfriend whom the Madonna character abandons in the opening minutes.

Movie Mysteries

Johnny Rotten quickly became punk's biggest star. His split from the Sex Pistols in early 1978 would be a direct result of his unwillingness to play along with the film that Malcolm McLaren was making, and in which the group would star, titled 'Who Killed Bambi?' In the script of the unmade film – which only concluded one day's shooting with director Russ Meyer – the narrator asks at the very end if success would spoil the one who had been sent to redeem rock 'n' roll: Johnny Rotten. No, the script concluded, it would be the other way round. Living up to his name, he would 'waste, spoil, smash, blow up and destroy success'.[51] As the titles rolled at the end of another film, Don Letts's *Punk Rock Movie*, it might have seemed an accurate summation of Rotten, for there he was, destroying a portable record player as the voice of an American woman, not seen on screen, intones, 'Johnny Rotten, Johnny Rotten, aren't you beautiful.' But Rotten did object to being portrayed – with the added indignity of having to do the portraying *himself* – as the creation of McLaren.

For over a year the film had consumed the energies of McLaren – and the large cash advances the Sex Pistols had received from various record companies. It would end up destroying the group and leaving McLaren temporarily ruined. The aborted 'Who Killed Bambi?' and its successor film, *The Great Rock 'n' Roll Swindle* (1980, dir. Julien Temple), would become the chief evidence used by Rotten – now using his given name, John Lydon – and the other surviving members of the Sex Pistols in a court case against McLaren, when the film script was presented as if it were a factual account of what actually happened. McLaren, the prosecution argued, drawing on scenes from the film scripts, was set upon the financial exploitation of the four young Sex Pistols from the outset. Most of the Pistols' earnings, it was revealed, had vanished into the two film productions.

When the verdict was reached in favour of Lydon, the order of the court stipulated that since the only assets that the remaining Sex Pistols had were wrapped up in *The Great Rock 'n' Roll Swindle* and its soundtrack, the only way to rescue any money out of the dispute was through the determined exploitation of the movie under the supervision of a court-appointed receiver. Following this turn of events, and with McLaren out of the picture, Richard Branson – head of the Pistols' British record company – established Virgin Films with the sole aim of acquiring the rights to *Swindle*. Once obtained, he quickly swung into action, exploiting this property with a great deal of relish. In what would almost count as a parody of the way the new movie-famous Elvis had been exploited two decades earlier, Branson's Virgin Records released the soundtrack to the not-yet-finished movie complete with an accompanying poster of its recently deceased star, Sid Vicious, now portrayed as a murdering 'action man' under the caption: 'From beyond the grave'.

Days after the court ruling that took the film out of his hands, McLaren returned to the Tin Pan Alley studio in Denmark Street where the Pistols had lived and rehearsed between late 1975 and

1977 and where their ghosts, if not the spirit of *Expresso Bongo*, still lingered. Wondering if anything had survived the chaos of the last two years, and no longer holding keys to the property, he kicked in the doors. On the walls were notes made by Steve Jones and Glen Matlock that had been there for more than three years; graffiti by Lydon, with caricatures of Vicious, Jones and McLaren, was everywhere. And out in the courtyard below, now dirty and sodden with rain, were the gigantic multicoloured letters that his friend Helen Wallington-Lloyd dragged around a soundstage to form the words 'rock 'n' roll' in a scene in the film that he no longer controlled.

Vicious, thanks to the posthumous release of *The Great Rock 'n' Roll Swindle* and a series of hit singles from the soundtrack, did indeed end up in a starring role in the Pistols' story from beyond the grave. Lydon would have to wait just a little bit longer to find a film role that he wanted to do, eventually making it to the big screen in a co-starring role alongside Harvey Keitel in *Copkiller* (1983).[52] Before that, however, his attempts to get into the movies would end up having an indirect (and novel) influence on his group Public Image Ltd (aka PiL).

In 1978, Lydon was, for a short while, the favourite to play Jimmy the mod, the lead role in the film adaptation of The Who's *Quadrophenia*. Lydon did numerous screen tests, but in the end the film's insurers took fright at the thought that if the central role went to someone who had acquired a reputation for attracting chaos and disorder, the whole production might collapse if he didn't turn up or was once again attacked in the streets. During this time there would be regular deliveries of rushes to Lydon's home in London's West End, which would arrive by courier in standard film cans. Once Lydon had fallen out of the running to play the part, he took inspiration from those film cans when he

After performing 'My Way' in the finale of *The Great Rock 'n' Roll Swindle* (1981), Sid Vicious takes out a revolver and opens fire on the upper-class audience who had come to laud him.

decided that the next PiL album should be packaged in movie cans. And so it was: *Metal Box* was released as a three-LP set in a film can stamped with the band's logo. Lydon never got to be in the movie, but he got to be in a film can.

Joe Strummer of The Clash would go on to be the one artist from the punk era to embrace the idea of taking dramatic roles in films, appearing in Aki Kaurismäki's *I Hired a Contract Killer* (1990), two Alex Cox movies, *Straight to Hell* and *Walker* (both 1987), and Jim Jarmusch's *Mystery Train* (1989), among others. Strummer – who in a certain light resembled a young Paul Newman – could look the part, and he did not have the kind of overpowering image that could effectively erase the identity he had to assume for a role. Yet he faced the same dilemma as many other rock stars who transitioned to the screen, namely, the kind of 'acting' that was often a part of playing rock – that ability to project oneself into the song and the live act – was not the same as acting on screen. 'Strummer had an actor's presence and timing,' wrote the film critic Howard Hampton, 'but when he took a stab at screen acting for real, he didn't have the same mesmeric dimension.'⁵³ In that, he was not alone, and, in common with numerous others, it was surely something to do with being a bit-part player in someone else's drama, rather than living out one's own through the music.

On the set of *Straight to Hell*, in which he played the hitman-bank robber Simms, Strummer was reportedly 'out-methoding' the rest of the cast – which included Dennis Hopper and Jim Jarmusch – by sleeping on the set dressed in character and practising twirling a revolver in idle moments. 'I think about acting 24 hours a day,' Strummer said. 'I've had an intense life, so I've got a lot of experience to draw on.'⁵⁴ The intensity of The Clash's music, as it happened, would have a direct – although not very obvious – influence on another film: Martin Scorsese's *Raging Bull*. During filming in early 1979, an irate Scorsese – who sported a Clash T-shirt on set – was 'twisted into a knot of bitterness, defiance and self-doubt', thinking it would be his last film after the relative flop of his previous release, *New York, New York*. Losing patience with director of photography Michael Chapman, who was taking too long to set up shots, he would retreat into his trailer and 'put on the Clash at top volume',

> and sit there, revved up by the music, pacing back and forth, counting the seconds. After forty-five minutes, he'd come storming out, yelling, 'It's more than one side of the Clash, Michael. What are you doing?' Then he picked up a folding chair and heaved it against the side of the trailer, making big dents and chipping the paint.⁵⁵

IN THE 1970S, the idea of using rock music in film in an autono-
mous way that almost gave it the status of a character was
developed in the films of Wim Wenders. From his earliest films
– including his graduation feature, *Summer in the City* (1970),
whose only sound comes from the music of The Kinks – rock 'n'
roll music had a profound influence on his ideas. Once he had
achieved a measure of success, Wenders spread out favours when
he could to help other up-and-coming film-makers, including
gifting Jim Jarmusch some leftover film stock, with which he went
on to make his breakthrough film, *Stranger Than Paradise*. Another
film-maker he helped was his British contemporary Chris Petit,
whose 1979 monochromatic classic *Radio On*, featuring stark
winter landscapes and vacant urban scenes remarkably illuminated on film by streetlights and electronic signs, evokes the
period with help from its soundtrack.

Shot in wintertime, the interior spaces of *Radio On* – freezing-
looking rooms where time seems suspended – complement the
empty landscapes from London to Bristol through which the
character of Robert drives, and the urban scenes he finds himself
in at either end of the trip as he investigates what has happened
to his brother, creating the image of a world enveloped in gloom.
It is a film overlaid with an almost epochal sense of isolation.
Along with its soundtrack of electronic and new wave music, it
remains, as an audiovisual work of art, a beguiling time capsule
of the immediate post-punk world. It was described, after
Wenders's 'road movie trilogy', as both the first British road
movie and as the last of the road films of the 1970s (a trend that
might be traced back to *Easy Rider*, although it dated from 1969).
The film was produced with help from with Wenders's production company Road Movies and had a substantial role for Lisa
Kreuzer, one of the stars of Wenders's *Alice in the Cities* (1974),

Chris Petit's *Radio On* (1979) was a road movie in the style of
Wim Wenders, and likewise made use of music from radios, jukeboxes
and tape machines, putting it at the centre of the story.

a film that was in some ways a forerunner of *Radio On*. However,
it endures as a film aside from those associations because it so
expertly conveys something of the essence of that strange period
in recent British history through its use of recorded music.

Although recorded rock music had, by the late 1970s, become
more commonplace on screen, Petit's film stands apart, both in
the fact that all of its music was roughly contemporaneous to the
period it was set in, and in the way that the music lives within
the places that make up the landscapes and environments of the
film. Aside from the use of Bowie's 'Heroes' over the opening
titles, the recordings that are used here are heard in 'natural'
contexts – songs on the radio, played on jukeboxes, on record
players and in the car that carries the central character of Robert,
a London DJ (David Beames), between the capital and Bristol.
Sometimes the music stops abruptly when one scene switches
to another, leaving the sound of the music behind in the place it
was coming from, or is heard in snatches and fragments when
the viewpoint shifts from the subjective (when Robert is driving

the car, listening to music) to the objective (when the car is seen moving through a landscape from a more distanced point of view). This is a trick used to interesting effect when the sound of Devo's rendition of The Rolling Stones' 'Satisfaction' – a sound that is machinic and at the same time jerkily spasmodic – cuts in and out as we alternately see the road from the driver's point of view, the sound of the music audible, and from outside the car, when the sound of the record disappears.

The sketchy plot of *Radio On* seems less important than the possibility that the film was viewed as an experiment in how music and image might be integrated on screen. Petit later said that the idea for the film began with the music (something reflected in the fact that the opening titles are actually a list of the songs used in the film) and from there proceeded to the problem of how this music might contribute to a journey in which the view from a moving car became a kind of mobile film screen itself.[56]

Before he sets out on his journey, Robert receives a package from his missing brother containing four Kraftwerk cassettes. The electronic sounds of Kraftwerk – alongside some of Bowie's *Low* (1977) and Robert Fripp's ambient 'Urban Landscape' (1979) – provide much of the soundtrack to Robert's road trip. Some have noted that the characteristically 'cold and emotionless' nature of synthesizer music was a departure for rock music in film, but one that lent itself to the idea of the 'imaginary cultural landscape' seen from the window of the car.[57] The interiors of the film, by contrast, featured more familiar kinds of rock music, most of it from the catalogue of London's punk and new wave label Stiff Records – Ian Dury, Wreckless Eric and Lene Lovich – and used much in the style of Wenders's road films of the 1970s, where it is an integral part of the settings the characters find themselves in, rather than overlaid onto a scene afterwards.

It is a device that was used expertly by Wenders, and by Petit here too, where it makes something more of the music than the music on its own might suggest by inserting it directly into a vision of a time, a place, a world in such a way as to give it life. A 1977 record, Wreckless Eric's 'Whole Wide World' – little heard today – is selected by Robert from the jukebox in a gloomy and near-empty pub, where he stands alone at a bar with a drink. In that moment, the song becomes that world, and as such the music is elevated into a timeless fragment of the period, simply by virtue of the fact that it is here *au naturel*, in its time and place – an example of how the particularity of rock 'n' roll can paradoxically allow it to transmit its emotional power across time and space.

7

VIDEO VORTEX

'Not everyone may be aware of it just yet,' reported the *New York Times* in July 1979, 'but we're teetering on the edge of the video disk era.'[1] Videodisc technology, in a format that was still unclear – perhaps it would be tape, or some kind of computer-readable software – promised to do what had only been truly possible before in cinema: the combination of sight and sound in high fidelity.

Before the year was out, the first video album – which is to say, a visual counterpart to a long-playing record album – had been made: *Eat to the Beat* by Blondie, featuring the same twelve tracks that were to be found on their 1979 album of the same name, had been filmed in studio and on location in New York and New Jersey with the director David Mallet at a reported cost of $100,000-plus.[2] It was 'more fun than touring', declared Debbie Harry, each day an adventure in yet another new location with friends in tow.[3] But when it was premiered in full at the New York new wave rock disco Hurrah in January 1980, it 'was immediately declared a disaster by the critics'.[4]

Perhaps it was the case – as many would come to say of music video as a genre – that subjecting the listener to additional layers of meaning in the form of film-director-inspired song interpretations was too much weight for the music to bear. The record industry seemed to be moving in the direction of something that would marry sound and vision, but the power of popular music was already partly in its ability to rouse the imagination and flood it with image-producing stimuli.

Such problems with the effect that video music might have on the listening experience did not concern an entertainment industry that stood to benefit from the expected revolution in home video. Music insiders were already organizing their first get-togethers to explore the numerous practical issues that the new medium was likely to present for the industry.[5] In November 1980, a gathering of mostly middle-aged men in suits took place at the Sheraton-Universal Hotel in Los Angeles, where bedrooms were remade as screening rooms, as two days of technical demonstrations and discussion got under way. Alone among the beige-suited executives and promotions men from the performing side of the music world was Todd Rundgren, by then acclaimed as much for his skills as a record producer as he was as a songwriter and performer.

Rundgren – along with Brian Eno and ex-Monkees member Michael Nesmith – had been one of very few rock figures to speak publicly about his interest in, and experiments with, the new technology and to take an interest in its artistic, rather than merely promotional, possibilities in the service of making and experiencing music.[6] For Rundgren, the potential of video became apparent after he had seen the work of the artist Nam June Paik in the early 1970s, which involved manipulated images displayed on multiple monitors arranged installation-style in gallery spaces. It was after this that the preternaturally curious Rundgren started buying equipment with the aim of setting up a video studio, even going so far as to explore the possibility of a 24-hour music channel using video satellite broadcasting.[7]

At the International Music Video Conference in the Sheraton-Universal, Rundgren was premiering his incomplete video interpretation of Japanese electronic composer Tomita's album *The Planets* (an arrangement of Gustav Holst's orchestral suite of 1914–16), a job that he had been selected for by Tomita's label, RCA Records, a major investor in home video technology.[8] The reason Rundgren – and not a conventional film or video director – had been chosen was simple: he was one of the few people in the country with an interest in music production who had also invested time and money in acquiring state-of-the-art video equipment. By then he had his own $2-million studio, Utopia Video, and had spent some time experimenting with the new medium. RCA, being in the business of selling entertainment, had a more basic interest, much less to do with art than with money. They had already invested heavily in developing video hardware technology and owned the patent on a new videodisc format named SelectaVision, but they lacked what was referred to at the time as 'software' – video content – that could demonstrate the potential of their product to customers and investors.[9]

What they really wanted to do was license the technology, not get involved in the creation of video content. In fact, when Pennebaker was contracted to film Bowie in 1973 for what became *Ziggy Stardust and the Spiders from Mars*, it was because Bowie was an RCA artist, and the film was intended – like Rundgren's Tomita project – to be a vehicle for demonstrating the company's new videodisc technology. As Rundgren told *Creem* magazine the month before the big Los Angeles industry event, his interest in video was not a matter of getting caught up in the novelty of the medium: it was a serious investment of time and money intended to develop the artistic potential of video, in which the Tomita video was a key exploratory step. 'It's totally scripted out,' he revealed.[10] Designing the imagery himself and bringing it to a rough form of completion suitable to accompany 25 minutes of music had been six months' work for Rundgren.[11]

Rundgren, though, was too far ahead of the industry in his thinking. He had personally sunk $150,000 into the Tomita project, but RCA agreed to pay only one-fifth of that for the rights to use the video for demonstration purposes. When he stood up to speak at the conference it was to pull up the record company for lacking the vision to finance the development of content and failing to invest in video artists who might help to open up the medium. 'RCA has spent $100 million developing the machine', he told the audience, 'and has not spent one percent of that to develop new software.'[12] The key problem, he would come to realize, was not only content creation but the means of delivery. Why bother with videodiscs and videocassettes?

The answer was surely to take the content straight to the most direct medium: television. Why should people buy discs at $25 each that they couldn't erase and reuse, when cable TV was already offering a possible solution? Cable would allow people to spend far less on content through channel and service subscriptions and have the ability to turn it on and off as they pleased. 'Video disk is hoping to sell 50,000 machines in a year,' he said, explaining how stupid an idea it seemed to be. 'There's no way that video disk marketing can keep up with cable . . . I mean, they're hooking up a million homes at a time.'[13] This was a problem that would take another two years to resolve itself.

Video technology and hardware began to become more commonplace as a tool and medium first in the visual arts in the 1960s. In the following decade, the impact of video for rock-related purposes developed slowly. The first rock film shot entirely on video was Frank Zappa's *200 Motels* (1971), centred around the life of a band on the road. Vincent Canby in the *New*

York Times found it an exhausting tableau of gags and sketches but was blown away by some of its innovative video tricks. 'I have no idea how these things are done but they are quite marvellous,' he wrote. After a while, though, they were also likely to be 'immensely distracting' to anyone with an interest in the music.[14]

Later in the decade, the importance of long-form video could also be seen in the independently produced tapes made by San Francisco's Target Video, which sought not only to document the city's burgeoning punk scene using a medium and technology that was relatively inexpensive, but to develop 'a theory of the medium of videotape'.[15] As well as nightclub and performance spaces, Target operated studio facilities and would become a focal point for artists and performers who were drawn in by the scene of the late 1970s, even acting as campaign headquarters for the San Francisco mayoral run undertaken by punk rocker Jello Biafra (frontman of Dead Kennedys) in 1980.[16] By mid-1980 it

An advert for Target Video published in the San Francisco magazine *Damage*.

was producing a magazine show that was available on cable TV in the Bay Area, Los Angeles and New York.[17]

Target's low-budget independent films were usually shown in public venues like clubs and small theatres, where they could work as part of an evening that blended the rock music content with other non-music independent film and video. It was not unusual to find short films that might best be described as 'promos' for the artists featured at these events, even if the films did not feature musicians performing or miming to the music in any way; they were usually described as 'films' and 'movies', no matter how long they were or whether they were film or video. There were few, if any, other outlets for such films, which eventually forced producers and film-makers to create their own distribution networks. A column in San Francisco's *Damage* magazine outlined what was at stake: it was about circumventing the corporations that controlled the flow of all information, and forming small independent groups to 'produce, show and distribute artists' work'.[18]

Notable among these rock shorts that were not simply clips of artists miming or performing was Bruce Conner's 'Mongoloid', an assemblage of found footage cut to the Devo song of the same name, and Alex de Laszlo's 'Human Fly', a three-minute film set to the eponymous Cramps song in which the band members act a scene from a kind of silent horror movie ('ghoulish escapades with The Cramps in the cellars of New York's Bowery', ran an ad from distributors One Way Films).[19]

Many of the long-form tapes that were made by Target were live performance films, such as the infamous 1978 film of The Cramps, *Live at Napa State Mental Hospital* (a free concert for patients), and would resurface decades later on DVD. As a producer and distributor, Target became pioneers of a form, the long-form music video, that would develop in the 1980s into a new medium that acquired its own sales chart in *Billboard* magazine as home video players caused an explosion in the sales of such tapes. But when we think of music video it is more common to have in mind the kind of short clips that were made for promotional purposes, and which also exploded – off the scale and reshaping the whole of popular music – through MTV, the new channel launched in August 1981, and later other channels and outlets.[20]

The question of when and where the MTV-style music video originated is a complicated one. As film historian David Ehrenstein has pointed out, the idea that the record industry had just, out of nowhere, hit upon a new form of creative communication was belied by the realization that its derivative and gimmicky video output in the first years of MTV actually had 'precedents stretching across the first seven decades' of twentieth-century cinema.[21]

Californian artist and film-maker Bruce Conner, whose work encompassed a variety of approaches from assemblage to sculpture and photography, was also making film collages set to records as early as *Cosmic Ray* (1960), which featured a soundtrack of Ray Charles performing 'What I'd Say'.[22] Something of a departure from the approach adopted in that film, insofar as it did not make use of found film, was the 1966 short *Breakaway*, which could have been intended as a study of the human body in motion but in light of subsequent history looks now like an early music promo, although *Breakaway* had been conceived and filmed with much greater skill and artistry than most promos ever would be.

The film features the sound and images of dancer, choreographer and singer Toni Basil (credited as Antonia Christina Basilotta), who earlier had a role in Dennis Hopper's *Easy Rider* (Conner had some involvement in that too, inspiring Hopper's editing of the film, and here in *Breakaway*, Hopper aimed lights as Conner filmed). Basil's record 'Breakaway', a midtempo, Motown-like tune written and produced by Ed Cobb, provides the soundtrack here, although the viewer never has the impression that she is dancing to that music. The record, rather, provides a tempo and the rhythmical cues against which Conner's innovative filmic experiment is constructed as a vision of Basil in continuous motion. But by contrast with later pop music videos that might seem to echo it, *Breakaway* emerged from a highly technical and collaborative process between Conner and Basil.

The film was shot 'at single-frame exposures as well as at 8, 16, 24, and 36 frames per second', and the use that is made of the results is mesmerizing.[23] Basil seems to be brought to life like a spirit Conner has conjured out of the darkness, akin to a

Toni Basil in Bruce Conner's 16 mm film *Breakaway* (1966),
a masterpiece of film, music and dance set to Basil's recording
of the song of the same name, and a forerunner of the music video.

movable doll that has been wound up and set off. The impression is underlined by the fact that the film begins with the motionless Basil, and when the song comes to an end the film continues by rewinding everything (images and music) back to the point of motionless origin once again. The stroboscopic motion through which we see full body shots of Basil dancing also make the film appear analogous to a primitive flipbook. In this film, Conner might be said to be 'dancing' with Toni Basil.[24]

As well as these films by Conner, and some of Kenneth Anger's work, we might also count as forerunners of the music video the 1960s promo clips of Peter Whitehead, such as The Rolling Stones' 'We Love You' (and many others filmed as 'inserts' for the British TV show *Top of the Pops* and other outlets), and Michael Lindsay-Hogg's shorts for The Who ('Happy Jack') and the Stones ('Jumpin' Jack Flash').

The roots of MTV can in fact be identified in a variety of sources: Richard Lester's Beatles films, in particular the sequences for the songs 'Can't Buy Me Love' (*A Hard Day's Night*) and 'Ticket to Ride' (*Help!*), cannot be overlooked, and neither can the Busby Berkeley musicals of the 1930s (such as *Gold Diggers of 1935*) nor the now long forgotten French-made Scopitone movie machines, which were essentially jukeboxes with a 26-inch back-projected movie screen fitted atop, holding up to 36 short films (often in colour).[25] Then there is the famous opening sequence of Pennebaker's *Don't Look Back* – the 'Subterranean Homesick Blues' alleyway scene – which was made specifically for Scopitone, even though by then, in 1965, the novelty of that device was already pointing towards failure, due in part to the unreliability of the complex mechanism required to serve up the 16 mm film loops and keep them in sync with the sound of the music. The music industry soon came to see Scopitone as 'ineffective at best, a liability at worst'.[26] The technology also had some competition in the early 1960s from Cinebox, an Italian-manufactured film jukebox (and both were preceded two decades before by a device called the Panoram, which played clips that were known as 'Soundies').[27]

In the 1970s, the BBC in Britain hosted a weekly music magazine programme called *The Old Grey Whistle Test*, an attempt to treat rock music culture as worthy of serious attention. It revolved around a mix of live studio performances by artists who had released new albums (whereas Top 40 singles were the province of the BBC's *Top of the Pops*) with interviews and film reports. But it also pioneered its own variant of the short music film, drawing on the private collection of a vintage film collector, Philip Jenkinson, who was hired by the show's producer Mike Appleton to put together clips that could accompany a track from a newly released album if the artist was unavailable to perform in the studio. One of the best-known of these clips appropriated footage from Arnold Fanck's 1931 film *Der Weisse Rausch* (The White Ecstasy), featuring skiers descending Alpine slopes, cut to a track from Mike Oldfield's *Tubular Bells* (1973).[28] Elsewhere on British TV in the 1970s, *Top of the Pops* and other national and regional shows became outlets for promo clips. It was not unusual, in fact, to see clips used to fill short gaps in the schedules on commercial daytime television. Some record companies, notably Virgin, also made clips to be shown in their own stores on specially installed screens (this was the origin of a 1977 Sex Pistols promo for 'Pretty Vacant').

Elsewhere, other innovators were doing their own thing. In San Francisco, The Residents, a fringe avant-rock concept band, were formed by aspiring film-makers who discovered that the magnetic tape used for recording music was cheaper than film, and that music provided a less expensive medium through which they could realize their ambitions.[29] Nonetheless, they made a short 16 mm film clip inspired by German Expressionist cinema to go with their cover of 'Land of 1,000 Dances' (1975) and sent it to record companies as a kind of music-film demo. The mind-boggling film – from a larger satirical work called *Third Reich 'n Roll* – played with Nazi and KKK symbolism, and showed the group members scuttling around dressed in 'robes' and pointy Klansman-style hats made out of newspaper while 'banging on trash cans and oil drums in sped-up motion'.[30] It looks like someone had come across some strange tribal ritual and filmed it.

The World Is Full of MTV

For some of those who emerged at the turn of the 1980s, such as Duran Duran, there was an awareness that many of the biggest and longest-running UK hits of the recent past – from Queen's 'Bohemian Rhapsody' (1975) to The Boomtown Rats' 'I Don't Like Mondays' (1979) – had been sustained by their regularly replayed videos, particularly clips that at the time had been regarded as novel uses of the medium.[31]

In the late 1970s, Michael Nesmith – whose group The Monkees' career had been tied up with being on screen since the start – began making clips, simply as a way of avoiding having to stand in front of a microphone, pretending to sing. He began to script movie-like scenarios for his songs.[32] During the process of editing one of these, which was called 'Rio', he came to the realization that the clip was doing something unusual: it was overturning the grammar of film. Instead of images driving the narrative content, it was the songs that drove the narrative. 'It didn't make any difference that the images were discontinuous,' he said. 'It was hyper-real. Even people who didn't understand film, including me, could see this was a profound conceptual shift.'[33]

Nesmith had the idea of putting together a television channel that played only music clips and made a 30-minute pilot show that he called *PopClips*. The show was taken up by cable TV channel Nickelodeon and was broadcast weekly during 1980 and early 1981. It would ultimately act as a trial for the format that MTV soon popularized.[34] When MTV started, it was within the 'narrowcasting' system of cable television provision.[35] The market for cable was largely found in 'predominantly white suburbs and rural communities', since many urban population centres were 'not even wired for cable'.[36] It was something that would shape the early content of an MTV that was directed towards white audiences, setting up the conditions in which the rigid formatting, which aped radio formats – still at this time serving particular audiences – would be torn down by performers like Michael Jackson and Prince.

Prior to MTV's launch, market testing was undertaken with prospective audiences in those markets where it would be available. A slate of 150 rock and pop artists were to be audience-rated for interest. The channel had begun with the aim of aping the radio format known as AOR (album-orientated rock), which in the segregated world of American popular music meant that the target audience would be served the same kind of safe and unthreatening rock music to which the label AOR was attached. There would be no R&B, no oldies from the first two or more decades of rock 'n' roll, and almost no content from before 1977 – in other words, before the channel's target audience were old enough to be paying attention to music. This was, in other words, a profoundly market-driven concept whereby the cable operators were acutely aware of who their subscribers were and knew the demographics of the homes into which they piped in content. The expectation was that MTV would reach around 2.1 million homes initially, and it would not be available in places such as Manhattan (where it was recorded) or Los Angeles (the centre of the U.S. music industry).

Starting with what MTV executive Bob Pittman later remembered to be '250 videos' – perhaps close to the sum total of what then existed – the channel displayed a preference for content that would not offend corporate sponsors.[37] This was, after all – in an echo of the conservatism of 1950s TV – advertising-supported programming. 'The fevered spirit of teen rebellion against family, school and state, which energized rock music from Buddy Holly to the Clash,' said *Film Comment*, looking back at the first year or so of the channel, 'is sorely lacking at MTV.'[38]

Within a couple of years, however – and through relentless campaigning in TV ad slots that featured music stars of the day to encourage audiences in parts of the country where the channel was not yet available to write to local cable providers with the demand, 'I Want My MTV' – it would go on to become the medium through which megastars of the 1980s such as Madonna, Michael Jackson and Prince conquered the world. Because MTV came to possess a wider and eventually national reach in the USA in a way no radio station could (owing to the limitations imposed on radio transmitters), it gradually found itself playing music – based on clips that were available – that otherwise found it difficult to get an airing on radio. Devo was one such band. These Midwest weirdos who were once described as a 'self-contained concept band' – they took control of every aspect of their sound, look and appearance and the means through which it was disseminated – had from the beginning of their existence been

A magazine advert for MTV, 1988, published in *Spin* magazine.

interested in making films.[39] The influence of The Residents on their videos seemed clear, with Devo's videos 'a riotous jumble of found footage, masked freaks, and sci-fi mash-ups'.[40]

The spark for Devo's interest in video was a *Popular Science* article from 1974 about laserdiscs. 'We were making music-driven narratives, short films,' Mark Mothersbaugh said of the group's early days, and they hatched a plan to 'do a collection of 'em once a year on laserdisc'.[41] Some of these short films were made to accompany their debut album, *Q: Are We Not Men? A: We Are Devo!* (1978), including the still astonishingly inventive-looking clip for their jerky robotic version of The Rolling Stones' '(I Can't Get No) Satisfaction'; by the early 1980s, in videos such as 'Whip It' (wearing their trademark 'energy dome' flowerpot hats), they were using the new medium to underline a cartoonish theatricality that otherwise might only have been conveyed by the

An advert for Devo, 1978, featuring images from some of their early videos.

covers of their records. If nothing else, Devo's MTV-driven success was proof that in the landscape of this new national visual radio, being weird or unusual was probably enough to give you an edge. The same might be said of Talking Heads' David Byrne. The video for the Talking Heads song 'Once in a Lifetime' (1981), which Byrne co-directed with Toni Basil, transforms the singer into a kind of possessed evangelist, his body seemingly thrown around as if he were a puppet. With its funky bass and African-inflected percussion, the single didn't fit easily into either rock or R&B programming and as such never really made a break-through on radio: was it a rock song, or was it something else? Were the musicians black or white? Listening audiences were unsure what to make of it. But the video was another matter, and MTV lapped it up.[42]

But while Devo and Talking Heads broke through with video specifically because they had a carefully developed visual sensibility that lent itself to the medium, MTV was still largely sticking with a format designed to appeal to the white AOR market segment. The fact that black R&B and non-rock music – such as dance music – found it impossible to make it onto a channel that was capable of creating huge surges in record sales seemed to many to be steeped in a racially motivated desire to deny airspace to black music. In this period the fate of Michael Jackson would become symbolic of the struggle of black artists to crash through the new racial and musical barrier that MTV had established. Jackson would not be the first black artist to be played on MTV – the more rock-orientated Prince had been playlisted with '1999', as were British teenage reggae group Musical Youth with 'Pass the Dutchie' (both 1982) – but he would be the most significant.

Jackson's breakthrough on MTV was the video for 'Billie Jean' in early 1983, a clip that showcased his abilities as a dancer and exploited the visual medium to the fullest to complement the music. Its success on the channel exposed him to an entirely new audience – the predominantly white and rock-orientated audiences that were still its main subscribers. By the time MTV aired Jackson's 'Thriller' video later that year, black artists were beginning to make up much more of the playlist. 'Thriller' itself was unlike any video MTV had shown to date: it was almost fourteen minutes long in its full version, and in terms of production values – the cinematography, casting, choreography and budget of half a million dollars – it stood alone. Rather than being directed by a novice film-maker or someone who made commercials, 'Thriller' was directed by John Landis, a bona fide Hollywood director, whose *An American Werewolf in London* (1981) Jackson had been a big fan of. 'Thriller' brought some of the same visual quality

Michael Jackson on the set of the short
Martin Scorsese-directed film for 'Bad' (1987).

and special effects to this mini movie in which Jackson, on his way home from seeing a horror film, finds himself surrounded by zombies before suddenly transforming into one himself.

The public unveiling of 'Thriller' was also unlike anything that had been seen before. It was treated as an event, with its own theatrical premiere in Los Angeles and a host of worldwide TV reveals before it was made available to be playlisted like any other video clip. It also spawned its own 'making of' film with a long-form video that became the best-selling home video of all time. One of Jackson's other blockbuster videos, 'Bad' (1987), also made use of established film expertise – it was directed by Martin Scorsese – and also wore its movie influences proudly: in this case, *West Side Story* was the influence for a short film that revolved around street-fighting gangs. What these videos did was let the world see Jackson dance, over and over again – something that was probably infinitely more watchable than the standard fare of music videos, which for many did not bear repeated viewing.

THE UNVARNISHED business aspect of MTV as an outlet for record company product went along with other changes that would define the 1980s, reshaping the music industry for a while as much as television had in 1950s America. The decade was a time of blatant commercialism and 'selling out' on a grand scale. It was an era when songs advertised Hollywood films, and the films advertised the songs. It was also the era of reinvention for a whole generation of artists who suddenly realized that if MTV meant anything, it was that they weren't washed up yet.

Especially memorable as specimens of the era were some of the videos that 'starred' the battle-scarred survivors of the

1960s and '70s, now older and on the cusp of second life in this, the video age. Where self-destruction had in the past been almost a default objective in rock – that idea about hoping to die before getting old didn't come out of nowhere – by the 1980s it seemed to have been replaced by almost the exact opposite: self-preservation and that new phenomenon, 'detoxing', a kind of urge towards mental and physical purification. The examples seemed endless: the newly sober Aerosmith, led by the duo of Joe Perry and Steven Tyler (who joked that he must have 'snorted half of Peru' in the previous decade), enjoyed an MTV-aided comeback hit when they appeared in the video for Run DMC's cover of their 1975 hit 'Walk This Way'. This period of their re-invention coincided with them adopting a kind of identity that separated them as survivors of the excessive 1970s, a period when Perry and Tyler adopted the name – seemingly without irony – the 'Toxic Twins'. If they couldn't live it like the old days, they could still present the simulacra of it as its grizzled survivors.

Likewise, a 1986 *Spin* magazine feature on Peter Gabriel, who had crossed into the new decade even bigger than he had been before thanks to a series of inventive videos, noted that while the singer had retreated from the public eye after suffering 'a series of personal and professional crises of confidence' in the 1970s, he made it through to the MTV era by 'becoming a disciple of John Lilly's sensory-deprivation tanks, where in the perfect darkness of saline-solution-filled confines' he was able to 'dream without boundaries'.[43]

Notable among the ageing rockers to embrace the new MTV age was the unlikely figure of Lou Reed, whose most memorable video outing of 1984, 'I Love You, Suzanne', was one in which the hard-won public persona that had been established over two decades or so of unrelenting self-destructiveness was demolished in approximately three minutes of eye-boggling video reinvention. The clip begins with Reed disembarking from a motorcycle to make a call in a phone booth. Within a minute or so of this introduction, we can only look on in wonder as he seems to morph into the John Travolta of *Saturday Night Fever*, but in leathers and shades rather than white suit and medallion. Reed high-kicks and pirouettes as he leaps from a nightclub stage into the audience, where the eponymous Suzanne, looking like a *Vogue* cover star, beckons him to dance. If it was a body double doing these moves, then it was hard to tell: the video editor had done such a good job of turning the Lou Reed everybody knew into Lou Reed, king of the nightclub dance floor, that the transition was seamless.

But on the other hand, perhaps he was just playing himself and this new video age Lou was no act. It was an idea that was borne out in some profiles of the time. 'The New Lou's got a wife, a house in the country, and a new Harley in the driveway,' wrote Scott Cohen in a 1986 *Spin* piece: 'The Old Lou avoided people, places, and things. The New Lou's in shape, looks great, and takes it to the hoop. The Old Lou took anti-vitamin pills. Down for Lou was up. Today's Lou breathes easy, does tai chi, and is sugar-free.'[44] The MTV audience was representative of a new and younger generation who were weaned on the music of the video age – music accompanied by visuals – and in this new rock landscape figures like Lou Reed could become avatars of the age simply by moving on screen, thereby rendering what they had been in previous incarnations, not available for easy video recall, largely irrelevant. In the temporality of 1980s rock, the 1960s – now getting on for twenty years earlier – was another world. As far as Reed was concerned, it was a fact underlined by his appearance in an advertising campaign for Honda motorcycles that not

The Long Ryders, rising stars of the alternative rock scene, pictured under the gaze of video director Tim Newman in an advert for Miller beer from 1986. The idea that a behind-the-scenes video shoot could advertise a product besides the music itself characterized an era when MTV, film and advertising mixed freely.

only seemed to follow on seamlessly from his reinvention in 'I Love You, Suzanne' but ended up adding enough cool to the once artistically questionable job of commercial endorsement that it opened up a route between product ads, MTV videos and Hollywood for aspiring film-makers.[45] In Lou's Honda starring role, the scene is Manhattan's Lower East Side, amid the hustle and bustle of the streets that inspired countless of his songs. The day is just beginning to slip into night as the sound of his 1973 hit 'Walk on the Wild Side' plays. A wall covered with poster advertisements is glimpsed amid the crowds – 'Lou Reed Live', one reads – and we catch what looks like a split-second shot of the man himself, wearing his customary shades, but the grainy images and jump cuts might be playing tricks on the eye. Finally, the camera pans to Reed sitting on a scooter outside the Bottom

Line club – once the haunt of Andy Warhol's entourage and the characters celebrated in 'Walk on the Wild Side' – and he delivers his one line: 'Hey, don't settle for walking.' *No, buy a Honda* is the unspoken message. Even Lou's old friend Warhol was on MTV, both as the host of his own show, *Andy Warhol's Fifteen Minutes* (1985–7) – its title a nod to his famous quip that in the future everyone would be famous for fifteen minutes – and as a director of videos for groups like The Cars.

What MTV videos represented, when all was said and done, were adverts – 'the marriage of Hollywood's pandering impulses to rock's lust for assimilation', to use the words of one critic.[46] Wim Wenders, whose films had used rock music in ways that might be regarded as templates for the music video, was at first hooked on the new channel, seeing in it, as so many had, effectively a new kind of 'radio' – one that simply added moving images. It was an infatuation that did not last. 'It's just another step towards a total inflation of imagery, to a point where people lose a feeling of integrity, of truth in images,' he said.[47] *Spin* – a publication born in the video age – took aim at MTV in its '35 Years of Rock'n'Roll' issue in 1990. 'The problem with rock'n'roll today is someone let too much light in,' wrote Legs McNeil in a piece reflecting on how the myth of Jim Morrison had been fuelled by darkness, danger and mystery. 'With MTV, commercial advertising and corporate sponsors, somehow all the daylight has destroyed the mesmerizing darkness.'[48]

The success of MTV, in fact, spilled over into the movies that were being made from the 1980s onwards, not only because many aspiring film directors built up their reputations and show reels with music video but because of the way that mainstream film began to use music as a promotional tool and an element of picture-making (via the often crude application of pop music on top of the image, abandoning the pre-rock practice of music underscoring the action on screen); this was often little more than a gimmick designed to draw in audiences. As a result, the 1980s were also a boom time for the film sound-track album and single releases; an age of 'heavily merchandised rock culture'.[49]

In 1984, a record number of film soundtracks sold in the millions – more than the two previous best years, 1978 and 1980, combined – with seven number-one singles coming from film soundtracks, including the best-selling single of the year, Prince's 'When Doves Cry'. In keeping with the 1980s as an era when commercial imperatives seemed to overtake artistic ones, such hit singles were essentially adverts for the movies they were featured in, complete with MTV-style videos that featured movie scenes cut in to more-or-less standard performance clips.[50] These became tired and clichéd very quickly. But with record companies, film studios and artists all prospering from the cross-pollination, it was a trend that continued throughout the decade.

Screen Stars of the 1980s

Some musicians used success in the MTV era as a springboard into film in a more determined way, seeing in it a means of extending the range of expression. David Byrne's performance in Jonathan Demme's *Stop Making Sense* (1984), regarded by some as a high-water mark of filmed live performance, singled out Byrne from the other Talking Heads even more than his appear-ance in their 'Once in a Lifetime' video had. The film established Byrne's flair for visual communication as a live performer, with an ability to project himself from the stage to the big screen in a way that few had managed to achieve before. The film made the oddness and weird tics that had always made him one of the least clichéd of rock frontmen the centrepiece of the film. Demme himself also put something on screen that drew attention to the performers and was able to bypass the usual formulae of concert performances translated onto film.

There are no fans, no backstage scenes or interviews. Instead, the film takes shape slowly through the musicians who emerge – first, Byrne on his own – onto an empty stage that only gradually becomes occupied. Byrne is joined by the other three long-standing Talking Heads, and then by the rest of the expanded group that they had morphed into by the early 1980s. Wearing an outsized suit and moving like no one else in rock 'n' roll, Byrne gained the kind of star recognition that saw Warner Bros. back him as the director of *True Stories* (1986), a musical based around a series of satirical vignettes and which also spawned a Talking Heads soundtrack album of the same name. In the film, the songs were sometimes performed by the actors instead, marking another departure from what might have been expected.

David Byrne (right) with Talking Heads in *Stop Making Sense* (1984).

The most successful musician in making the journey from music to video and then film was Prince. Albert Magnoli's *Purple Rain* (1984) was a semi-autobiographical tale of the rise of a Prince-like musician ('The Kid') fighting his way through the cut-throat club scene of Minneapolis. It served as an example of the mutually beneficial relationship that had come to exist between film soundtrack albums and the movies themselves. Driven by the box-office success of the film, the album sold 8 million copies in the USA alone between its release in July and the end of the year.[51] In the movie's opening week, *Purple Rain* was the biggest hit at the U.S. box office, and it ended the year as the ninth-highest-grossing movie of 1984.[52]

One surprising thing about the film was that it was even produced in the first place. Although Prince's record company, Warner Bros., agreed to finance it with a generous $7 million budget, Prince was still far from the pop star he would become in the wake of the film, having only broken the Top Ten with the album *1999* and the single 'Little Red Corvette' in 1983. It was a gamble on Prince becoming the perfect embodiment of an era when it was now possible to take what he had been doing already – blending R&B, dance and rock music – to a bigger audience than had been possible before MTV helped to create an audience that saw beyond such genre distinctions. If the movie could tap into the visual style and aesthetics of the era – if it could become like a movie-length MTV video – then there would be great scope for broadening Prince's appeal.

In *Purple Rain*, the Prince character seems trapped by his own unwillingness to move beyond a repertoire littered with darkly sexual dance numbers that do not always meet with the approval of audiences or promoters. As the more soap opera elements of the character's back story develop, he also repeatedly returns to

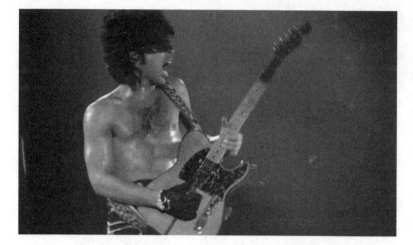

Prince in *Purple Rain* (1984), the first of a series of big-screen roles that would see the artist build his own film soundstage at his Paisley Park complex and take up the role of director in a number of films.

a piece of music that he cannot get out of his head – which by the end of the film has become its anthemic rock number, 'Purple Rain'. The story might have been said to describe the trajectory of Prince's career – from his third album *Dirty Mind* in 1980 to the mainstream success he would achieve through the film and its title song – pretty accurately. The scenes showing Prince onstage in performance are the most memorable parts of the movie. In turn, whole musical sequences, such as the one soundtracked by 'When Doves Cry', were lifted straight out of the movie and used as promo video clips, underlining again the way that music and cinema were feeding off each other.

Prince went further than most in trying to move between music and film. In 1986 he directed and starred in *Under the Cherry Moon* (1986), a 1940s-style musical that did not match the success of his debut but still spawned some of his best music in the form of the soundtrack album, *Parade*. The film that was taken to be a more obvious follow-up to *Purple Rain* was *Graffiti*

Bridge (1990), again directed by Prince, this time the rivalry between 'The Kid' and Morris Day of The Time that had served as one of the main plotlines of the first film seemed less plausible since Prince had so effortlessly eclipsed his former real-life rival in the years since. Some of the movie was shot in Prince's own Paisley Park studio complex in Chanhassen, Minnesota, which as well as housing a number of recording studios and a nightclub also contained a specially built soundstage for film projects. Like *Under the Cherry Moon*, however, it failed to repeat the success of *Purple Rain*; it seemed that in trying to be something he was not – a romantic lead actor – Prince was only undermining his real appeal. 'The boldest moment in the movie is the star's effort to direct himself in a big death scene, which he flubs,' wrote one critic. 'He allows himself to fall – mortally wounded – in such a way that his shoes are in the center of the frame, and they're more riveting than he is.'[53]

Prince was more successful in directing himself in the concert film *Sign o' the Times* (1987, also made at his own studios), which blended performance footage with 'between-song playlets' that provided a kind of narrative that glued it all together.[54] As far as music video as a medium itself went, there was a brief period in which the promo clip began to expand and acquire movie-like ambitions. Julien Temple, chief documentarist of the Sex Pistols, established himself as a prolific director of promo videos by the mid-1980s and made the twenty-minute film *Jazzin' for Blue Jean* (1984) with David Bowie. It took a standard three-minute song, Bowie's 'Blue Jean', and placed it within a story in which Bowie played the parts of 'Screaming Lord Byron' – a nod to his 1970s 'characters' – and a doppelgänger fan named Vic.[55] Like Jackson's 'Thriller' it popped up in theatres, running as the opening feature with Neil Jordan's movie *The Company of Wolves* in Britain. Other artists did similar long-form films, including Ray Davies of The Kinks – who wrote and directed a one-hour film musical for TV, *Return to Waterloo* (1984) – and Pink Floyd, who hired director Alan Parker to make a film musical of their album *The Wall* (1982), which pre-dated the success of MTV but was not that far removed from a long MTV-style video. The The's album *Infected* (1987), with a clip made for each song at a cost of $500,000, followed the example set by Blondie's *Eat to the Beat*, although it used a number of directors – including Tim Pope – rather than being the work of a single film-maker.[56] The group's UK record company, CBS, was happy to stump up such an amount in the hope that it would break The The into the American market. Matt Johnson, the artist behind The The, was happy to see it as an extension of his songwriting and said that he regarded his songs as 'very cinematic'. The series of videos was a perfect way to further convey *Infected*'s overarching theme, which he described as 'the symptoms and causes of the fall of the Western Empire'.[57]

Perhaps the most curious product of the collision between film and rock came in the form of the debut album by Big Audio Dynamite, the group formed by Mick Jones – who had left The Clash in 1984 – and punk rock documentarian and prolific video director Don Letts. Taking inspiration from hip-hop DJs, who plundered old records for sounds that could be mixed into new and unexpected combinations on twin turntables, they lit upon the idea of making an album in which sounds and dialogue from movies would be the source of samples that were then blended with a conventional rock band composed of guitars, drums and keyboards. The greatest achievement of this idea was the single 'E=MC²' from their debut album *This Is Big Audio Dynamite* (1985), which was their tribute to the films of the British director Nicolas Roeg. The song was written after Jones and Letts – both long-standing Roeg fans – had been to a screening of his film *Insignificance* (1985). 'I approached the lyrics like film treatments,' Letts later said, explaining that the song actually references all of Roeg's movies, albeit in a cryptic fashion. 'I called it an homage to Roeg. All the samples were from *Performance*.'[58]

The song, of course, had an accompanying video, directed by Roeg's son, Luc. It featured clips from every Roeg movie except the one that supplied the voices that were so deftly used in the song (those were the voices of Mick Jagger and James Fox, lifted from Roeg's *Performance*). This was not the kind of lazy interplay between film and music that had so come to characterize the video age but rather a more nuanced blending of two worlds, mediated in song and by the coming together of a musician (Mick Jones) and a self-taught film-maker (Don Letts) in a rock band.

The Rolling Stones starred in Hal Ashby's *Let's Spend the Night Together* (1983). Ashby was a rock 'n' roll freak who seemed to partake in the backstage perks more than Mick Jagger, and reputedly directed the opening scenes attended to by paramedics after collapsing from exhaustion before the start of the concert.

8

DO IT AGAIN

As early as 1966, The Beatles were already trying to figure out how they might avoid what they perceived as their impending obsolescence as the four lovable characters immortalized in *A Hard Day's Night*. The challenge they faced was in how to escape the screaming teenagers and discover a route into a kind of artistic freedom that might accommodate their emerging differences as individuals who were maturing and acquiring the things that go along with adulthood and respectability: wives, children, homes, wealth beyond their youthful dreams.

In the minds of the press and the public, more significance had been attached to the fate of The Beatles than any of their predecessors, never mind the contemporaries who would never achieve the same status as cultural icons who transcended the music world. In them, a generation who could only dream of taking their place had vested a whole host of 'dreams, hopes, energies' and 'disappointments'.[1] It was something that became more of a burden to them as they aged.

While the level of their success set The Beatles apart from their contemporaries, bringing them greater fame and more riches, they seemed to be, paradoxically, less free to do what they wanted. They had reached the point where success came to represent a limitation. Their record-breaking appearance at Shea Stadium, New York, in 1965, seen in the TV film *The Beatles at*

Shea Stadium (first aired by the BBC in March 1966), had been drowned out by the sound of screaming fans, with the band unable to hear themselves. Within that context, it is little surprise that The Beatles of Michael Lindsay-Hogg's *Let It Be* (1970) – filmed during the recording sessions for their final album in 1969 – are seen at a point of personal and professional transition. John Lennon had already released an album with Yoko Ono, the previous year's experimental *Unfinished Music No. 1: Two Virgins*, the pair appearing nude on the album sleeve to indicate the symbolic rebirth. The other members of the group – George Harrison in particular – were beginning to doubt the benefits of being subsumed by The Beatles' overpowering collective image.[2] Lindsay-Hogg's film documents the recording of what would become the *Let It Be* album, and immediately lent itself to the sense that this was the end of the line for The Beatles. The music we see performed, including the famous 'last concert' on the rooftop of their Savile Row Apple Corps building, and the interaction between the band members, betray a kind of collective exhaustion. The impromptu rooftop performance during the middle of the day would become almost 'the last collective memory' of the group.[3]

By the time the film was showing in cinemas, Paul McCartney had released his first solo album, and review copies distributed to the press came complete with a so-called 'self-interview' in which he signalled the end of the band, declaring that he was finished with 'the personal differences, business differences, musical differences' and preferred the company of his own family.[4] At the end of the year, he had their business partnership dissolved in the High Court. By this time, as we have seen in *Let It Be*, The Beatles seemed like much older men than the Goonish lads of *A Hard Day's Night*. Then, they were young men chased across the land by ever-present teenage mobs; now, they exuded a kind of existential weariness. Their bearded and moustachioed faces looked worn out by the accelerated lives they had been living during the decade they were about to leave behind. Lennon told *Rolling Stone* magazine that studio rehearsals seen in the film were really done under duress. 'It was a dreadful, dreadful feeling in Twickenham Studio, and being filmed all the time.'[5]

Some of the critics thought it was the right time for it to end. It 'was now an absurd idea for four married men approaching 30' to still be in a rock group together, wrote Tony Palmer in *The Observer*.[6] And so, The Beatles – with Lennon and Starr the oldest at 29, McCartney aged 27 and Harrison aged 26 – 'retired' as Beatles to concentrate on more mature pursuits. The media seemed to be calling time, too, on The Beatles' dastardly counterparts, The Rolling Stones. 'Mick Jagger', declared *The Times* in a 1968 look at youth culture, was 'an ancient of the pop world'.[7] Jagger was 25 years old but had clearly lasted longer than he was meant to. So, he did what rock 'n' roll stars before had done: he starred in a film. The image of a washed-up Jagger-like singer could be seen in *Performance* (filmed in 1968 but not released until 1970).

Jagger plays a reclusive rock star, Turner, trapped in a decadent downward spiral, no longer bothering the public but instead playing head games with gangsters and hangers-on. 'Turner is terminally jaded,' wrote Mick Brown in a study of the film, 'he has exhausted the possibilities of his art, grown tired of its rewards and bored with its diversions.'[8] Such might have been the fate of the average rock star facing a future for which there was really no roadmap. But Mick Jagger, as well as starring in *Performance* and as the eponymous Australian outlaw of *Ned Kelly* (1970), kept reappearing as . . . Mick Jagger. Far from retiring, he continued long past the time when most of those in his world who had reached his age had called it a day.

Ten years later, a few months before he was gunned down outside his apartment in New York, John Lennon couldn't make sense of why The Rolling Stones had not yet dissolved as The Beatles had. 'Why are these guys still together? Can't they hack it on their own? Why do they have to be surrounded by a gang?' he asked.[9] The Stones had recently released their fifteenth (or, in America, what counted as their seventeenth) album, *Emotional Rescue*. The following year they would embark on one of the most successful tours in the history of the music business and release a new album of songs that contained leftovers from sessions dating as far back as the early 1970s. The record, *Tattoo You*, was their most successful album for years, and the tour that went with it would supply the material for the Hal Ashby film *Let's Spend the Night Together* (1982). Ashby, one of the most acclaimed directors of the New Hollywood, was a Rolling Stones fanatic. Before agreeing to film them on tour, he had already been working with Jagger to try to bring Gore Vidal's novel *Kalki* (1978) to the screen. Jagger owned the movie rights.[10] 'In another life', Peter Biskind wrote, Ashby 'would have loved to have been Mick Jagger'.[11]

Ashby's Stones film, unlike those made by Robert Frank or the Maysles brothers, was to be more of a straight concert film than a documentary about the band on the road. Without the kind of *cinéma vérité* moments that had made those earlier films significant, some might have said that Ashby merely delivered a boring document that revealed little more than how big the Rolling Stones juggernaut had become by 1981. But if there was nothing much beneath the surface, or at least nothing behind the veil that it was deemed prudent to reveal, that itself told a story about where rock was now.

Where his contemporary Scorsese had delivered in *The Last Waltz* a concert film that was about the sense of something that *seemed* at the time to have been around a long time – filmed in a dimly lit theatre with dangling candelabra hanging over the besuited Band as the lights were about to go down one final time – Ashby's film couldn't have been in more contrast. The film begins in the daylight of a summer afternoon with Jagger and his bandmates running onstage at the Sun Devil Stadium in Tempe, Arizona, in front of joyous fans who are there for a day's entertainment. Ashby's camera sweeps over the stadium, capturing the spectacle from a helicopter as balloons are released into the blue sky. The scenes were directed by the hard-living Ashby from a gurney with an IV drip dangling from his arm, as he lay in a trailer that was receiving the images from the various camera positions: as a result of 'partying way beyond his capabilities' with the Stones, the director had collapsed just before the concert began.[12] But whatever had been going on offstage did not make it to the screen this time. Instead, the sole focus would be the apparently ageless band.

With his restless scurrying around, cavorting and vamping, Jagger embodied a youthful exuberance that was amazing to behold. As if to lend substance to the idea that The Rolling Stones had paradoxically grown younger with the passing years, even the mostly static Bill Wyman – at 45 the oldest of the group – sported a tracksuit. Keith Richards, too, seemed to have emerged revitalized from the darkest days of the 1970s, when his run-ins with the law threatened the existence of the band. The only hint of anything that could be described as unhealthy in *Let's Spend the Night Together* were the perma-cigarettes that dangled from the mouths of Richards and Ron Wood. If the style and tone of the film gave nothing like the sense of an ending that marked

Scorsese's *The Last Waltz*, it was nonetheless a film that revealed the Stones to have turned a corner; they now occupied a different place from the band who were seen in 1970's *Gimme Shelter*, a film that would be forever defined by the atmosphere of death and chaos that made it one of the most remarkable films about the 1960s.

Prior to the start of the tour, Jagger had been working on Werner Herzog's film *Fitzcarraldo*, in which he had been cast in a substantial dramatic role. But the production ran into serious delays on location in Peru and Jagger was forced to abandon the role (although he can be seen in Les Blank's documentary about the making of that troubled production, *Burden of Dreams*).[13] Speaking to the press at around the time of the release of Ashby's film, Jagger reflected on finding himself still fronting the Stones at the ripe old age of 38, and the fact that the instant fame he had found almost twenty years earlier had made for an odd and 'very adolescent' kind of life. 'Sometimes you wonder how it'd have been if you'd been involved in something that would have expanded your brain a little more,' he said.[14] By the time you get to thirty in rock 'n' roll, he added, 'you start to understand how idiotic you've been. Then you start to think, "Well, I can still play the part – but I'll be an actor; this isn't really me."'[15]

It is less clear that the same could have been said for the others, with Richards openly hostile to some of Ashby's crew and less willing to put on a show for the sake of keeping up appearances.[16] *Let's Spend the Night Together*, however, presents the band as Jagger had intended, as entertainers who put on the biggest rock show on the planet, on the cusp of a new era for rock as concert tours grew increasingly towards the mega scale, producing a different kind of experience that was as much about size and spectacle as mere music. Although it was on the surface a simple concert film, it featured the kind of comprehensive camera coverage of the subject that made it possible for the viewer to feel at times as if they were by the side of the stage, behind the performers, or flying high over the audience. Something else that enabled the Stones to keep things looking fresh after all this time was the fact that they would be under-rehearsed, warming up and becoming less ragged as the tour moved towards its end. The film captures an enjoyable level of unpredictability, with Richards, Wood and saxophonist Ernie Watts sometimes all plunging into a solo at the same time but going along with the flow as it took them 'into a careening, full-tilt ensemble improvisation'.[17]

The longer The Rolling Stones went on, mapping out the terrain for something greater than an ageing gang still playing rock 'n' roll, the more the potential life span of everyone that came after them could be extended. And the longer it went on, in an era when seemingly everything was filmed and photographed, it was usually captured on film. One such example was Scorsese's Rolling Stones concert film *Shine a Light* (2008). As a film, it arrived at a time where such releases had become so commonplace that it was hard to see anything in them beyond the ability to deliver more product for equally ageing fans, for whom the music of the Stones was no doubt one of the ways they were able to hang on to their youth. It is an unremarkable film apart from the new light it shines on the peculiarities of the times, when the aged Stones could be feted by world leaders. We can only marvel when Jagger and the band are introduced by the former u.s. president Bill Clinton, then, at sixty years old, a bit younger than the founding members of the band.

To see the Stones onstage in the later stages of their career – certainly from a distance, or through bleary eyes – it might have been hard to tell that it was not The Rolling Stones of the late 1960s up there onstage. Scorsese and a crew of notable cinematographers, though, had captured it all up close and in high definition, unafraid – as one assumes the band themselves were – to make a virtue of their longevity. 'Mr Jagger whirls, leaps, struts, wiggles his tiny hips and sashays around like an androgynous tart prowling a street corner at 3 a.m.,' said one complimentary review.[18] His body seemed to defy the truth of temporal longevity that he wore on his aged face, suggesting nothing so much as 'a double exposure of Dorian Gray and his infamous portrait, at once defiantly youthful and creepily gaunt'.[19] Alongside him was Richards, his friend since childhood, described as resembling 'an old madam chewing over her secrets'.[20]

Who, at the end of the 1960s, would have foreseen that it would come to this?

Metal Fatigue

No film encapsulated the nature of aged, squabbling rockers unable to call it a day more than Rob Reiner's *This Is Spinal Tap* (1984), the spoof documentary that came to be regarded by many it indirectly lampooned as the greatest – and, strangely, the truest – account of the many pitfalls of life in a rock band. The impression the film leaves on any viewer familiar with rock film is of a kind of funhouse mirror through which we are now able to see anew films made years before it was even conceived, many of which have since come to be seen for their 'Tap-like' moments or that might accurately be described as 'Spinal Tap-ish'.

The genius of *Spinal Tap* was in the way that it revealed the prolonged adolescence of the rock life to be, in fact, a fundamental and irredeemably absurd paradox: the older and more successful you were, the more your prima donna-ish ways were indulged in rock. The movie tells the story of a fictional English rock band, survivors of the 1960s who have passed through a number of embarrassing phases and undergone name changes but have still managed to keep going into early middle age, convinced of their own credentials as great survivors. In one scene, as the band members rest between shows, a radio in their hotel suite comes to life, playing a song they had recorded some twenty years earlier. As they gather round with their younger female companions – who we sense are too young to remember or know anything about this past – the convivial mood is cut short when the voice of a DJ pipes up over the fading strains of the song: 'and that was The Thamesmen, all the way from 1966. They later changed their name to Spinal Tap and can now be found languishing in the Where Are They Now category.'

Spinal Tap are led by David St Hubbins (Michael McKean) and Nigel Tufnel (Christopher Guest), the twin poles of creative energy who – like Jagger and Richards or Lennon and McCartney (or any number of other rock pairs) – have known each other since they were schoolboys. They form a fragile partnership, carrying the group through its many changes and with simmering jealousies and long-festering grudges barely kept in check. As opposites they were, in the words of hapless bassist Derek Smalls (Harry Shearer), like fire and ice. Smalls reveals that he, mediating between the two, was 'like lukewarm water'. But here, in 1982, Spinal Tap are back on the road in America, a tour that quickly becomes a disastrous affair, with technical mishaps on-stage – such as Derek becoming trapped in a womb-like pod that 'gives birth' to him during their song 'Rock 'n' roll Creation' – and countless bust-ups when they are not playing. The first clue they have that they are no longer as important as they might have thought is when their record company delays the release of a new album, *Smell the Glove*, because of its sexist cover, which depicts a woman on all fours wearing a dog collar and having a gloved hand thrust into her face. The censure seems to confuse Nigel, who complains, 'well, so what? What's wrong with being sexy?' 'Sex-*ist*, -IST . . . not sexy,' David and the band's cricket bat-wielding manager, Ian Faith (Tony Hendra), point out.

The offending album cover is eventually replaced with a new design – an all-black sleeve with no text and no images – which we see being delivered to them shrink-wrapped in cellophane. The band members bemusedly examine copies. 'It's like a black mirror,' Nigel observes. 'There's something about this that's so black, it's like . . . how much more black could this be, and the answer is none. None more black.' As the tour limps on to decreasing audience interest under the guidance of Derek's girlfriend Jeanine – who consults astrological charts to try to fix the bad vibes that seem to be following them – they arrive in Seattle to discover that their gig for the night has been downgraded because of lack of interest. Instead of playing the local arena, they must make a humiliating appearance at a nearby air force base, the nature of which they are unaware of until they arrive to be greeted by an officer, Lieutenant Hookstratten, who is under the impression they are named Spinal *Tarp*. Clearly, they are total unknowns to him.

As the group stand around nonchalantly, chewing gum and looking bored, he explains that the gig is to entertain the troops on their once-a-month 'at ease weekend' and then quickly shuffle offstage so that the evening's main entertainment – a puppet show – can commence. Looking at his watch, Hookstratten explains the situation with all the precision of normal military protocol, as if expecting everyone to synchronize watches: 'I would like to get the playing on by nineteen-hundred hours, if that's satisfactory,' he says. 'I make it now about eighteen-hundred-and-thirty hours.' 'So, what's that,' a confused Derek asks, 'about fifty hours?' '120 hours . . .?' the equally baffled David wonders. 'That's about thirty minutes,' Hookstratten says, 'about half an hour, give or take just a few minutes. I don't want to rush you.'

Michael McKean, who played David St Hubbins and co-wrote the script, recalled watching any rock movies they could to get ideas of how to 'furnish Spinal Tap with a believable past' that could allow them to improvise their parts once the cameras where rolling.[21] Harry Shearer had a part in one of those movies, *One Trick Pony* (1980), written by and starring Paul Simon, which helped them see the durability of such tales of rock survival, with Simon's character providing a convincing illustration of an artist clinging to the past and unwilling to call it a day 'no matter how clearly the market suggests he do so'.[22] In fact, *One Trick Pony* – as well as being one of those never-say-die, on-the-road portraits – sees Paul Simon play an ageing singer (by 1980 measures) called Jonah Levin, in a first intimation of the culture of ageing that would soon define each new generation of performers in post-1960s rock. The fact that Jonah hasn't had a hit record since the mid-1960s and won't give up is seen by his estranged wife as all the proof she needs that he has become trapped in a kind of prolonged adolescence. 'It's been fifteen years,' she says accusingly, like a mother telling off a wayward son. 'In six years, you'll be forty years old. And you've gone directly from adolescence to middle age.' But time and age seem irrelevant to Jonah. He says, 'in sixteen years I'll be fifty. In twenty-six years, I'll be sixty. In a mere sixty-six years I'll be one-hundred.' She shakes her head. 'Grown man living in a kid's world. Kids play rock and roll. Kids listen to it.' Out on the road, Jonah's band, who are very slick in a measured, jazz-rock, Steely Dan kind of way, are greeted with mildly appreciative applause from an audience at the end of their set, opening for the younger and much wilder B-52's. As Jonah and his band leave the stage, The B-52's run on to be greeted by scenes of wild ecstasy in the audience. Later, in the tour bus, Jonah and his band play a game called 'Rock 'n' roll Deaths' for twenty dollars a shot. If it's your turn and you can't name a dead rocker, then you lose – you're out. After a few rounds of name-throwing Jonah's bass player John (played by Tony Levin) finally gets to the most obvious one of all. 'Elvis!' he exclaims in mock triumph. 'Yeah. He's dead,' says a weary-sounding Jonah. It's almost as if they all know that the only way to really make it – and to find a way out of this life – is to die before your star fades.

Of all the guises that rock took on once it entered into its third decade, none would be as durable as the one that supplied *Spinal Tap* with its inspiration: heavy metal. By the time that *Metallica: Some Kind of Monster* (2004) was being filmed, the group had been around for longer than the Stones when they were greeted with amazement at the idea that such old men would still be touring in 1981. That, indeed, was the year of Metallica's formation, since when – as the titles of this movie reveal – they had become one of the best-selling acts of all time.

Shot in a low-quality camcorder style, which lends the sense of the viewer intruding on matters that might otherwise be kept private, the drama in this novel variant on the rock documentary is driven by what is essentially a family argument, or more precisely the breakdown of a marriage.[23] The marriage in this case is between the band's two figureheads, James Hetfield and Lars Ulrich. After more than two decades of spending too much time together, they can no longer keep a lid on their dissatisfaction with the way things have turned out, and now – during the

Metallica with James Hetfield (seated), therapist Phil Towle
(standing, in glasses) and Lars Ulrich (far right in blue shirt), in *Metallica:
Some Kind of Monster* (2004), taking a break from fighting with each other.

sessions for their first studio album in six years – the question is
whether they can keep in touch with the music and their original
motivations long enough to avoid the implosion of Metallica.

Metallica's devil-may-care attitude could be summed up in
the T-shirts they sold to their ever-increasing legion of fans,
which bore slogans like 'Alcoholica' or 'Metal Up Your Ass' and
would become the 'standard attire of a generation of high school
kids'.[24] It was an attitude that fed into a sound defined by unrelenting speed and aggression. But the past twenty years had
flown past so quickly that they now found themselves very rich
and very successful, but not very happy with the price they had
to pay for it. When bass player Jason Newsted leaves near the
beginning of the film, they bring in a new player, Robert Trujillo,
and deposit a million dollars into his bank account as a welcome
gift, just to ensure that he doesn't feel too underprivileged. In
another scene, Ulrich staggers drunkenly through a selection
of some of the modern art he has amassed, giving it one last

goodbye as he prepares to sell it for $13 million at the Christie's auction house – not because he needs the money, but because it no longer means what it did to him when he first found himself newly wealthy.

As relationships become more strained between Ulrich and Hetfield, the band decide to hire some help: 65-year-old group therapist Phil Towle, whose past experience included working with Chicago street gangs. 'Therapy', in a manner of speaking, was once the kind of thing done in another era by record producers. But that was before the performers vastly outstripped these former authority figures in wealth and power. *Some Kind of Monster* follows the group's near collapse and then rebirth as singer-guitarist Hetfield returns to recording sessions following a long spell in rehab. When he introduces himself as newly sober and more interested in the well-being of his family than in Metallica, the certainties of the old group dynamics are once again knocked sideways. He is now only willing to spend four hours a day in the studio; the rest of his time has to be given over to 'mending a marriage that was shattered by alcohol' and 'the rock 'n' roll lifestyle'.[25]

Ulrich, unable to believe the guy he has known for so long is sitting around speaking the language of therapy and going on about needing to have *trust* in him before they can repair their relationship, explodes. 'Fuck. Fuck. Fuck. FUCKKKK!' he screams in Hetfield's face. It was, as one profile of the band claimed, 'possibly the most intimate, most honest, most emotionally authentic exchange that these two men have ever experienced'.[26]

But Metallica survived and continue to thrive. Others too, seemingly held together by failure rather than fractured by success, offer further proof of metal's almost inbuilt desire to never give up. The stars of *Anvil: The Story of Anvil* (2008) are the lifelong friends and bandmates Steve 'Lips' Kudlow and Robb Reiner (the latter having almost the same name as the director of *Spinal Tap*), a Canadian metal band whose peak in the early pre-Metallica 1980s seems to belong to a distant past. Now more than a quarter of a century down the road, they have sunk into semi-obscurity yet remain determined to keep their rock 'n' roll dream alive. *Anvil* is probably the first rock documentary where failure – persistently and doggedly disregarded – becomes a key feature of a group's sense of itself and its perverse sense of identity and destiny.

Anvil's last survivors, Lips (guitar and vocals) and Robb (drums), are now in their fifties and struggle to hold down jobs that are a long way off what they had hoped for. 'When I work at Choice Children's Catering,' says Lips as he prepares to load up a van, 'they don't even know that my band exists.' But the film sees them begin to mount one final comeback attempt. Supplemented with new and younger members, they embark on a tour of Europe so disastrous that it might have come out of *Spinal Tap*. It earns them no money, but still they continue. Next they want to make another album with their 1980s producer, Chris Tsangarides, committing themselves to doing whatever it takes to raise the cash to pay him. Robb tries working as a tele-sales adviser but fails after one day.

As a story of persistence in the face of failure, *Anvil* was more than matched by *Last Days Here* (2011), a portrait of someone even more obscure: the near-unknown Bobby Liebling, who had once fronted an American Black Sabbath-like metal band in the 1970s and '80s known as Pentagram (the film's title alludes to the band's compilation of 1970s recordings, *First Daze Here*, 2001). Near the beginning of what is a remarkable portrait of extremes, we see an image of utter abjection as the frazzled and greying frontman reclines on a couch in what we learn is the 'sub-basement' of his elderly parents' home. Looking aged beyond his years, his body wracked by decades of drug abuse, he appears, one observer noted, like 'an extra from *The Walking Dead*'.[27] Liebling, though, has help, in the form of a fan-turned-manager who discovered and helped to release a cache of unreleased Pentagram recordings before arranging for this film to be made about his comeback. When those first scenes were shot, Liebling was 53 years old.

Despite the attention, he doesn't seem to care. It doesn't matter if he is alive or dead, he tells the film crew, but he'll 'stick around' anyway, just for them – just so they can make their film. Upstairs in the house, Liebling's mother and father are seen to be constantly worried about their son, who has never had anything like a hit record but still keeps telling them that one day he will end up in the Rock and Roll Hall of Fame. 'If he didn't have a dream,' his mother says, 'he'd probably kill himself.' When she adds that all she wants for him is to find 'a good woman', the implausibility of it is enough to provoke guffaws: here he is, a derelict drug addict barely existing and looking closer to the grave than to some rebirth. But it is exactly what happens.

A transformation begins midway through the story of Liebling's return to music when he begins seeing a younger female fan, who eases him back into an independent life in which he is free of crack cocaine and away from the safety of the sub-basement of the parental home. When quizzed about the difficulties that might be encountered given the three decades that separate them in age and experience, she says, 'In his heart, I think he will always be young.' Suddenly, Bobby is looking forward with optimism. 'I wanna live,' he tells his manager. 'I can't keep doing this child shit forever. I've been Peter Pan my whole life.' By the film's end, a startling metamorphosis has taken place. Liebling and his girlfriend, Hallie, appear before us in their small, bright apartment having breakfast with their daughter. It has been three years since we first met the ex-singer and he is now 56 years old. Unbelievably, he seems to have achieved the remarkable feat of both growing up and at the same time becoming visibly more youthful and revitalized, the ravages of time seemingly reversed.

NO VERSION of a metal reinvention was more curious than that of Ozzy Osbourne, who was reborn as the undisputed star of *The Osbournes*, an MTV-produced reality TV show that from 2002 to 2005 brought the daily struggles of the former bat-biter and Black Sabbath frontman to living rooms around the world. 'Be warned, these are not the Waltons,' *The Times* said in a listing for the fly-on-the-wall show, 'the family bickers and swears constantly in their crucifix-adorned house.'[28] While his albums had continued to sell by the million through the 1980s and '90s, there was never an inkling that Ozzy could become a screen star. His last headline-grabbing TV appearance, in fact, was probably when he was splashed across news reports in America during the early days of his solo career for urinating on the Alamo memorial while wearing a dress.

The Ozzy we see in *The Osbournes*, though, is the previously unseen domestic version, still clad mainly in black all day but now in his fifties and having to contend with a household that seems to thrive on chaos. 'Gus, Jim, Bill . . . whatever your fucking name is,' he says to the family cat as it investigates what he is up to in the kitchen, 'Don't go near my chicken, you understand? Fuck off! Because your name's gonna be "Dead" if you touch this chicken.' When not contending with the various pets that have free rein in his home, he has to contend with his wife and manager, Sharon Osbourne, who might actually be the wilder of the two – she dumps rubbish in the neighbours' garden as revenge for them playing loud music – and must try to exert some kind of fatherly influence over the teenage Jack and Kelly, reminding them of how privileged they are. 'You haven't been standing in front of 30 billion decibels for 35 years,' he tells Kelly when she complains that he is not listening to her.

Within the programme's thirty-minute format, such moments – skilfully selected and edited – made for compulsive television as the former Prince of Darkness was shown grappling with everyday life at home after decades on the road, making for more of a soap opera than its reality TV counterparts. The show was the biggest hit in MTV's history, winning the Osbourne family a further $13 million deal for a second series before the first had finished airing. While the show can be seen as part of the reality

Ozzy Osbourne (above) and family became a reality-TV hit in *The Osbournes*.

TV phenomenon that took off around the turn of the new century, it seemed to reach places that others did not. Osbourne's fame seemed to immediately render other examples of this new television format, such as *Big Brother* and *Survivor*, 'utterly redundant'.[29] The great advantage that it had over the shows that featured little-known celebrities or unknowns was that its star was already a larger-than-life, almost cartoon version of rock's live-fast-die-young ethos. Here he was, not only *not* dying before he got old but presenting a version of his act that was all about laying bare the effects of thirty-odd years of hard living.

Whether or not *The Osbournes* had contrived to extract the maximum comedy from the contrast between Ozzy's image and the apparently confounding reality of his life as seen on TV, it was simply undeniable that seeing the bumbling icon, senses apparently damaged by decades of rock 'n' roll excess, absorbed by some pointless quest or struggling with the remote control, was the realization of a genius idea. As with all reality television, it was the little and apparently insignificant things that were blown up into the stuff of the everyday. Sharon, a cut-throat manager in the rock world, keeps him in line when necessary, usually with some choice expletives or the kind of admonishment one might be more accustomed to directing at a child or a pet. Thus when a startled-looking Ozzy stumbles out of a room to greet her in one episode, it is with a request for her help as he declares that he has been robbed. 'Someone has been in my room and taken away my beers . . . away from my room.' 'I don't think so, darling,' she replies, 'Who would do that?' Before the groaning rocker is able to formulate a response, she continues: 'Who could possibly do that? Who's the beer thief? YOU! *You're the beer thief.*'

Songs of Experience

Rock film, which had been taken into new territory in the 1960s by the Maysles brothers and Pennebaker in their direct cinema films about rock culture, was a significant precursor of reality TV. Likewise, Andy Warhol's *Chelsea Girls* (1966), featuring Nico alongside other Warhol 'superstars', was a slice of the same kind of 'doing nothing' that would come to define the twenty-first-century TV phenomenon. Running for more than three hours over two screens, the film plunged viewers into the mundane reality of a group of what avant-garde film-maker Jonas Mekas, presenting the film in New York, described as 'lovers, dope addicts, pretenders, homosexuals, lesbians and heterosexuals' living at the Chelsea Hotel in New York.[30] Its depiction of bohemian life at the Chelsea was considered obscene enough to attract the attention of vice detectives when the film played outside New York.[31] 'At its best, *Chelsea Girls* is a travelogue of hell,' said a review in the *New York Times*,

> a grotesque menagerie of lost souls whimpering in a psychedelic moonscape of neon red and fluorescent blue. At its worst it is a bunch of home movies in which Mr. Warhol's friends, asked to do something on camera, can think of nothing much to do.[32]

The film ends with the camera focused on the then still glamorous Nico for long minutes as colour flashes across her face and the music of The Velvet Underground plays.

In 'Chelsea Hotel', a BBC *Arena* documentary made in 1981, Nico – who by this time had found something to do – is seen once again in the place where she had lived in the 1960s, her blonde hair replaced by the dyed dark colour she favoured by then, as she sits in a room singing 'Chelsea Girls', a song she originally recorded in 1967.[33] Accompanied by a lone electric guitar played by a young man, the song is darker and grittier by comparison with the overly sweet, string-laden original version. 'Aside from the people that are now in heaven or hell, or not staying here,' she told director Nigel Finch, 'I guess I am the person, the Chelsea Girl.' By the 1980s, however, Nico had travelled far from those days, particularly in a musical sense.

Susanna Nicchiarelli's 2017 biographical movie *Nico, 1988* tells the story of the final year of Nico's life as she and her band tour Europe playing to half-empty halls. After passing under the radar for most of the previous two decades, Nico (played by Trine Dyrholm) has relocated to the apparently sunless surroundings of post-industrial Manchester, in the north of England, from where her new manager Richard (John Gordon Sinclair)

Trine Dyrholm as Nico in *Nico, 1988*.

helps her put together a band that will enable her to tour once again. The events of Nico's Manchester years were also the basis of James Young's book *Nico: Songs They Never Play on the Radio* (1992), and on screen they provide the basis for a perceptive study of fame slowly burning itself out over time.[34]

The late 2010s saw a return to what might be called 'rock biopics', yet most of them – although many were very successful – really do not provide any insights into why rock persisted against all expectations. *Bohemian Rhapsody* (2018, about Queen) and *Rocketman* (2019, about Elton John) are films that follow the well-worn 'star is born' path, charting the trajectory of an unknown to their greatest success. Insofar as these kinds of films are bound up in details and events – and reach conclusions – that are overly familiar to the viewer, their only real novelty lies in the way that they try to bring to life and offer up a simulacrum of people and places that existed in the past. Rami Malek as Freddie Mercury looks and acts the part in *Bohemian Rhapsody*, but with more than half a decade compressed into around two hours, it is not a film that could ever get beyond such surface correspondences. What makes *Nico, 1988* one of the few rock biopics that succeeds is the fact that its story concerns the fall and decline of an icon into a period of their life where the details are sketchy. It almost illustrates the fact that what rock requires to translate most successfully into film in terms of compelling stories is the ability to reveal something hitherto unseen, a sense of mystique.

During her brief involvement with The Velvet Underground – it lasted less than a year – Nico had been seen as a kind of 'mannequin' inserted into the group to enhance its visual presence, a role that was little different than the one she had already grown tired of after many years working as a fashion model.[35]

Her 1968 album *The Marble Index* marked the real beginning of the musical journey that ends with the events of *Nico, 1988*. A short, self-authored 'bio' that appeared in a 1982 book about Edie Sedgwick – another Warhol acolyte – reveals that Nico accepted her obscurity with a dose of humour, even quoting a disparaging review in the short paragraph that sums up her career since the Warhol days. 'In the Sixties I was modelling and acting and singing,' she wrote: 'Since then, I have been the author of songs and a singer of "dirgelike songs themselves full of girlish Gothic imagery and spacy Romanticism" (John Rockwell, *New York Times*, 1979). I have a new album coming out.'[36] The Nico of The Velvet Underground was not the real Nico, or at least not the one she wanted to be. This much was also the point of Susanne Ofteringer's documentary film *Nico Icon* (1995), which attempts to trace its subject's passage from *Vogue* model to a proto-goth figure clad in black and singing those aforementioned dirge-like compositions. 'She started at some point having a real resentment of her good looks,' Paul Morrissey says in the film. 'She hated the fact that people thought she was beautiful. She thought it was some disgrace to be beautiful.'[37]

While Nico's appearance in 1966 and '67 still betrayed the influence of the modish fashions that she had discovered in London, it hid the eerie, hollow sound of a voice that suggested something altogether different. In the gloomy lament of 'All Tomorrow's Parties' her voice conveyed an image of New York as the empty stage for endless rehearsals that preceded nothing so much as the inevitable end, as life just ticked away. The words of the song, written by Lou Reed, were characteristic of the kind of urban realism that became his subject and were clearly associated with him as the song's author, but in spirit Nico was already there. Her brief musical fame through this early association with

Warhol and The Velvet Underground – which made her an icon of the era – makes what came after all the more surprising.

The harmonium-driven post-apocalyptic soundscapes of songs like 'Frozen Warnings' from 1968's *The Marble Index* are remarkably evocative today, not necessarily of time and place but as singular examples of rock's visionary ambition as it was played out towards the end of the 1960s. The title of the album was taken from William Wordsworth's autobiographical poem *The Prelude*, in which 'the marble index' refers to a bust of Sir Isaac Newton that he encountered as a young man and which represented to him the 'index' of a restless, questing mind. Nico's *Marble Index*, likewise, was to be seen as a voyage into uncharted territory. And it was: there was nothing else in like it in rock music. Yet at the same time, it could only have been the product of rock as a mode of romantic, artistic expression.

It was not until the post-punk era that Nico's brand of 'gothic romanticism' would seem to be a little more in tune with the times. 'I am a nihilist, I like destruction,' 1980s Nico says in grainy video footage resurrected in *Nico Icon*, before she is shown performing her own gloomy rendition of The Doors' 'The End', accompanied only by the sound of her harmonium. It is a sound of desolation, a howling wind, and befitting of the song's title. This is the Nico of *Nico, 1988*, now far removed from the Chelsea Girl. By then almost fifty, she would have been the oldest female rock artist there had ever been until that point. Onstage, Trine Dyrholm as Nico performs 'All Tomorrow's Parties' with a glass of red wine in one hand, a cigarette in the other, an image of the artist in the midst of self-destruction.

The final tour that provided the basis of this tale of her downward spiral was motivated, *Nico, 1988* suggests, by the desire to find or recapture a sound that she thought was out there

Nico (centre) and Iggy Pop (foreground) in a 1968 film
made to accompany some songs from her *Marble Index* album.

somewhere. She carried around a tape recorder in the hope of catching again something that had remained with her since her childhood in Germany at the end of the Second World War. It was the sound of 'Germany being bombed', she tells a radio interviewer in once scene. The sound of 'war ending, of the city burning. It was a sound that really wasn't a sound, it was many things at the same time. It was . . . the sound of defeat.'

SPEAKING IN 2006 during a period when she had been under the gaze of documentarist Steven Sebring since the end of the 1990s, when she had returned to performing after almost two decades, Patti Smith declared Peter Pan as an early ideal. 'He achieved everything I wanted to achieve,' she said, 'which was to never grow up.'[38] In her memoir *Just Kids* (2010), Smith even recalled telling her mother as an eleven-year-old that she 'was of the clan of Peter Pan and we did not grow up'.[39] For people like her, born in the 1940s, the best way to avoid growing up, of course, was to get into rock 'n' roll.

In rock 'n' roll, though, her model was more often said to be someone whose face she sometimes sported on a T-shirt: an early notice in the *Village Voice* made the connection, describing Smith as an 'androgynous Keith Richards look-alike'.[40] It was partly a physical resemblance – borne out in photographs of Smith from the early 1970s and seen in Sebring's documentary, *Patti Smith: Dream of Life* (2008) – but also a matter of attitude. Her 'eye for icons', biographer Dave Thompson wrote, 'was already trained upon those artists who were, for want of a less cliched expression, too fast to live'.[41] Beyond rock icons, they also included non-musical figures who for some cultural historians appear in the genealogy of 1960s rock.[42] These were writers such as Arthur Rimbaud and William Blake, predecessors whose republished works Smith would later write prefaces or introductions for.[43]

There were not too many female rock stars before Patti Smith. One might count Grace Slick of Jefferson Airplane, Janis Joplin and Nico. Other women artists who came out of the 1960s, such as Joni Mitchell, were unique but did not embody the idea of rock as something that was lived as much as it was performed. Smith couldn't be Peter Pan in the way that the male rock stars were – suspended on some timeless plane of adolescence – without giving up other things. And it is partly because she gave up her life performing and then returned to it decades later that *Dream of Life* is rather a different film than past portraits of rock performers had been. The template that had been established by films such as *Don't Look Back* was to pull back the curtain on an artist at a particular time and place, or at least limited by time and events.

This idea of getting behind or inside the mind of the artist could be achieved even with fairly limited access to the subject – as was the case with *Don't Look Back* – and later through the use of archival material and interviews with people who were connected to the subject at hand. In the digital era it also became easier to shoot more 'footage' because of the nature of the medium and the seemingly unlimited storage capacity for filmed material. For *Dream of Life*, Sebring filmed Smith over a twelve-year period beginning in 1995. It was at that point that she resumed her life as a writer and performer, following a sixteen-year break when she more or less vanished from public life to raise a family (although she did release one album in 1988, also titled *Dream of Life*, but there was no return to performance). This makes both Smith – as a figure in rock music – and the film quite unique, and symbolic of the nature of a rock culture that had come to be defined by ageing artists.

The reasons why this was the case were complex but had much to do with the fact that the media and music industry landscape of the post-1980s period stifled rock's ability to reinvent itself. The business was in using new digital media to raise back to life the music of the past now that new media had created space for it, and to attract new audiences that had not even been alive when much of the music was first released. While this helped to largely kill off rock as the self-generating cultural force it had become in the between the mid-1960s and early 1980s, it also, paradoxically, gave new life to artists from that era.

Dream of Life is a portrait not only of one of those artists whose work spanned both the old and the new eras, but of how time and age had become a primary subject of their work. An elegiac tone is set from the beginning when Smith's rhythmic, poetic voice – revealing her fidelity to the word as the source of innocence – plays over a series of impressionistic, fragmentary images. The effect can be hypnotic, indeed 'dreamlike', pulling through the depths of Smith's memory words that compress the past events of a life into a crystallized moment of birth. 'Life is an adventure of our own design, intersected by faith and a series of lucky and unlucky accidents,' she says: 'I was born in Chicago, mainline of America, in the centre of a blizzard, after World War Two. In 1967 I moved to New York City and met Robert Mapplethorpe. In 1969 we moved to the Chelsea Hotel.' Smith's iconic status is assumed in the film's form, which lacks any sense of narrative time, eschewing the kind of context that someone unfamiliar with Patti Smith could easily latch on to. The fact that it was filmed over such a long period of time is not at all evident. Yet it is about time and age. People from her past, such as actor-playwright Sam Shepard, appear without any

Patti Smith in her room full of souvenirs and mementoes in *Patti Smith: Dream of Life* (2008). The first of a new kind of rock/film collaboration, *Patti Smith* was filmed over twelve years, although the final result shows little evidence of the passage of time.

acknowledgement on screen or in voiceover. Shepard was another survivor of the bohemian New York of the late 1960s and early 1970s, and our sense from *Dream of Life* is that it is because so many who were close to Smith died in those sixteen years, when she was living a private life, that her work has become concerned with commemoration more than anything else. The Patti Smith seen in this film is a conduit for others who are no longer around, and for the other times and places where their spirits may be found.

In London she takes photographs at William Blake's gravestone, an aspect of her work found in the books of haunted Polaroids she publishes, whose subjects are often the empty rooms or abandoned objects of the departed. Old images of Smith living at the Chelsea Hotel reveal a person for whom meaning becomes attached to things from the past, now souvenirs and mementos – the opposite of the kind of things that populate the disposable present, one might say. When Sebring cuts from an old image showing a room in the Chelsea Hotel to the present day, it is to a scene that underlines a continuity with that past: in both rooms, for example, there is a photo of Bob Dylan. This sense is there in other photographs and mementos, too: she holds up a child's dress and tells us that in it she can see her whole childhood. Such belongings tell us about someone for whom life – unlike so many of her romantic and rock 'n' roll predecessors – is for the long haul.

If Smith did not quite make it in the Peter Pan stakes, she does nonetheless appear to look unchanged throughout the film, which, considering she was fifty years old when filming started and 62 when it ceased, suggests that the passage of time, as in a dream, is illusory or non-existent. In fact, the film seems to be an attempt to allow us to enter into *her* dream of life.

IN THE 2010S, rock film began to move into a space that can only be described as quasi-documentary. These films, beginning with *Dream of Life*, are not documentaries in the conventional sense but are really works of self-presentation. One of the most original of these is *20,000 Days on Earth*, a film about Nick Cave that is actually an artfully constructed portrait of a day in the life of the artist. As the title implies, it is the 20,000th day of his life – a number that would put him somewhere approaching 55 years old. The film, a collaboration between Cave and British film-makers Jane Pollard and Iain Forsyth, makes no attempt to conform to rock film expectations. It is not about his enduring or emerging from trials or battles with bandmates, but about the work of being Nick Cave and the method behind the art. Towards that end, the film-makers prepared for their role like literary biographers, ploughing through Cave's journals and looking for the evidence that confirmed their observation of Cave as someone ageing but not giving in to it.[44]

A dazzling title sequence opens the film: a bank of television monitors, arrayed like the kind of setup through which security personnel may be supposed to observe the daily lives of urban dwellers on CCTV cameras, fill up with images of a life. From birth to the present, the flickering monitors accelerate us through a succession of images that represent significant events or periods in Cave's life, all glimpsed fleetingly. A series of digits in the corner of the screen count upwards from zero, marking the passing days in the life of the artist and hurrying along to the present. Within seconds we are into the thousands of days, and soon we can recognize familiar images of Cave taking shape on the many screens. There he is with his band The Birthday Party, the group with which he first came to public attention (1978–83), as well as with Kylie Minogue (1996) and PJ Harvey (1990s) – collaborators

In homage to a scene from *The Man Who Fell to Earth*, Nick Cave examines himself in the mirror in *20,000 Days on Earth* (2014).

and muses. And then, as the counter on screen reaches 19,999 days, the title sequence ends, cutting to a black screen.

The 20,000th day begins with Cave waking up in a bed that occupies a clean and uncluttered room. The scene resembles a stage set, rather than anything that could be described as a real domestic setting. An alarm clock goes off by the bedside table, but our subject is already awake, alert. In the bathroom he examines himself in the mirror, a scene that takes after a similar one in *The Man Who Fell to Earth*, when David Bowie (as Newton) plucks out the contact lenses that conceal his alien eyes and thus his real identity. Cave's voice cuts across the scene to say, 'I awake, I write, I eat, I write, I watch TV. This is my twenty-thousandth day on earth.'

Time, and the effects of time on the past, on memory and on the art of rock 'n' roll as an art of the self, are the real subjects of this film, and Cave represents how age and the repetition of doing it again and again – going to his office and sitting in front of a typewriter – become the core of a disciplined identity. Ideas are sketched on notecards and then dated with a rubber stamp, the day, month and year now permanently inked and an index to what was occupying his mind at that precise moment in time.

As an exercise in self-examination, if not indirectly an exploration of how rock survives by the tricks and strategies it finds for playing itself in new ways, 20,000 *Days on Earth* also points to the porousness of time and experience, and the fact that at any given moment the past may come flooding into the present. We see Cave in conversation with a psychotherapist, talking about his father and some of the early life experiences that remain with him in memory. Then there is the ghostly appearance of figures from his past, who become conduits for things on his mind – the actor Ray Winstone, Blixa Bargeld from the Bad Seeds and Kylie Minogue – who turn up as passengers in his car and help him navigate his way into the thoughts that preoccupy him. Twenty thousand days amount to many years, and we find that Cave is naturally preoccupied with the passing of time. The slightly younger and still glamorous-looking Minogue represents his worries about ageing and being forgotten; Bargeld, the benefit of time and wisdom to self-discovery and creative endeavour; and Winstone, the problems that age presents for living a life that is essentially an exercise in role-playing. Winstone tells him it was difficult to 'reinvent' himself in the film business after he had reached the age of fifty. 'I can't reinvent myself. I don't want to, either,' Cave replies. Rock stars, he says, do indeed create themselves, but they must be 'godlike' and impervious to anything but their own vision, their own quest. 'You can't have them changing every second week because there's something new.'

In writing and performance, he embodies the very myth that he creates through music, lyric and image, along with everything else that becomes bound up in the phenomenon of rock stardom. The fact that life – or the accumulation of experience – ends up in one way or another sustaining the myth is clear when we see Cave going through documents and images from his past, assisted by the staff of what appears to be an archive facility, with screens and projectors, as if he is preparing for an exhibition of his life. It is simply a further means of self-examination in which they – like the therapist – help sift through the contents of his archives and material objects that will trigger his recollections. As we reach the end of the film, the camera becomes weightless and carries the viewer upwards into the night sky – departing from the earth as Cave's 20,000th day draws to an end – as he stands by the sea below in his home town of Brighton, its night lights reflected on the surface of the water. 'In the end, I'm not interested by that which I fully understand,' he says over these images. 'This shimmering place where imagination and reality intersect, this is where all love and tears and joy exist. This is the place. This is where we live.'

EPILOGUE:
LOOK BACK

The latest in Martin Scorsese's growing list of rock movies, *Rolling Thunder Revue: A Bob Dylan Story by Martin Scorsese* (2019), opens with a title sequence whose images are lifted straight from Georges Méliès' short silent film *The Vanishing Lady* (1896): a Victorian magician, played by Méliès himself, performs a disappearing trick, aided by a little cinematic knowhow, and the body of the lady disappears before our eyes. It is only after watching Scorsese's film and suspecting that things are not quite what they seem that we recall this seemingly incongruous title sequence, and we wonder what he has done with the subject of his film, Bob Dylan.

We suspect that, whatever it is, he did not act alone. Dylan's desire to remain elusive and to frustrate the various inquisitors that have dogged him throughout his career (and who cropped up repeatedly in Pennebaker's *Don't Look Back*) would precede and extend beyond the outright acceptance of his multifarious nature as seen in Todd Haynes's 2007 film *I'm Not There* (which might have been subtitled 'Whoever You Think I Am'), in which Dylan is played by half a dozen actors whose number include Cate Blanchett. Within that context, the trickery of *Rolling Thunder Revue*, which at first sight seemed to be little more than the resurrection of footage that was shot for Dylan's own vanished directorial debut in the movies, *Renaldo and Clara* (1978), should not come as a surprise.

In *Rolling Thunder Revue*, Scorsese and Dylan try to maintain the mystique by wrapping the older documentary evidence of a tour that took place in 1975 and '76 inside yet more Dylanesque slipperiness. The film's full title, in case anyone misses it, includes the words 'A Bob Dylan Story by Martin Scorsese' (which itself echoes *This Is Spinal Tap: A Rockumentary by Marty DiBergi*, a film inspired by Scorsese's own *The Last Waltz*).

Among the most amusing 'revelations' in the film are the secrets behind Dylan's sudden adoption of white face paint during the 1975–6 Rolling Thunder Revue tour from which the live footage is culled. Everywhere in the film too, we see him with his white face paint, a kind of theatricality that seemed to be totally alien to the Dylan of ten years earlier. We learn that Scarlet Rivera, the dazzling violinist who starred in Dylan's touring band at the time, introduced him to her boyfriend at the time, Gene Simmons, the fire-breathing, face-painted leader of 1970s rockers Kiss. As if the idea of Dylan taking his cue from Kiss is not suspicious enough (though who knows? The two men actually wrote a song together decades later), we then see the actress Sharon Stone reminiscing about meeting Dylan on the tour. An archive image of a young Stone flashes before our eyes, and there she is wearing a Kiss T-shirt. Dylan, she tells Scorsese, later told her that he wrote the song 'Just Like a Woman' (released some ten years earlier) for her. Up flashes another old photo of Dylan, this time signing an autograph for her before a concert. The average Dylan fan will, by this point, be very suspicious about this recreation of the Rolling Thunder Tour. But it doesn't end there. Take the scene with Dylan and Allen Ginsberg at the grave of Jack Kerouac (which appeared in *Renaldo and Clara*), reading to the departed writer. Could the choice of this scene, which was surely the inspiration for the one in *This Is Spinal Tap* where the ageing English

A scene from *The Rolling Thunder Revue: A Bob Dylan Story by Martin Scorsese* (2019), to give the film its full title, in which actress Sharon Stone (above) recalls meeting Bob Dylan during his Rolling Thunder Revue tour.

rockers turn up at Elvis Presley's gravesite and attempt to sing 'Heartbreak Hotel', have been a reciprocal nod to that 1980s classic of rock film? Rest assured, by now there will be websites and articles teeming with the details of the deception that Scorsese has perpetrated, but we might wonder if that, indeed, is partly the intention.

'I'm trying to get to the core of what this Rolling Thunder thing is all about, and I don't have a clue,' Dylan tells a voice behind the camera near the start of the film:

DYLAN: Because it's about nothing. It's just something that happened forty years ago. And that's the truth of it.
INTERVIEWER: Why don't we go down that road?

DYLAN: Okay. I don't remember a thing about Rolling
Thunder. I mean it happened so long ago I wasn't even
born, ya know. So whaddya wanna know?

Rolling Thunder Revue is, by any measure, a post-*Spinal Tap* rock
film; but then again, we realize that this kind of trickery and
deception has been part of who Bob Dylan has been from the
very beginning. In 1965, right in the middle of the time when
journalists at press conferences would expect Dylan to expound
on the meaning of life, one asked him if there was anything that
he would sell himself out for. 'Ladies' undergarments', came the
reply. How they laughed. Yet, look again: there he is in 2004,
actually physically appearing in an Italian TV commercial for the
lingerie emporium Victoria's Secret, the sound of the song 'Love
Sick' – from the critically acclaimed and commercially successful
album *Time Out of Mind* – ringing out as shaky images of Dylan
fade into images of scantily dressed models.

It stands to reason that only someone unfamiliar with Dylan
would expect *Rolling Thunder Revue* to be like those rock documentaries that exist as a means to repackage 'lost footage'. As
Dylan himself says at one point in the opening exchange, 'life
isn't about finding yourself, it's about creating yourself.'

And a thought occurs while watching this film: rock, at a certain point – sometime towards the end of the 1960s – acquires
(and maybe requires, for its own longevity) a kind of mystique;
it encourages its own mythology. But what role does film play
in this? Clearly, for those who had some idea about what they
were doing and what the medium could do for them, film could
only add to the development of the larger myth around rock 'n'
roll. Yet the camera often invaded the space of rock's self-styled
mystique and made it look ridiculous: the most obvious example

of this was Presley, who by the end of the 1960s had so lost sight of the person he was in 1956 that he was entrusting his persona to film directors like Norman Taurog, 'a Hollywood veteran best known for *Boys Town* with Spencer Tracy in 1938'.[1] Not only was Taurog 'old Hollywood' and unsympathetic to rock 'n' roll, he was half-blind. But, as Peter Biskind wrote, 'there was nothing anomalous about a blind director' back in the 1930s and '40s – they were just there to 'make sure the actors hit their marks while the camera was running'.[2]

And it is because Dylan and Scorsese (born in 1941 and '42, respectively) are contemporaries who shared a commitment to the idea that rock 'n' roll was not just about music but about a certain way of life, or how it could be represented on screen, that *The Rolling Thunder Revue* succeeds. It works as a film of our time, two decades into the twenty-first century – a time when we can be easily overwhelmed by the availability of images of the past through the exponential increase in media content, including a vast proliferation in the screen presence of popular music far exceeding the scope of a book like this – because it is an example of how to exist within that culture. As such, it also succeeds as a work that sustains rock's artistic longevity at a time when appearing on screen, even for the aspiring rock stars of the twenty-first century, has become so commonplace as to be unremarkable.

AFTERWORD:
FANS

Rock on screen today, and for much of the last two decades, has been increasingly about how it thrives in a culture that arises in and through the lives and obsessions of its fans. The idea of a world without The Beatles sets the scene for Danny Boyle's *Yesterday* (2019), an alternate history movie in which the most famous and successful popular music act of all time exists only in the memory one confused person, Jack Malik (Himesh Patel), an aspiring singer-songwriter.

After a flop appearance at a big music festival that might have sealed his arrival on the music scene, he is resigned to the fact that it is just not going to happen for him. 'This is the end of our long and winding road,' he says, quoting – as he always seems to do – the most suitable Beatles reference for the occasion. With him is Ellie (Lily James), a childhood friend who is now also his manager and biggest fan, who tries to ease the pain of the moment by saying that next time he will be playing to a bigger crowd. Jack and Ellie return to normal life until one evening when Jack is cycling home: everything around him is plunged into darkness and he collides with a bus.

As we watch Jack fly through the air in slow motion, the sound of The Beatles' 'A Day in Life' – the section of the record with the ingenious glissando that throws the dreaming and waking parts of the lyric into collision – is heard escaping from John Lennon's trippy visions into Paul McCartney's sober verse. Jack lands on the ground with a thud, and immediately the lights all around come back on – and, as we suddenly see Earth from outer space, all around the globe, too. After waking in hospital, he senses something is not quite right when Ellie doesn't groan or pull a face as he plays his old game of conversing with her through Beatles songs. Will she still be there to look after him when he's sixty-four?, he wonders. 'I don't know. I'll think about it . . . why sixty-four?'

Once released from hospital and back home, Jack discovers that all his Beatles albums have vanished, and even the Internet hive mind throws up no trace of them. (The Rolling Stones, however, still exist.) Not yet fully aware of what is going on, he tries to remember some of their songs – as if to prove to himself that he has not lost his mind – and begins writing titles of songs on post-it notes. He meets with Ellie and friends, where he is presented with a new guitar. Taking it out of the case, he sits down and plays 'Yesterday', to gasps and looks of disbelief. 'When did you write that?' 'Paul McCartney wrote it . . . you know, The Beatles?' They all look puzzled.

In a last-ditch attempt to catch Ellie out at what he suspects is a trick being played on him, Jack trudges in the pouring rain in the dark night to find out once and for all if she really, genuinely, has no idea who The Beatles are. 'Genuinely,' she says. 'Okay,' he replies, 'then I'm in a really, really, really complicated situation.' It is not so much that he realizes that he now has the sole responsibility for ensuring this music doesn't die – meaning he has to perform and record the songs of The Beatles – but that this is his ticket to the life he always wanted: a life of singing and performing. As the story plays on, Jack contrives to carve out a successful career travelling the world and singing the songs of the unknown Beatles. The cosmic bargain for this seeming gift,

In Danny Boyle's *Yesterday* (2019) striving singer-songwriter Jack Malik (Himesh Patel) realizes that he is the only person who has any knowledge or memory of The Beatles and sets about trying to remember and then steal their songs to achieve stardom.

we learn at the mushy end of the film, is that John Lennon is not dead but rather lives out his life quietly in a small seaside cottage where he does what he did before The Beatles existed: he paints.

In a world awash in the sounds of the past – of every era of music that was ever recorded – it seems an absurd idea that anything like The Beatles could just vanish. But *Yesterday*, in a curious way, is also a film very much about now, and not only the state of rock music in the twenty-first century but the ways that its screen life has gradually shifted to focus on the part the music plays in the lives of those to whom it means the most.

No form of popular culture can exist without an audience, but with few exceptions in the first two to three decades of rock's life on screen, the fans – although ever-present in one way or another – did not usually make it as subjects themselves. One of the films to be told from the point of view of the fans was another Beatles-related film, *I Wanna Hold Your Hand* (1978), a comedy about a group of friends trying to meet The Beatles in 1964 after they first arrived in America. Even in *A Hard Day's Night*, whose entire premise is that The Beatles spend all their lives fleeing from a chasing mob, the fans are really just part of the scenery, a backdrop against which we get to see how funny, in a Goonish-way, these Beatles really are.

In *Woodstock* and *Message to Love*, two films that are in large part about what happens when a vast, city-sized population suddenly appears out of nowhere in battlefield-like conditions to celebrate rock 'n' roll, the fans are also really just part of the scenery. Sure, they made the events possible, but they are more or less anonymous participants in the films that resulted from the events, people with no real discernible inner life. Their visual presence lends the kind of detail that helps to underline the scale and cultural significance of the events.

But other smaller and more obscure films were sometimes about the fans; films such as *Groupies* (1970) and *Permissive* (1970, also about groupies) reveal how the culture that was growing up around rock was taking form in the lifestyles of fans as much as the performers. If the performers had by the late 1960s made rock 'n' roll a way of life, it was equally so for some of their most passionate fans. Such films, though, often represented the point at which the glamour of the star trip can quickly fade into seediness.[1] Robert Frank's little-seen Rolling Stones behind-the-scenes tour film, *Cocksucker Blues* (1972), is often held up as the ultimate expression of rock decadence on film, although in truth the film has more to do with the boredom of touring and the routine nature of the fast living it depicts than it has to do with what its title – taken from an unreleased Stones track – might suggest.[2]

The transition of the fans seen in early 1960s rock films to the groupie figures of the 1970s marked a definite cultural shift. 'Tales of the groupies are often lurid,' noted a full-page advert for a *Rolling Stone* magazine special report from 1970, 'They are an index of emerging contemporary values in the United States.'[3] The so-called Plaster Casters, who made casts of the penises of their rock star favourites, would lug around a suitcase of the 'statuettes' that they made to impress potential conquests.[4] In return for playing model to the Plaster Casters, the musicians would receive T-shirts that read 'The Plaster Casters of Chicago'.[5] When we see the Plaster Casters in *Groupies* they clearly represent a more privileged set of VIP fans who had access to the stars. But they existed alongside other, more desperate-looking counterparts, female and male groupies who are seen hanging around backstage looking to be introduced to whatever travelling rock circus had arrived in town.

As an aspect of the increasing prominence given to fans in screen visions of rock, versions of the female groupie have appeared more recently within what are essentially nostalgic depictions of an era that seems lost to time – in *Almost Famous* (2000) and *The Banger Sisters* (2002), for instance. But in Tony Palmer's *Bird on a Wire* (1974), filmed on Leonard Cohen's 1972 European tour, the real thing is glimpsed in one particularly memorable scene when a German actress looking like an older version of the 'Penny Lane' character in *Almost Famous* turns up in the melancholic bard's dressing room to try to claim him for the night. 'Why don't you come home with me?' she says.[6] 'Will you? Please?' Palmer's camera has been a bit lost in the commotion of the crowded room until, out of nowhere, the woman appears in front of Cohen, who seems taken aback at how forthright she is. 'I really appreciate the offer,' he says with a smile and the best of manners, 'but it's hard to come on to a girl in front of a camera.'[7] Even the caricatures of Wayne and Garth in *Wayne's World* (1992), in their backstage reverence of Alice Cooper – *'we're not worthy'*, they declare in exaggerated adulation

– could be seen as another version of this groupie-like sacrifice to the rock gods.

Then there are the films that bring us closer to rather different obsessives whose engagement is on a more intellectual level, such as A. J. Weberman, the self-styled inventor of 'Dylanology'. *The Ballad of AJ Weberman* – which bears a title that has the ring of an early Bob Dylan song – is about the relationship that the eponymous fan struck up with his hero in the 1960s. Weberman achieved enough fame through his connection to Dylan that he appeared as a celebrity himself on various New York public access and cable TV shows (some of which are used in this film help to illustrate his story). Weberman was equal parts detective and conspiracy theorist, a boundless fanatic who saw in Dylan's growing withdrawal from the public in the late 1960s a lifelong challenge – one that fed his own indefatigable desire to reveal what he thought was the 'real' Dylan. Dylan was using drugs, he argues, suggesting it is the key to his entire oeuvre. Weberman rummaged through Dylan's trash, making off with bags full of the stuff that he and a group of Dylanology students would examine for clues. As the excitable Weberman tells us in this strange account of the outer limits of rock fandom, it provided key insights into what was going on in Dylan's mind. 'I get right down to the nitty-gritty of things,' he says, as if it is 1966 all over again. 'I get into Dylan's thoughts.' We can imagine that Dylan might have wanted – as we learn Weberman's wife had – to take out a restraining order to keep him away.

Along with one of his sidekicks, a singer named David Peel – once of David Peel & The Lower East Side, who recorded for Warner Bros. records and appeared in the film *Medicine Ball Caravan* (1972) – Weberman returns to the scene of the original crime, where he first stumbled upon the idea of rummaging through Dylan's bins, and they perform their homage to ... A. J. Weberman. *The Ballad of AJ Weberman* shows the fan at the centre of his own little world – Brooklyn, the East Village – through which a gaggle of eccentric supporters flit in and out like caricatures drawn for a Coen brothers movie. There's the friend with absurdly painted eyebrows who provides him with a place to stay rent-free, and others like Aaron 'The Pieman' Kay – Weberman's sometime co-conspirator in tormenting celebrities – who recounts throwing pies in the faces of famous people, alongside various other wacky characters who insist that A. J. is simply a misunderstood genius. 'I thought I was Verlaine to his Rimbaud,' says Weberman, no closer to reality than he was all those years before.

A fan seemingly more in tune with reality than Dylan's one-time tormentor is Rob, the record store owner and lead character in Stephen Frears's movie *High Fidelity*. Records are his life, and in more ways than the obvious one of putting food on the table, something revealed in his reaction to yet another failed romance. As Rob sits on the floor of his apartment, the camera draws back and we see that the floor has almost entirely vanished under piles of LPs, rising to varying heights like towers. A model city of music. He is engaged in some serious thinking about his life when one of his employees, named Dick, turns up at the door. 'I guess it looks as if you're reorganizing your records,' Dick says, taking a look around and realizing that he is probably intruding on some kind of emotional breakdown. Rob motions for him to stay:

DICK: Whats this, though ... chronological?
ROB: No.
DICK: Alphabetical?
ROB: Nope ...

DICK: What?

ROB: *Autobiographical.*

DICK: No fucking way.

ROB: Yeah . . . I can tell you how I got from Deep Purple to Howlin' Wolf in just twenty-five moves. And if I wanna find the song 'Landslide' by Fleetwood Mac, I have to remember that I bought it for someone in the fall of 1983 pile but didn't give it to them for personal reasons.

DICK: That sounds . . .

ROB: Comforting?

DICK: Yes.

Then there's the fan whose unwillingness to put rock 'n' roll aside for more adult pursuits leads him to confront an upside-down reality. When *Blackboard Jungle* first played in cinemas in 1955, audiences left behind them a trail of destruction, with newspaper headlines decrying the end of all civilized values. The idea that rock was a rebellious force that expanded out from the music into a way of being is, in part, the premise of Richard Linklater's *School of Rock* (2003), in which the roles established in *Blackboard Jungle* are hilariously reversed.

Where the new teacher in *Blackboard Jungle*, Mr Dadier, was mocked and had his masculinity challenged as soon as he walked through the school gates on his first day by students who looked like street toughs, here, when the new teacher, Dewey Finn (played by Jack Black), going by the name of Mr Schneebly, walks into the school it is to be greeted by students who are demanding disciplined instruction. But unlike Mr Dadier, this teacher has not come from another school. He has come from a rock 'n' roll band. Dewey, we discover, is an aspirant but failing guitar hero with a penchant for hopeless gestures.

As the film begins, we see Dewey as himself, diving from the stage of a small club where his band are playing at the climax of the last number – an exuberant gesture anticipating the acclaim of the audience – but he miscalculates badly. Instead of catching him, the crowd part and look on as he falls flat on his face. Dewey drinks it off, but the band fire him. Out of desperation, he impersonates his nerdy roommate Ned Schneebly, a substitute teacher, in order to take advantage of an opportune gig teaching at a private school for children of the well-to-do, where the disciplinarian principal Ms Mullins (Joan Cusack) seems unable to talk to the children without it all ending in tears. Dewey soon finds himself standing in front of a classroom full of obedient children who expect him to teach them something useful. After he tries and fails to write his name on the board – he can't spell 'Schneebly' – he says, 'you know what? Just call me Mr. S.'

When he looks around the classroom, he can see that the children have questions on the tip of their tongues for the new teacher. At the front of the class, one of them, Summer (Miranda Cosgrove), is wearing an expression that says: I want to speak. '*Tinkerbelllll . . .?*' Dewey says mockingly. 'Summer,' she replies sharply, correcting him, 'Thank you, Mr S. As class factotum, would you like to know what our class schedule is?' Sinking into his chair, he tells his class to sit still and keep quiet because he has a hangover. 'Does that mean you are drunk?' one of them asks. 'Noooo . . . it means I was drunk yesterday. Now be quiet and have recess.'

But this does not sit well with the kids. Summer has an instinct for order and tries to bring Mr Schneebly back to the normal class schedule. Forget about it, Dewey tells her, it is going to be recess *all the time*. He still doesn't realize that he is, in a manner of speaking, younger than them. Looking around for

Mr Schneebly, also known as Dewey Finn (Jack Black), teaches the kids how to stick it to the man in *School of Rock* (2003).

wayward spirts, he spots a kid at the back with untidy hair, whose name, he quickly discovers, is Freddy. 'What do you like to do, Freddy?' 'I dunno, burn stuff?' he replies. 'Just go out and have recess,' Schneebly says, after looking like he was giving it consideration. 'My parents don't spend $15,000 a year for recess,' Summer pipes up, 'How do we get gold stars if we just have recess?'

Dewey can't make sense of what is going on. Forget about all that learning crap, gold stars, merits and demerits, he tells them, because it's all a waste of time, and he is the living proof of it: they'll always be tripped up by *The Man* – by every person who has ever told them they can't do as exactly as they want. Sensing that they don't have any idea what he is talking about, he adds, 'Oh, you don't know The Man? He's everywhere. In the White House, down the hall. Ms Mullins? – *she's The Man!*' Almost losing control of himself, Dewey exclaims, with the passion of the demented believer, the fan who becomes what he worships, 'there used to be a way to *stick it* to The Man, and IT WAS CALLED ROCK 'N' ROLL.'

Mr S. reaches an accommodation with these seekers of gold stars and merits. Soon he is standing in front of a carefully etched genealogy of rock 'n' roll history, something that as a lifelong fan he has learned well enough to school the kids in the basics of the art, all the while preparing them to enter a local Battle of the Bands contest as his backing band, through which he will once again exact his revenge on The Man.

IF ROCK CULTURE spawned fans who became groupies in the 1960s and '70s, it was equally true that it gave us the rock journalist. In Pennebaker's *Don't Look Back*, the newspaper hacks famously do not have much affinity with the subjects they are charged with writing about. A photographer taking photos of Joan Baez, who was travelling with Bob Dylan on his tour, takes out a notepad and asks her name. When she says her name and he does not know how to spell it, she has to repeat it and eventually say, 'Joan Baez . . . B-A-E-Z.' 'Strewth!' the photographer says, 'I didn't recognize you, I'm so sorry. I've been looking for you all day.'

Those kind of journalists – not remotely fans of the music – were supplanted in the 1970s by a very different kind of figure, the rock critic. In *Almost Famous* (2000, dir. Cameron Crowe), set sometime in the mid-1970s, we get a glimpse of how much had changed in rock culture since the world of *Don't Look Back*. It tells the story of a guileless young music writer, William Miller (Patrick Fugit), a thinly veiled stand-in for Crowe himself, who is as eager to meet his hero Lester Bangs (Philip Seymour Hoffman) – the gonzo rock critic of rock magazines *Rolling Stone* and *Creem* – as he is to meet the people that Bangs writes about. The role of the rock critic, Bangs tells him, is to hold the phoney rock stars up to the light and show them for the frauds they are. By the time William meets him, Bangs – still commissioning articles for *Creem* – has lost whatever enthusiasm he once had for the rock scene. 'So, you're the kid who's been sending me those articles,' he says to William:

> BANGS: Your writing is damn good. It's just a shame that you missed out on rock 'n' roll.
> WILLIAM: I did?!
> BANGS: Oh, yeah, it's over.
> WILLIAM: Over?
> BANGS: Over. You got here just in time for the death rattle, the last gasp, the last grope.
> WILLIAM: Well, at least I'm here for that.[8]

Beneath the cynical exterior, Bangs senses a kindred spirit in William's unwillingness to let this news dent his enthusiasm. He decides that the best thing he can do is give him some advice. As the young writer takes out his notebook and pen, Bangs looks at him. 'You *cannot* make friends with the rock stars.' William nods, waiting for more, as Bangs begins to go through some of the apparent fringe benefits that make up for the pitiful rewards of the life of the rock critic. 'They'll buy you drinks. You'll meet girls . . . they'll try to fly you places for free . . . offer you drugs.' William smiles at the thought of it all. 'I know. It sounds great,' Lester admits,

> But they are not your friends. These are people who want you to write sanctimonious stories about the *genius* of

the rock stars, and they will *ruin* rock 'n' roll and strangle
everything we love about it . . . Ninety-nine per cent
of what passes for rock 'n' roll now – silence is more
compelling.

Having got that off his chest, he calms down and takes pity on
his young fan. 'I can pay you thirty-five bucks. Gimme a thousand
words on Black Sabbath.'

In Todd Haynes's *Velvet Goldmine* (1998), the rock-fan-as-
journalist takes a different direction insofar as the newspaper
reporter, Arthur Stuart (played by Christian Bale) finds himself
plunged back into his own adolescent obsession with the intertwined lives of rock stars Brian Slade and Curt Wild. Just as Bowie
killed off Ziggy Stardust at the final concert of his 1973 London
tour – singing Jacques Brel's 'My Death' before he departed – so
too, in *Velvet Goldmine*, does Brian Slade. In fact, Slade fakes his
own death as a way of slipping free of the character that he – like
his real counterpart – had been playing as he rode a wave of
success, here named Maxwell Demon. The story of Slade and
Wild's career peak of the 1970s is mediated through Arthur's
attempt to use the journalistic skills he has acquired in the inter-
vening ten years or so to track down Slade, whom he eventually
finds alive performing under another name.

There was something of a real-life counterpart to that detective story in *Searching for Sugar Man* (2012), an engrossing tale
of a near unknown performer, Sixto Rodriguez, who recorded
in the late 1960s and early '70s and had attained some measure
of success in South Africa and Australia but remained almost
unknown in his native America. *Searching for Sugar Man* tells
the story of the desire of two South African fans to find out what
happened to this forgotten figure, whom they believe to be dead,

only to find him alive and well and living in Detroit. In fact, from the late 1990s to the present, there have been so many films that might be described, either wholly or in part, as rock 'detective' movies that it could make up a subgenre of the form.

From the aforementioned *Velvet Goldmine* and *Searching for Sugar Man* to Stephen Woolley's *Stoned* (2005), which is a dramatic retelling of the events surrounding the death of Brian Jones of The Rolling Stones, one might add David Mamet's *Phil Spector* (2003) and Vikram Jayanti's *The Agony and Ecstasy of Phil Spector* (2013) – one a dramatization and the other a documentary – about Spector's trial and conviction for murder in 2009. Then there is Nick Broomfield's documentary *Kurt and Courtney* (1998) and Gus Van Sant's drama *Last Days* (2005), two films about the death of Kurt Cobain. Another film pair worth a mention in this respect is Aaron Aites and Audrey Ewell's documentary *Until the Light Takes Us* (2008) and Jonas Åkerlund's film *Lords of Chaos*

In *Searching for Sugar Man* (2012) – one of many recent rock films that could be described as a 'detective story' – some fans go in search of the mysterious Sixto Rodriguez, a singer-songwriter who seemed to have vanished from the face of the earth after making albums in 1970 and 1971 that made him 'more popular than the Rolling Stones' in South Africa, but almost unknown everywhere else.

(2018), concerned with the deadly effects of the Norwegian black metal movement in the 1990s, tales of deaths and arson attacks that had their origins in the rise of a musical culture unlike anything seen anywhere else. Of the two, *Until the Light Takes Us* is the more compelling, telling the story of the events through the testimonies of two of its main witnesses, the incarcerated Varg Vikernes of Burzum (serving time for murder and arson) and Fenriz of Darkthrone.

Equally, there are the explorations of places haunted by the ghosts of rock 'n' roll past: Stephan Kijak's documentary *Stones in Exile* (2010), about the places that created just the right kind of ambience for The Rolling Stones to produce one of their most revered albums, *Exile on Main Street* (1972), and Davis Guggenheim's *From the Sky Down* (2011), which follows U2 as they return to the Berlin studio where they made one of their landmark albums, *Achtung Baby* (1991). The multi-part series about the Grateful Dead, *A Long Strange Trip* (dir. Amir Bar-Lev, 2017), contains many moments of this kind, including one particularly affecting scene where singer-guitarist Bob Weir returns to the site of a Grateful Dead outdoor show – a field that now stands empty and overgrown with wild grass. Now, there is nothing there but what is in his head, the ghosts of that past, his dead bandmate Jerry Garcia, and the sense of rock's elegiac endings being as numerous as its rebirths. Garcia lived only for the moment and had no real interest in posterity, Weir says, but now, standing here, he has to disagree. 'I don't think that what we see as time can put an end to what we had. I think it was, is, and will be there. Those moments were more alive than anything that a heart pumps out, that's what we were living for . . . that's eternity.'

Far less sombre is the low-budget documentary *Rock n Roll London* (2006), in which Art Wood (brother of the more famous

Rolling Stone Ronnie Wood) takes viewers on an amusing and informative journey through the places that would become key to the emergence of the likes of The Rolling Stones, The Who and others in the early 1960 London rock and blues scene. But more than that, it is also a trip to the haunts that shaped his own experience as an unwitting survivor of it all as leader of the once popular Artwoods. Tales of mods smashing up bars and encounters in dressing rooms with music legends like Howlin' Wolf are punctuated with asides to the camera telling us that this was stuff all that happened 'hundreds of years ago' or even 'about a million years ago', revealing Wood's astonishment that both he and the places – historical relics and hidden spaces – are still standing and that someone is still interested enough to be pointing a camera at him and asking that he reveal his secrets for posterity.

An essential truth about the unlikely longevity of rock is revealed when he sits down in the pub where The Kinks cut their teeth, The Clissold Arms near Muswell Hill in north London, with their former drummer, Mick Avory. 'My plan', Avory tells Wood, 'was to do it for a couple of years, make a pile of money, and buy a castle.' As if this was a reasonable dream, Wood responds, '*I know!* No one knew it was gonna go on this long . . . I sold all my stuff. It would be worth a fortune now.'

Is it so far-fetched that Mick Jagger and Keith Richards would end up down on their luck and running a chandlery store called Some Like It Yacht ('for all your chandlery needs'), as imagined in the BBC TV comedy *Stella Street* and portrayed by fans Phil Cornwell and John Sessions? Or, indeed, that another fan, J. D. Ryznar, could concoct an online video series called *Yacht Rock* that plays on the fact that an interchangeable roster of musicians and producers were the people behind the smooth 1970s rock sounds of Steely Dan, Toto and The Doobie Brothers, whose records sometimes featured 'guys on boats on the cover' (or sang, like Christopher Cross, about sailing) and were ripe for comic treatment as characters in personal situations?[9]

What such films confirm is that rock music as a cultural form endures not just through its artistic reinventions, and the often mythical lives of its stars and the times and places that made them – and bring them to our screens – but in virtue of the ways the music, as culture, finds a place for itself in what was always the supplementary medium of the screen, which it first used as a means of extending its life when Elvis Presley moved into the movies in 1956. But as screen media becomes ever more expanded in our digital world, so too the life of rock on screen finds new themes and new stories to fill up the seemingly limitless space.

REFERENCES

1 EXPLODING TOMORROW

1 Charlie Gillett, *The Sound of the City: The Rise of Rock and Roll*, 2nd edn (Boston, MA, 1996), p. 31.
2 Ed Ward, Geoffrey Stokes and Ken Tucker, *Rock of Ages: The Rolling Stone History of Rock and Roll* (Harmondsworth, 1987), p. 111.
3 David Halberstam, *The Fifties* (New York, 1993), p. 477.
4 Ibid., p. xii.
5 Ibid., pp. 185, 195.
6 Jake Austen, *TV-a-Go-Go: Rock on TV from 'American Bandstand' to 'American Idol'* (Chicago, IL, 2005), p. 16.
7 'Rocksploitation' is the term used by David Ehrenstein and Bill Reed in their book *Rock on Film* (London, 1982).
8 Ted Ownby, 'Foreword', in Joel Williamson, *Elvis Presley: A Southern Life* (Oxford and New York, 2015), p. 10.
9 Stanley Booth, *Rhythm Oil: A Journey through the Music of the American South* (Boston, MA, 2000), p. 50.
10 Robert Gordon, *It Came from Memphis: The Unturned Roots of Rock and Roll* (London, 1995), p. 46.
11 Hugh Barker and Yuval Taylor, *Faking It: The Quest for Authenticity in Popular Music* (New York, 2007), p. 140.
12 Booth, *Rhythm Oil*, p. 49.
13 Louis Cantor, *Dewey and Elvis: The Life and Times of a Rock 'n' Roll Deejay* (Urbana and Chicago, IL, 2005), p. 143. Although see Larry Birnbaum, *Before Elvis: The Prehistory of Rock 'n' Roll* (Lanham, MD, 2013), p. 6, who is sceptical of it having been Elvis's choice, given his initial preference for syrupy ballads, and argues that he probably recorded it on Sam Phillips's suggestion.
14 Ibid., p. 7.
15 Max Norris, 'Waiting, Waiting for Their Elvis', *Daytona Beach Morning Journal*, 9 August 1956, quoted in 'Aug. 9, 1956: Reporters

Look Down Noses Covering Elvis in Daytona Beach',
www.floridahistorynetwork.com, accessed 16 October 2019.

16 Ibid.

17 William McPhillips, 'Elvis Hits Town and Teen-Agers Turn Out',
San Francisco Chronicle, 4 June 1956, p. 20.

18 Peter J. Levinson, *Tommy Dorsey: Livin' in a Great Big Way* (Boston,
MA, 2005), p. 288.

19 Ibid., p. 290.

20 Ibid., p. 288.

21 Halberstam, *The Fifties*, p. 475.

22 Richard F. Shepard, 'Presley Signed by Ed Sullivan', *New York Times*,
14 July 1956, p. 33.

23 Ibid.

24 Richard Meltzer, 'Elvis Exhumed!' (excerpt), in *A Whore Just Like
the Rest: The Music Writings of Richard Meltzer* (Boston, MA, 2000),
pp. 248–9.

25 In the documentary *Hollywood Rocks and Rolls in the 50s*, dir. Kent
Hagen (Multicom Entertainment Group, 1999).

26 James L. Neibaur, *The Elvis Movies* (London, 2014), p. 30.

27 David E. James, 'Rock 'n' Film: Generic Permutations in Three
Feature Films from 1964', *Grey Room*, 49 (Fall 2012), p. 9.

28 Gillett, *Sound of the City*, p. 43.

29 Michael Sragow, 'Introduction', in Ehrenstein and Reed,
Rock on Film, p. 10

30 Gillett, *Sound of the City*, p. 206.

31 Milton Bracker, 'Experts Propose Study of Craze', *New York Times*,
23 February 1957, p. 12.

32 'Rock 'n' Roll Exported to 4 Corners of Globe', *New York Times*,
23 February 1957, p. 12.

33 Bosley Crowther, 'Frenzy 'n' Furor Featured at the Paramount',
New York Times, 23 February 1957, p. 13.

34 Paul Ackerman, 'Square Circles Peg Rock and Roll Idiom
as a Beat to Stick', *Billboard*, 4 February 1956, p. 1.

35 Ibid.

36 Alexander R. Hammer, 'Fad Also Rocks Cash Registers',
New York Times, 23 February 1957, p. 12.

37 Ibid.

38 Bill Simon, 'Term R&B Hardly Covers Multi-Material So Grouped',
Billboard, 4 February 1956, p. 55.

39 Nick Tosches, *Country: The Twisted Roots of Rock 'n' Roll*
(Boston, MA, 1985), p. 81.

40 Ibid., p. 73.

41 Ibid.

42 Nick Tosches, *Hellfire: The Jerry Lee Lewis Story* (London, 1989), pp. 145–6. On the matter of this event see also the account in Bruce Pegg, *Brown Eyed Handsome Man: The Life and Hard Times of Chuck Berry* (New York and London, 2002), pp. 89–90.

43 Rick Bragg, *Jerry Lee Lewis: His Own Story* (Edinburgh, 2015), p. 265.

44 Ibid.

45 Gary Lachman, 'The Crowned and Conquering Child', in *Kenneth Anger: Magick Lantern Cycle*, DVD booklet (British Film Institute, London, 2009), p. 8.

46 Elenore Lester, 'From Underground: Kenneth Anger Rising', *New York Times*, 19 February 1967, p. 103.

47 On what changed, see Peter L. Kauff, 'Filmrock', *Billboard*, 14 November 1970, p. R-20.

48 James, 'Rock 'n' Film', p. 8.

49 Lester, 'From Underground', p. 103.

50 Ibid.

51 Lachman, 'Crowned and Conquering Child', p. 14.

52 Page later released it as *Lucifer Rising and Other Sound Tracks* (LP, self-released, 2012).

2 UNTAMED YOUTH

1 Michael L. Jones, *The Music Industries: From Conception to Consumption* (Basingstoke, 2012), p. 82.

2 Quoted in Harvey Kubernik, *Hollywood Shack Job: Rock Music in Film and On Your Screen* (Albuquerque, NM, 2006), p. 43.

3 Peter M. Nichols, 'A Chance to Relive The Beatles' First Visit to the United States', *New York Times*, 17 October 1991, p. C22.

4 Mark Ribowsky, *He's A Rebel: Phil Spector, Rock and Roll's Legendary Producer*, updated edn (Cambridge, MA, 2006), pp. 157–9.

5 Ibid., p. 159.

6 Ibid., p. 161.

7 Mick Brown, *Tearing Down the Wall of Sound: The Rise and Fall of Phil Spector* (London, 2007), p. 163.

8 Ibid.

9 This was one argument against rock films in general made by the rock critic Dave Marsh. See his article 'Schlock Around the Clock' in *Film Comment*, XIV/4 (July–August 1978), p. 9.

10 See Jesse Schlotterbeck, 'A Hard Day's Night as a Musical Biopic of the Post-Studio Era', *Quarterly Review of Film and Video*, xxxiii/6 (2016), pp. 567–79.

11 Penelope Gilliatt, 'Beatles in Their Own Right', *The Observer*, 12 July 1964, p. 25.

12 'Official Beatle Mania', *The Guardian*, 11 July 1964, p. 1.

13 'Beatles – Teenagers' Witch Doctors', *The Guardian*, 21 May 1964, p. 11A.

14 Cyril Dunn and Peter Dunn, 'The Roots of Beatlemania', *The Observer*, 10 November 1963, p. 29.

15 Robert Zemeckis (dir.), *I Wanna Hold Your Hand* (Universal Pictures, 1978), at 1 hr 16 mins.

16 Mark Blake, *Pretend You're in a War: The Who and the Sixties* (London, 2014), p. 149.

17 Pete Townshend, 'For the Love of Mod', *The Times* (Arts and Music), 18 March 2011, p. 6.

18 Blake, *Pretend You're in a War*, p. 156.

19 Pete Townshend, *Who I Am* (London, 2012), p. 74.

20 Barry Miles, 'Miles Interviews Pete Townshend', *International Times*, 13–26 February 1967, p. 5.

21 Ibid.

22 Gustav Metzger, 'Auto-Destructive Art: Demonstration by G. Metzger', South Bank, London, 3 July 1961. Texts from a flyer.

23 Tony Palmer, 'Fireworks with Fury', *The Observer*, 15 October 1967, p. 24.

24 Ibid.

25 Jagger's and Richards's recollections on this are voiced in Brett Morgen (dir.), *The Rolling Stones: Crossfire Hurricane* (Tremolo Productions, 2012), at approx. 13 mins 40 secs.

26 The incident was blown out of all proportion, according to the account given in Bill Wyman, *Stone Alone: The Story of a Rock 'n' Roll Band* (Cambridge, MA, 1997), p. 303.

27 Brett Morgen (dir.), *The Rolling Stones: Crossfire Hurricane* (Milkwood Films/Tremolo Productions, 2012), at approx. 19 mins.

28 Anthony Burgess, *You've Had Your Time: Being the Second Part of the Confessions of Anthony Burgess* (New York, 1990), p. 26.

29 Ibid.

30 Dave Wallis, *Only Lovers Left Alive* [1964] (Richmond, MA, 2015).

31 Andrew Loog Oldham, *2Stoned* (London, 2003), p. 155.

32 David Kalat, *The Strange Case of Dr Mabuse: A Study of the Twelve Films and Five Novels* (Jefferson, NC, and London, 2005), p. 276.

33 Oldham, 2Stoned, p. 156.
34 See the account given in James Riley, *The Bad Trip: Dark Omens, New Worlds and the End of the Sixties* (London, 2019), pp. 37–44.
35 Jack Sargent, *Naked Lens: An Illustrated History of Beat Cinema* (London, 2001), p. 137.
36 Oldham, 2Stoned, p. 279.
37 Ibid., p. 278.
38 Steve Appleford, 'Andrew Loog Oldham on Rolling Stones Film *Charlie Is My Darling*', *Los Angeles Times*, 20 November 2012, www.latimes.com.
39 Nigel Finch (dir.), *25×5: The Continuing Adventures of the Rolling Stones* (BBC *Arena* special, 1989).
40 Christopher Sandford, *The Rolling Stones: Fifty Years* (London, 2012), p. 179.
41 Sargent, *Naked Lens*, p. 138.
42 Kubernik, *Hollywood Shack Job*, p. 49.

3 ALTERED STATES

1 Peter Biskind, *Easy Riders, Raging Bulls: How the Sex 'n' Drugs 'n' Rock 'n' Roll Generation Saved Hollywood* (London, 1998).
2 James Monaco, *American Film Now: The People, the Power, the Money, the Movies* (New York, 1984), p. 254.
3 Ibid., p. 261.
4 Keith Beattie, *Documentary Screens: Nonfiction Film and Television* (Basingstoke, 2004), p. 86.
5 Ibid.
6 Jamie Diamond, 'Albert Maysles' Camera Sees and Says it All', *New York Times*, 13 February 1994, p. H11.
7 Charles Warren, 'Cinema Direct and Indirect: American Documentary, 1960–1975', in *American Film History: Selected Readings, 1960 to the Present*, ed. Cynthia Lucia, Roy Grundmann and Art Simon (Malden, MA, 2016), p. 57.
8 William Grimes, 'Richard Leacock, Pioneer of Cinéma Verité, Dies at 89', *New York Times*, 26 March 2011, p. A21.
9 D. A. Pennebaker interviewed in Harvey Kubernik, *Hollywood Shack Job: Rock Music in Film and On Your Screen* (Albuquerque, NM, 2006), p. 10.
10 Clinton Heylin, *From the Velvets to the Voidoids* (London, 1993), p. 15.
11 Vincent Canby, 'Chelsea Girls in Midtown Test', *New York Times*, 1 December 1966, p. 56.

12 Elenore Lester, 'So He Stopped Painting Brillo Boxes and Bought a Movie Camera', *New York Times*, 11 December 1966, p. 169.

13 Ibid.

14 Andy Warhol and Pat Hackett, POP*ism: The Warhol Sixties* (New York, 1980), p. 183.

15 Ibid.

16 Ibid., p. 181.

17 Richard Witts, *Nico: Life and Lies of an Icon* (London, 1993), p. 90.

18 Gene Youngblood, *Expanded Cinema*, 50th anniversary edn (New York, 2020), p. 103.

19 Ibid.

20 Grace Glueck, 'Syndromes Pop at Delmonico's: Andy Warhol and His Gang Meet the Psychiatrist', *New York Times*, 14 January 1966, p. 36.

21 Victor Bockris and Gerard Malanga, *Up-Tight: The Velvet Underground Story* (London, 1983), p. 7.

22 Ibid.

23 Simon Rycroft, *Swinging City: A Cultural Geography of London, 1950–1974* (Abingdon, 2016), p. 66.

24 Ibid.

25 Mark Harris, *Pictures at a Revolution: Five Movies and the Birth of the New Hollywood* (New York, 2008), p. 88.

26 Ibid.

27 Rycroft, *Swinging City*, p. 68.

28 Penelope Gilliatt, 'London Life – A Foreign View', *The Observer*, 19 March 1967, p. 24.

29 Edward Lucie-Smith, 'Pop Culture and the World of Fashion', *The Times*, 15 February 1966, p. 13.

30 John Anthony Moretta, *The Hippies: A 1960s History* (Jefferson, NC, 2017), p. 118.

31 Ibid.

32 Herbert Gold, 'Where the Action Is', *New York Times*, 19 February 1967, p. 50.

33 Blair Jackson, *Garcia: An American Life* (New York and London, 1999), p. 131.

34 Scott MacFarlane, *The Hippie Narrative: A Literary Perspective on the Counterculture* (Jefferson, NC, and London, 2007), p. 146.

35 The report is excerpted in the documentary series *Long Strange Trip: The Untold Story of the Grateful Dead*, dir. Amir Bar-Lev (Double E Pictures and AOMA Sunshine Films, 2017), ep. 1, at approx. 36 mins.

36 Gold, 'Where the Action Is', p. 1.

37 Bockris and Malanga, *Up-Tight*, p. 48.

38 Quoted in James Henke and Parke Puterbaugh, *I Want to Take You Higher: The Psychedelic Era, 1965–1969* (San Francisco, CA, 1997), p. 25.

39 Tom Wolfe, *The Electric Kool-Aid Acid Test* (London, 1989), p. 218.

40 Lawrence Schiller, 'A Remarkable Drug Suddenly Spells Danger', *Life*, 25 March 1966, p. 29.

41 Ibid.

42 Ray Manzarek, *Light My Fire: My Life with The Doors* (London, 1999), p. 93. Between graduating from the UCLA film school and starting The Doors, Jim Morrison lived at Jakob's Venice Beach house.

43 Joel Selvin, *Summer of Love: The Inside Story of LSD, Rock and Roll, Free Love and High Times in the Wild West* (New York, 1994), p. 119.

44 Kurt von Meier, 'Love, Mysticism, and the Hippies', *Vogue*, 15 November 1967, p. 160.

45 Barney Hoskyns, *Waiting for the Sun: The Story of the Los Angeles Music Scene* (London, 1996), p. 143.

46 Ibid., p. 140.

47 See *The Complete Monterey Pop Festival* (The Criterion Collection, 2017), 3-disc DVD/Blu-ray box set, which includes the original movie, a disc of outtakes and also separate, longer performances of The Jimi Hendrix Experience and Otis Redding.

48 D. A. Pennebaker, *Monterey Pop* DVD commentary, quoted in Glenn Abel, 'Monterey Pop', *Hollywood Reporter*, 25 November 2002, p. 12.

49 Hoskyns, *Waiting for the Sun*, p. 143.

50 See 'Interview with Eric Burdon', in *Hendrix on Hendrix: Interviews and Encounters with Jimi Hendrix*, ed. Steve Roby (Chicago, IL, 2012), p. 330.

51 Renata Adler, 'Monterey Pop Views the Rock Scene', *New York Times*, 27 December 1968, p. 44.

52 Ibid.

53 Jerry Hopkins, *The Jimi Hendrix Experience* (New York, 1983), p. 130.

4 MAKING MOVIES

1 Scott Cohen, 'Iggy: A Brief History of Iggy's Pop's Formative Years', *Spin* (August 1980), p. 63.

2 Alfred G. Aronowitz, 'The Doors Seek Nirvana Vote Here', *New York Times*, 25 November 1967, p. 44.

3 The 'Unknown Soldier' film clip was shot by Mark Abramson. See Stephen Davis, *Jim Morrison: Life, Death, Legend* (London, 2004), p. 230.

4 Steven Travers, *Coppola's Monster Film: The Making of 'Apocalypse Now'* (Jefferson, NC, 2016), p. 121.

5 Ibid., p. 150.

6 Michael Herr, 'Khesanh', *Esquire*, 1 September 1969, and 'Conclusion at Khesanh', *Esquire*, 1 October 1969.

7 Ibid.

8 Alfio Leotta, *The Cinema of John Milius* (Lanham, MD, 2019), p. 48.

9 This is the 1975 version of the *Apocalypse Now* script. It is archived in the Margaret Herrick Library of the Academy of Motion Picture Arts and Sciences, Los Angeles, sourced for use here at https://indiegroundfilms.files.wordpress.com, accessed 20 May 2021. Another source that cites this version of the screenplay, and this same scene (but does not repeat the lines exactly as I have here) is Todd Decker, *Hymns for the Fallen: Combat Movie Music and Sound after Vietnam* (Oakland, CA, 2017), p. 93.

10 James Riordan and Jerry Prochnicky, *Break On Through: The Life and Death of Jim Morrison* (London, 1991), p. 501.

11 Bill Wyman, *Stone Alone: The Story of a Rock 'n' Roll Band* (Cambridge, MA, 1997), p. 490.

12 Ibid., p. 501.

13 Philip Norman, *Mick Jagger* (London, 2012), p. 292.

14 'Sympathy for the Devil', *International Times*, 14–29 January 1970, p. 5.

15 Norman, *Mick Jagger*, p. 292.

16 Ibid.

17 See Alexander Howarth, 'A Walking Contradiction (Partly Truth and Partly Fiction)', in *The Last Great American Picture Show*, ed. Thomas Elsaesser, Alexander Howarth and Noel King (Amsterdam, 2004), pp. 84–5.

18 In 'The Zapruder Footage', *The Late Show*, BBC Two, England, 22 November 1993. Also re-broadcast under the title 'Kennedy Zapruder'.

19 James Monaco, *American Film Now: The People, The Power, The Money, The Movies* (New York, 1984), p. 153.

20 Vincent LoBrutto, *Martin Scorsese: A Biography* (Westport, CT, 2008), p. 112.

21 As recounted in Andy Greene, 'Sex, Drugs and Scorsese: The Making of the Woodstock Documentary', *Rolling Stone*, 11 June 2009, p. 22.

22 Ibid.

23 Peter Fornatale, *Back to the Garden: The Story of Woodstock* (New York, 2009), p. 276.

24 Ibid.

25 Foster Hirsch, 'Reviews: *Woodstock*', *Film Quarterly* (Spring 1971), p. 54.

26 Peter Biskind, *Easy Riders, Raging Bulls: How the Sex 'n' Drugs 'n' Rock 'n' Roll Generation Saved Hollywood* (London, 1999), p. 150.

27 John Williams, 'Interview with Martin Scorsese', *The Guardian*, 5 June 1975, p. 10.

28 Peter Brunette, ed., *Martin Scorsese: Interviews* (Jackson, MS, 1999), p. 19.

29 Richard Schickel, *Conversations with Scorsese* (New York, 2011), p. 350.

30 Don Simpson, a friend of Scorsese's in the early 1970s, quoted in Biskind, *Easy Riders, Raging Bulls*, p. 15.

31 Schickel, *Conversations with Scorsese*, p. 349.

32 Ibid., p. 351.

33 Ibid., p. 350.

34 Mark Harris, *Pictures at a Revolution: Five Movies and the Birth of the New Hollywood* (New York, 2008), p. 359.

35 David Browne, *Fire and Rain: The Beatles, Simon and Garfunkel, James Taylor, CSNY, and the Lost Story of 1970* (Boston, MA, 2011), p. 35.

36 Digby Diehl, 'Rock Invades Hollywood', *New York Times*, 21 January 1968, p. 24.

37 Ibid.

38 Karen Dillon, 'Wim's Desires', *Spin* (July 1992), p. 46.

39 David Thompson, ed., *Altman on Altman* (London, 2006), p. 66.

40 Gayle Sherwood Magee, *Robert Altman's Soundtracks* (Oxford and New York, 2014), p. 69.

41 Ibid., quote p. 68.

42 Peter Conrad, *Modern Times, Modern Places: Life and Art in the 20th Century* (London, 1998), p. 566.

43 Peter L. Kauff, 'Filmrock', *Billboard*, 14 November 1970, p. R-20.

44 Conrad, *Modern Times, Modern Places*, p. 566.

45 Wim Wenders, *Emotion Pictures: Reflections on the Cinema*, trans. Sean Whiteside with Michael Hofmann (London and Boston, MA, 1986), p. 31.

46 Kauff, 'Filmrock', p. R-20.

47 Ibid.

48 Barney Hoskyns, *Across the Great Divide: The Band and America*, revd edn (London, 2003), p. 221.

49 Terry Curtis Fox, 'Martin Scorsese's Elegy for a Big-Time Band', in *Martin Scorsese*, ed. Brunette, pp. 79–83.

50 Marc Raymond, *Hollywood's New Yorker: The Making of Martin Scorsese* (Stony Brook, NY, 2013).

51 Hoskyns, *Across the Great Divide*, p. 336.

52 Levon Helm and Stephen Davis, *This Wheel's on Fire: Levon Helm and the Story of The Band* (Chicago, IL, 2000), p. 258.

53 Ibid., p. 257.

54 Hoskyns, *Across the Great Divide*, p. 240.

5 THE AFTERMATH

1 Barbet Schroeder (dir.), *More* (Les Films du Losange, 1969).

2 Mark Blake, *Pigs Might Fly: The Inside Story of Pink Floyd* (London, 2017), p. 132.

3 See for example Jonathan B. Vogels, *The Direct Cinema of Albert and David Maysles* (Carbondale, IL, 2005), pp. 74–99.

4 Ethan Russell (with Gerard van der Leun), *Let It Bleed: The Rolling Stones, Altamont and the End of the Sixties* (New York and Boston, MA, 2009), p. 164.

5 Vogels, *Direct Cinema*, p. 77.

6 The film was broadcast only once, on 30 November 1969. It can now be found as a DVD in the 40th anniversary edition of the *Bridge Over Troubled Water* album (Sony Music/Columbia Records, 2009).

7 Robert Hilburn, *Paul Simon: A Life* (New York, 2018), p. 149.

8 Ibid., p. 150.

9 Tony Palmer, 'Figures on the Festival', *The Observer*, 6 September 1970, p. 6.

10 Stephen Holden, 'Peace Signs (and Other Kinds): Watching Hippies Self-Destruct', *New York Times*, 24 December 1996, p. C17.

11 Palmer, 'Figures on the Festival', p. 6.

12 Peter Wilby, 'Glastonbury Waits for a Dose of Celestial Fire', *The Observer*, 20 June 1971, p. 3.

13 Jon Pepper, 'The Hippies' Vale of Avalon', *The Guardian*, 20 December 1969, p. 7.

14 Nick Mason, *Inside Out: A Personal History of Pink Floyd* (San Francisco, CA, 2017), p. 130.

15 Ibid.

16 Blake, *Pigs Might Fly*, p. 168.

17 Ibid., p. 167.
18 Mason, *Inside Out*, p. 173.
19 Tony Palmer, '3 Mile Roll of Rock', *The Observer*, 6 August 1972, p. 1.
20 Jerry Hopkins, 'Beatle Loathers Return: Britain's Teddy Boys', *Rolling Stone*, 103, 2 March 1972, pp. 1, 14, 16.
21 The quotations are from backstage interviews in the film.
22 See Ed Ward, Geoffrey Stokes and Ken Tucker, *Rock of Ages: The Rolling Stone History of Rock and Roll* (Harmondsworth, 1987), p. 210.
23 Ibid.
24 Vincent Canby, 'Film: Eat the Document', *New York Times*, 1 December 1972, p. 31.
25 Ibid.
26 For more on this snapshot of the scene at the end of the 1960s, see Sharon Monteith, 'From the Human Be-In to Helter Skelter', in *American Culture in the 1960s*, ed. S. Monteith (Edinburgh, 2008), pp. 68–9.
27 Fredric Jameson, *Postmodernism; or, The Cultural Logic of Late Capitalism* (London and New York, 1991), p. 19.
28 Ibid.

6 THE NEW PEOPLE

 1 Peter Roberts, 'Burlesque in Mime', *The Times*, 7 March 1968, p. 7.
 2 Michael Wale, 'David Bowie: Rock and Theatre', *The Times*, 24 January 1973, p. 15.
 3 Michael Wale, 'David Bowie, Festival Hall', *The Times*, 10 July 1972, p. 7.
 4 Richard Williams, 'Stars of Rock', *The Times*, 2 September 1972, p. 11.
 5 Quoted from Paul Trynka, *David Bowie: Starman* (London, 2011), p. 175.
 6 D. A. Pennebaker, 'How I Met Ziggy Stardust and Survived', essay included in the 30th anniversary DVD release of *Ziggy Stardust and the Spiders of Mars: The Motion Picture* (Parlophone Pictures, 2003), n.p.
 7 Keith Beattie, *D. A. Pennebaker* (Champaign, IL, 2011), p. 36.
 8 Pennebaker, 'How I Met Ziggy Stardust'.
 9 Quote from Peter Doggett, *The Man Who Sold the World: David Bowie and the 1970s* (London, 2011), p. 238.
10 Ibid.

11 Anthony O'Grady, 'David Bowie: "Rock and Roll is Dead"', RAM (Rock Australia Magazine), 26 July 1975, at www.rocksbackpages. com, accessed 25 July 2020.

12 Robin Denselow, 'David Bowie on Record', *The Guardian*, 13 June 1974, p. 10.

13 Howard Sounes, *Seventies: The Sights, Sounds and Ideas of a Brilliant Decade* (London, 2006), p. 259.

14 R. J. Cardullo, *Interviews with English Filmmakers: Powell to Pawlikowski* (Albany, GA, 2018), p. 103

15 Neil Spencer, 'Don't Look Over Your Shoulder, but the Sex Pistols Are Coming', *New Musical Express*, 21 February 1976, p. 31.

16 Ibid.

17 Julien Temple, 'A Picture of Punk', *The Times* ('The Eye' supplement), 4 June 2005, p. 6.

18 See Charles M. Young, 'Rock Is Sick and Living in London: A Report on the Sex Pistols', *Rolling Stone*, 20 October 1977, p. 75.

19 Steve Severin in Mark Paytress, *Siouxsie and the Banshees* (London, 2003), p. 46.

20 Don Letts (dir.), *The Punk Rock Movie* (Notting Hill/Punk Rock Films, 1978).

21 Vivien Goldman, 'The Great Pistols Movies Fiasco', *Sounds*, 29 July 1978, at www.rocksbackpages.com, accessed 7 January 2021.

22 Vivienne Westwood quoted in Len Richmond, 'Buy Sexual', *Forum* (June 1976), p. 21.

23 Miguel Cullen, 'Don Letts Interview', *Daily Telegraph*, 26 August 2010, www.telegraph.co.uk.

24 Goldman, 'The Great Pistols Movies Fiasco'.

25 Erica Echenberg, 'Snapshot: Opening Night at the Roxy', *The Guardian* ('Review' section), 7 July 2006, p. 2.

26 Goldman, 'The Great Pistols Movies Fiasco'.

27 Ibid.

28 Barry Miles, *London Calling: A Countercultural History of London Since 1945* (London, 2010), p. 374.

29 Clinton Heylin, *From the Velvets to the Voidoids: A Pre-Punk History for a Post-Punk World* (London, 1993), p. 71.

30 Ibid., p. 76.

31 Nina Antonia, *The New York Dolls: Too Much Too Soon* (London, 1998), p. 86.

32 Debbie Harry, *Face It: A Memoir* (New York, 2019), p. 102.

33 Jim Fields and Michael Gramaglia (dir.), *End of the Century: The Story of the Ramones* (Magnolia Pictures, 2003).

34 Debbie Harry, Chris Stein and Victor Bockris, *Making Tracks: The Rise of Blondie*, 2nd edn (Cambridge, MA, 1988), p. 30.

35 Jonathan Buchsbaum, 'A la Recherche des Punks Perdus', *Film Comment*, XVII/3 (May–June 1981), p. 44.

36 Richard Hell, *I Dreamed I Was a Very Clean Tramp: An Autobiography* (New York, 2013), p. 147.

37 Heylin, *From the Velvets to the Voidoids*, pp. 117–18.

38 Buchsbaum, 'A la Recherche des Punks Perdus', p. 44.

39 Jim Jarmusch, *Interviews*, ed. Ludvig Hertzberg (Jackson, MA, 2001), p. 27.

40 Ibid.

41 Buchsbaum, 'A la Recherche', p. 43.

42 Ann Bardach and Susan Lydon, 'A Cool Blonde and a Hot Band', *New York Times Magazine*, 26 August 1979, p. 19.

43 Harry, Stein and Bockris, *Making Tracks*, p. 7.

44 Bardach and Lydon, 'A Cool Blonde', p. 20.

45 Paul Newland, *Don't Look Now: British Cinema in the 1970s* (Bristol, 2010), p. 255.

46 Filmwax Radio, 'Ep 385: Amos Poe segment' (interview), 23 November 2018, www.youtube.com, accessed 15 November 2019.

47 See Jonathan Everett Haynes, 'Downtown Godard', in *Downtown Film and TV Culture, 1975–2001*, ed. Joan Hawkins (Bristol, 2015), p. 64.

48 Vera Dika, *The (Moving) Pictures Generation: The Cinematic Impulse in Downtown New York Art and Film* (New York, 2012), p. 72.

49 Michael Goddard, 'No Wave Film and Music Documentary', in *The Music Documentary: Acid Rock to Electropop*, ed. Robert Edgar, Kirsty Fairclough-Isaacs and Benjamin Halligan (New York, 2013), p. 119.

50 Harry, Stein and Bockris, *Making Tracks*, p. 149.

51 Quoted in 'Interview with Julien Temple', *Slash*, III/3 (April 1980), p. 19.

52 *Copkiller*, directed by Roberto Faenza and starring Harvey Keitel and John Lydon (Aura Film, 1983). Confusingly, the film has also been released under two other titles: *Corrupt* and *Order of Death*.

53 Howard Hampton, 'Rock and Roll: Mise en Scène', *Film Comment*, XLIII/6 (November–December 2007), p. 32.

54 Simon Banner, 'Hell on Reels', *Spin* (August 1987), p. 73.

55 Peter Biskind, *Easy Riders, Raging Bulls: How the Sex 'n' Drugs 'n' Rock 'n' Roll Generation Saved Hollywood* (London, 1998), p. 392.

56 See Adam Scovell, 'Chris Petit on *Radio On*', *Sight and Sound*,
    22 August 2019, www.bfi.org.uk, accessed 27 January 2020.
57 Paul Newland, *British Films of the 1970s* (Manchester, 2015), p. 74.

7 VIDEO VORTEX

1   John Rockwell, 'Rock Is Edging into Video', *New York Times*, 29 July
    1979, p. D24.
2   Jim McCullaugh, 'Chrysalis Scores Vidcassette Beat', *Billboard*,
    27 October 1979, p. 1.
3   Debbie Harry, Chris Stein and Victor Bockris, *Making Tracks: The
    Rise of Blondie*, 2nd edn (Cambridge, MA, 1988), p. 149.
4   Michael Shore, *The Rolling Stone Book of Rock Video* (London, 1985),
    p. 73.
5   The International Music Video Conference, held in Los Angeles,
    15–18 November 1979, was the first event of its kind. See *Billboard*,
    6 October 1979, p. 10.
6   Rockwell, 'Rock Is Edging into Video', p. D24.
7   Rob Tannenbaum and Craig Marks, *I Want My MTV: The Uncensored
    Story of The Music Video Revolution* (New York, 2012), p. 18.
8   Cary Darling, 'Looking Ahead – Video Music: Tomorrow Is Here
    Today', *Billboard*, 15 December 1979, p. 56.
9   Bruce C. Pilato, 'Adventures in Video With Todd Rundgren',
    The Mix, v/4 (April 1981), p. 18.
10 Toby Goldstein, 'Todd Rundgren: Video-Tripping with the Perfect
    Master', *Creem* (October 1979), p. 62.
11 Ibid.
12 Pilato, 'Adventures in Video', p. 19.
13 Ibid., p. 20.
14 Vincent Canby, 'Frank Zappa's Surrealist *200 Motels*', *New York
    Times*, 11 November 1971, p. 60.
15 Nicholas Rombes, *A Cultural Dictionary of Punk, 1974–1982*
    (New York, 2009), p. 281.
16 Glen Phillips, ed., *California Video: Artists and Histories*
    (Los Angeles, CA, 2008), p. 194.
17 Joe Rees, 'Information Wars', *Damage*, 1/6 (May 1980), p. 36.
18 'Items: Video by XTV', *Damage*, 1/2 (August–September 1979), p. 39.
19 The advert is in *Damage* magazine, 1/11 (December 1980), p. 10.
20 For the launch of MTV see Tannenbaum and Marks, *I Want My MTV*.
21 David Ehrenstein, 'Pre-MTV', *Film Comment*, XIX/4 (July–August
    1983), p. 41.

22 Dara Birnbaum, 'Three Women, Three Films: Bruce Conner in the 1960s', in *Bruce Conner: It's All True*, ed. Rudolf Frieling and Gary Garrels (Berkeley, CA, 2016), p. 50.

23 Ibid., p. 51.

24 Ibid.

25 Amy Herzog, 'Illustrating Music: The Impossible Embodiments of the Jukebox Film', in *Cool: Music Videos from Soundies to Cellphones*, ed. Roger Beebe and Jason Middleton (Durham, NC, and London, 2007), p. 46.

26 Ibid., p. 47.

27 On Scopitone and Soundies, see Herzog, 'Illustrating Music', pp. 30–58.

28 See Peter Mills, 'Stone Fox Chase: *The Old Grey Whistle Test* and the Rise of High Pop Television', in *Popular Music and Television in Britain*, ed. Ian Inglis (London and New York, 2016), pp. 55–69. The Mike Oldfield/Leni Riefenstahl film clip can be seen at 'Tubular Bells – Mike Oldfield (HD)', www.youtube.com, uploaded 4 November 2011.

29 Recounted in Don Hardy (dir.), *Theory of Obscurity: A Film about the Residents* (DoF Media, 2015).

30 Shore, *Rolling Stone Book of Rock Video*, p. 65.

31 Tannenbaum and Marks, *I Want My MTV*, p. 8.

32 Shore, *Rolling Stone Book of Rock Video*, p. 67.

33 Tannenbaum and Marks, *I Want My MTV*, p. 11.

34 The historical development is discussed in R. Serge Denisoff, *Inside MTV* (Abingdon and New York, 2017).

35 Ibid., p. 42.

36 Ibid., p. 47.

37 Tannenbaum and Marks, *I Want My MTV*, p. 44.

38 Arlene Zeichner, 'Rock 'n' Video', *Film Comment*, XVIII/3 (May–June 1983), p. 39.

39 Shore, *Rolling Stone Book of Rock Video*, p. 61.

40 Saul Austerlitz, *Money for Nothing: A History of the Music Video from the Beatles to the White Stripes* (New York and London, 2007), p. 24.

41 Chris Willman, 'The Secret History of Devo', *Spin* (August 2010), p. 76.

42 Zeichner, 'Rock 'n' Video', p. 39.

43 Timothy White, 'Gabriel', *Spin* (September 1986), quotes on pp. 53, 70.

44 Scott Cohen, 'Lou Reed Don't Live Here Anymore', *Spin* (July 1986), p. 50.

45 Randall Rothenberg, *Where the Suckers Moon* (New York 1995), p. 211. The genesis and impact of the Lou Reed Honda commercial is discussed at length, see pp. 209–12.

46 Howard Hampton, 'Scorpio Descending: In Search of Rock Cinema', *Film Comment*, xxxiii/2 (March–April 1997), p. 36.

47 Katherine Dieckmann, 'Wim Wenders: An Interview', *Film Quarterly*, xxxviii/2 (Winter 1984–5), p. 7.

48 Legs McNeil and Tom Baker, 'Morrison: Long, Long Ago, in a Place Far Away When Rock 'n' Roll Was Dangerous', *Spin* (August 1990), p. 28.

49 Vincent Canby, 'Prince's Cherry Moon Lacks a Glow', *New York Times*, 13 July 1986, p. H19.

50 Paul Grein, 'Big Hits from the Big Screen', *Billboard*, 22 December 1984, p. TA-6.

51 Ibid.

52 Brian Raferty, '*Purple Rain*, the Oral History', *Spin* (July 2009), p. 60.

53 Canby, 'Prince's Cherry Moon Lacks a Glow', p. H22.

54 Armond White, 'Rock's Rebellion', *Film Comment*, xxiv/6 (November 1988), p. 32.

55 David Buckley, *Strange Fascination: David Bowie, The Definitive Story* (London, 2005), p. 364.

56 Jim Bessman, 'Longform Focuses The The's Image', *Billboard*, 20 December 1986, p. 37.

57 Ibid.

58 'The Making of E=MC2 by Big Audio Dynamite', *Uncut* (August 2009), p. 34.

8 DO IT AGAIN

1 Tony Palmer, 'After The Beatles Left Home', *The Observer*, 24 May 1970, p. 29.

2 See Steve Matteo, *The Beatles' Let It Be* (New York and London, 2010), pp. 20–24.

3 Ibid., p. 3.

4 Ed Ward, Geoffrey Stokes and Ken Tucker, *Rock of Ages: The Rolling Stone History of Rock and Roll* (Harmondsworth, 1987), p. 462.

5 Jann S. Wenner, *Lennon Remembers* (London, 2000), p. 101.

6 Palmer, 'After The Beatles Left Home', p. 29.

7 Sheila More, 'The Restless Generation: 2', *The Times*, 11 December 1968, p. 7.

8 Mick Brown, *Performance* (London, 2000), pp. 212–13.

9 John Lennon, *Playboy* interview (September 1980), quoted in Nick Kent, 'Back to Zero', *Spin* (August 1986), p. 45.

10 Nick Dawson, *Being Hal Ashby: Life of a Hollywood Rebel* (Lexington, KY, 2009), p. 246.

11 Peter Biskind, *Easy Riders, Raging Bulls: How the Sex 'n' Drugs 'n' Rock 'n' Roll Generation Saved Hollywood* (London, 1999), p. 172.

12 Dawson, *Being Hal Ashby*, p. 254.

13 See Brad Prager, *The Cinema of Werner Herzog: Aesthetic Ecstasy and Truth* (London, 2007), pp. 37–9.

14 Michiko Kakutani, 'Jagger, 39, Shows No Sign of Quitting', *New York Times*, 14 February 1983, p. C11.

15 Ibid.

16 Dawson, *Being Hal Ashby*, p. 254.

17 Robert Palmer, 'They Filmed as the Stones Rolled', *New York Times*, 6 February 1983, p. H15.

18 Stephen Holden, 'Only Rock 'N' Roll, But They're Still at It', *New York Times*, 4 April 2008, p. E12.

19 Ibid.

20 Ibid.

21 Michael McKean and Karl French, 'The A to Z of Spinal Tap', *The Guardian*, 22 September 2000, p. B4.

22 Ibid.

23 The film also spawned a book, Joe Berlinger and Greg Milner, *Metallica: This Monster Lives* (London, 2005).

24 Quotation from '35 Heaviest Metal Moments', *Spin* (August 1990), p. 47.

25 Chuck Klosterman, 'Band on the Couch', *New York Times Magazine*, 20 June 2004, p. 40.

26 Ibid., p. 42.

27 Jeannette Catsoulis, 'Last Days Here', *New York Times*, 2 March 2012.

28 Gabrielle Starkey, 'The Osbournes, MTV', *The Times* ('Play' supplement), 18 May 2002, p. 140.

29 Beth Bain, 'Reality Bites', *The Times* ('Play' supplement), 25 May 2002, p. 9.

30 Jonas Mekas quoted in Vincent Canby, 'Chelsea Girls in Midtown Test', *New York Times*, 1 December 1966, p. 56.

31 Anon., 'Chelsea Girls Film is Seized in Boston by Vice Squad Detectives', *New York Times*, 31 May 1967, p. 50.

32 Dan Sullivan, 'Andy Warhol's *Chelsea Girls* at the Cinema Rendezvous', *New York Times*, 2 December 1966, p. 45.

33 Nigel Finch (dir.), *Arena: Chelsea Hotel* (BBC, 1981).
34 James Young, *Nico: Songs They Never Play on the Radio* (London, 1992).
35 Richard Witts, *Nico: Life and Lies of an Icon* (London, 1993),
    pp. 147–8.
36 Jean Stein and George Plimpton, *Edie: American Girl*
    (London, 1982), p. 444.
37 Susanne Ofteringer (dir.), *Nico Icon* (Bluehorse Films/CIAK
    Filmproduktion, 1995).
38 Susan Hitch, 'Interview with Patti Smith', *Night Waves*, BBC Radio 3,
    28 November 2006.
39 Patti Smith, *Just Kids* (London, 2010), p. 10.
40 Dave Thompson, *Dancing Barefoot: The Patti Smith Story* (Chicago,
    IL, 2016), p. 77.
41 Ibid., p. 21.
42 See Camille Paglia, *Sexual Personae: Art and Decadence from Nefertiti
    to Emily Dickinson* (London and New Haven, CT, 1990).
43 See, for example, William Blake, *Poems: Selected by Patti Smith*
    (London, 2007), and Arthur Rimbaud, *A Season in Hell and The
    Drunken Boat*, trans. Louise Varèse, with a preface by Patti Smith
    (New York, 2011).
44 Eric Haynes, 'Riffs on the Documentary', *New York Times*,
    14 September 2014, p. AR12.

EPILOGUE: LOOK BACK

 1 Peter Biskind, *Easy Riders, Raging Bulls* (London, 1998), p. 18.
 2 Ibid., p. 19.

AFTERWORD: FANS

 1 Ron Dorfman and Peter Nevard (dirs), *Groupies* (Maron
    Films, 1970); Lindsay Shonteff (dir.), *Permissive* (Shonteff Film
    Productions, 1970).
 2 The subject is discussed at more length in John Scanlan, *Easy
    Riders, Rolling Stones: On the Road in America, from Delta Blues to '70s
    Rock* (London, 2015), pp. 134–7.
 3 The quotation is from an advert for *Rolling Stone* magazine that
    appeared in the *New York Times*, 12 February 1969.
 4 There is a quite detailed account of how the Plaster Casters would
    introduce themselves in Frank Zappa and Peter Occhiogrosso,
    The Real Frank Zappa Book (New York, 1999), pp. 104–6.

5 John Lombardi, 'The Jimi Hendrix Experience: Slowing Down and Growing Up', in *Hendrix on Hendrix: Interviews and Encounters with Jimi Hendrix*, ed. Steve Roby (Chicago, IL, 2012), p. 330.

6 Tony Palmer (dir.), *Bird on a Wire* (The Machat Company, 1974). The actress-groupie in the dressing room was Doris Kunstmann (b. 1944).

7 The concert that preceded the encounter was a highly charged affair, in which Cohen ended up out in the audience, cavorting with female fans. See Sylvie Simmons, *I'm Your Man: The Life of Leonard Cohen* (London, 2012), p. 246.

8 This dialogue is from the director's cut of *Almost Famous*, released on DVD as *Almost Famous/Untitled (Director's Edition)* (Columbia TriStar Home Entertainment, 2000).

9 Drew Toal, 'Sail Away: An Oral History of Yacht Rock', *Rolling Stone*, 26 June 2015, www.rollingstone.com.

SCREENOGRAPHY

FILMS

25×5: The Continuing Adventures of the Rolling Stones (Nigel Finch, 1989)
200 Motels (Tony Palmer and Frank Zappa, 1971)
20,000 Days on Earth (Iain Forsyth and Jane Pollard, 2014)
Alice in the Cities (Wim Wenders, 1974)
Almost Famous (Cameron Crowe, 2000)
American Graffiti (George Lucas, 1973)
Anvil: The Story of Anvil (Sacha Gervasi, 2008)
Apocalypse Now (Francis Ford Coppola, 1979)
Ballad of AJ Weberman, The (James Bluemel and Oliver Ralfe, 2006)
Bird on a Wire (Tony Palmer, 1974)
Blackboard Jungle, The (Richard Brooks, 1955)
Blank Generation, The (Amos Poe and Ivan Kral, 1976)
Blow-Up (Michelangelo Antonioni, 1966)
Bohemian Rhapsody (Bryan Singer, 2018)
Breakaway (Bruce Conner, 1966)
Cadillac Records (Darnell Martin, 2008)
Charlie Is My Darling (Peter Whitehead, 1966)
Chelsea Girls (Andy Warhol, 1966)
Chelsea Hotel (Nigel Finch, 1981)
Cocksucker Blues (Robert Frank, 1972)
Copkiller (Roberto Faenza, 1983)
'Cracked Actor', *Omnibus* (Alan Yentob, 1975)
The Cramps: Live at Napa State Mental Hospital (Joe Rees, 1981)
Desperately Seeking Susan (Susan Seidelman, 1985)
Don't Knock the Rock (Fred F. Sears, 1956)
Don't Look Back (D. A. Pennebaker, 1967)
Easy Rider (Dennis Hopper, 1969)
Eat the Document (Bob Dylan, 1972)
Elvis (John Carpenter, 1979)
Elvis on Tour (Pierre Adidge and Robert Abel, 1972)

End of the Century: The Story of the Ramones (Jim Fields and Michael Gramaglia, 2003)

Exploding Plastic Inevitable (Ronald Nameth, 1967)

Expresso Bongo (Val Guest, 1959)

Foreigner, The (Amos Poe, 1978)

Gimme Shelter (Albert Maysles, David Maysles and Charlotte Zwerin, 1970)

Girl Can't Help It, The (Frank Tashlin, 1956)

Glastonbury Fayre (Nicolas Roeg, 1972)

Go, Johnny, Go! (Paul Landres, 1959)

Grace of My Heart (Allison Anders, 1996)

Graduate, The (Mike Nichols, 1967)

Graffiti Bridge (Prince, 1990)

Great Balls of Fire! (Jim McBride, 1989)

Great Rock 'n' Roll Swindle, The (Julien Temple, 1980)

Groupies (Ron Dorfman and Peter Nevard, 1970)

Hard Day's Night, A (Richard Lester, 1964)

High Fidelity (Stephen Frears, 2000)

High School Confidential! (Jack Arnold, 1958)

I Wanna Hold Your Hand (Robert Zemeckis, 1978)

Jailhouse Rock (Richard Thorpe, 1957)

Jazzin' for Blue Jean (Julien Temple, 1984)

Jubilee (Derek Jarman, 1978)

Kings of the Road (Wim Wenders, 1976)

Kurt & Courtney (Nick Broomfield, 1998)

Lambert & Stamp (James D. Cooper, 2014)

Last Days Here (Don Argott and Demian Fenton, 2011)

Last Waltz, The (Martin Scorsese, 1978)

Let the Good Times Roll (Robert Abel and Sidney Levin, 1973)

Let It Be (Michael Lindsay-Hogg, 1970)

Let's Spend the Night Together (Hal Ashby, 1982)

London Rock and Roll Show, The (Peter Clifton, 1973)

Love Me Tender (Robert D. Webb, 1956)

Loving You (Hal Kanter, 1957)

McCabe & Mrs. Miller (Robert Altman, 1971)

Man Who Fell To Earth, The (Nicolas Roeg, 1976)

Mean Streets (Martin Scorsese, 1973)

Medicine Ball Caravan (François Reichenbach, 1972)

Metallica: Some Kind of Monster (Joe Berlinger and Bruce Sinofsky, 2004)

Message to Love: The Isle of Wight Festival (Murray Lerner, 1996)

Monterey Pop (D. A. Pennebaker, 1968)

More (Barbet Schroeder, 1969)
Nico, 1988 (Susanna Nicchiarelli, 2017)
Nico Icon (Susanne Ofteringer, 1995)
No Direction Home: Bob Dylan (Martin Scorsese, 2005)
Not Fade Away (David Chase, 2012)
One Trick Pony (Robert M. Young, 1980)
Patti Smith: Dream of Life (Steven Sebring, 2008)
Performance (Donald Cammell and Nicolas Roeg, 1970)
Permanent Vacation (Jim Jarmusch, 1980)
Permissive (Lindsay Shonteff, 1970)
Petulia (Richard Lester, 1968)
Pink Floyd: Live at Pompeii (Adrian Maben, 1972)
Pink Floyd: The Wall (Alan Parker, 1982)
Punk and the Pistols (Paul Tickell, 1995)
Punk Rock Movie, The (Don Letts, 1978)
Purple Rain (Albert Magnoli, 1984)
Quadrophenia (Franc Roddam, 1979)
Radio On (Chris Petit, 1979)
Return to Waterloo (Ray Davies, 1984)
Revolution (Jack O'Connell, 1967)
Rock Around the Clock (Fred F. Sears, 1956)
Searching for Sugar Man (Malik Bendjelloul, 2012)
Sex Pistols Number 1 (Julien Temple, Derek Jarman and
    John Tiberi, 1977)
School of Rock (Richard Linklater, 2003)
Scorpio Rising (Kenneth Anger, 1963)
Rolling Stones: Shine a Light (Martin Scorsese, 2008)
Sign o' the Times (Prince, 1987)
Simon & Garfunkel: Songs of America (Charles Grodin, 1968)
Stardust (Michael Apted, 1974)
Stop Making Sense (Jonathan Demme, 1984)
Straight to Hell (Alex Cox, 1987)
Stranger Than Paradise (Jim Jarmusch, 1984)
Summer Holiday (Peter Yates, 1963)
Summer in the City (Wim Wenders, 1971)
Sympathy for the Devil (aka *One Plus One*) (Jean-Luc Godard, 1968)
That'll Be the Day (Claude Whatham, 1973)
Tonite Let's All Make Love in London (Peter Whitehead, 1967)
The Trip (Roger Corman, 1967)
This Is Spinal Tap (Rob Reiner, 1984)
Twin Peaks: Fire Walk with Me (David Lynch, 1992)

Under the Cherry Moon (Prince, 1986)
Unmade Beds (Amos Poe, 1976)
Velvet Goldmine (Todd Haynes, 1998)
The Velvet Underground and Nico: Symphony of Sound
    (Andy Warhol, 1966)
Vinyl (HBO pilot) (Martin Scorsese, 2016)
Walker (Alex Cox, 1987)
Wanderers, The (Philip Kaufman, 1979)
Wayne's World (Penelope Spheeris, 1992)
What's Happening! (Albert and David Maysles, 1964)
Who's That Knocking at My Door (Martin Scorsese, 1967)
Wild One, The (Laslo Benedek, 1954)
Woodstock (Michael Wadleigh, 1970)
Yesterday (Danny Boyle, 2019)
Zabriskie Point (Michelangelo Antonioni, 1970)
Ziggy Stardust and the Spiders from Mars (D. A. Pennebaker, 1979)

TELEVISION

Dinah! (20th Century Fox TV, USA, 1977)
Ed Sullivan Show, The (CBS TV, USA, 1955, 1956)
Milton Berle Show, The (NBC TV, USA, 1956)
Old Grey Whistle Test, The (BBC TV, UK, 1973)
Smothers Brothers Comedy Hour, The (CBS TV, USA, 1967)
Stage Show (aka *The Dorsey Brothers Stage Show*) (CBS TV, USA, 1956)
Steve Allen Show, The (NBC TV, USA, 1956)
Today Show, The (aka *The Grundy Show*) (Thames TV, UK, 1976)

MULTI-PART SERIES

Andy Warhol's Fifteen Minutes (MTV, 1985–7)
Elvis (New World Television, USA, 1990)
Elvis: The Early Years (CBS TV, USA, 2005)
Long Strange Trip: The Untold Story of the Grateful Dead
    (Amazon Studios, 2017)
The Osbournes (MTV, 2002–5)
Stella Street (BBC TV, UK, 1997–2001)
Yacht Rock (www.yachtrock.com, 2005–10)

MUSIC VIDEOS

'Bad', Michael Jackson (Martin Scorsese, 1986)

'Billie Jean', Michael Jackson (Steve Barron, 1983)

'E=MC^2', Big Audio Dynamite (Luc Roeg, 1985)

Eat to the Beat, Blondie (David Mallet, 1979)

'Human Fly', The Cramps (Alex de Laszlo, 1978)

'(I Can't Get No) Satisfaction', Devo (Chuck Statler, 1978)

'I Love You Suzanne', Lou Reed (Tim Newman, 1984)

'I'm Not Sayin'', Nico (Peter Whitehead, 1966)

Infected, The The (Tim Pope et al., 1987)

'Land of 1,000 Dances', The Residents (The Residents, 1977)

'Mongoloid', Devo (Bruce Conner, 1977)

'Once in a Lifetime', Talking Heads (David Byrne and Toni Basil, 1981)

'Pass the Dutchie', Musical Youth (Don Letts, 1982)

'Rio', Michael Nesmith (William Dear, 1977)

'Thriller', Michael Jackson (John Landis, 1982)

'Unknown Soldier', The Doors (Mark Abramson/The Doors, 1968)

'Walk This Way', Run DMC and Aerosmith (Jon Small, 1986)

'We Love You', The Rolling Stones (Peter Whitehead, 1967)

'When Doves Cry', Prince and The Revolution (Prince, 1984)

ADVERTS

'Honda: Don't Settle for Walking', Lou Reed (Larry Bridges/
Wieden+Kennedy, 1983)

PHOTO ACKNOWLEDGEMENTS

The author and publishers wish to thank the organizations and individuals listed below for authorizing reproduction of their work.

All images from the author's collection, except:

Alamy: p. 187 (Everett Collection Inc); Getty Images: pp. 68 (Michael Ochs Archives), 86 (Mark and Colleen Hayward/Redferns), 113 (Warner Bros/Michael Ochs Archive), 130 (United Artists/Archive Photos), 172 (Erica Echenberg/Redferns), 209 (Ron Galella/Ron Galella Collection).

INDEX

Page numbers in *italics* refer to illustrations